Positive Political Theory I

## MICHIGAN STUDIES IN POLITICAL ANALYSIS

*Michigan Studies in Political Analysis* promotes the development and dissemination of innovative scholarship in the field of methodology in political science and the social sciences in general. Methodology is defined to include statistical methods, mathematical modeling, measurement, research design, and other topics related to the conduct and development of analytical work. The series includes works that develop a new model or method applicable to social sciences, as well as those that, through innovative combination and presentation of current analytical tools, substantially extend the use of these tools by other researchers.

General Editors: John E. Jackson (University of Michigan) and Christopher H. Achen (Princeton University)

Keith Krehbiel
*Information and Legislative Organization*

Donald R. Kinder and Thomas R. Palfrey, Editors
*Experimental Foundations of Political Science*

William T. Bianco
*Trust: Representatives and Constituents*

Melvin J. Hinich and Michael C. Munger
*Ideology and the Theory of Political Choice*

John Brehm and Scott Gates
*Working, Shirking, and Sabotage: Bureaucratic Response to a Democratic Public*

R. Michael Alvarez
*Information and Elections*

David Austen-Smith and Jeffrey S. Banks
*Positive Political Theory I: Collective Preference*

Gregory Wawro
*Legislative Entrepreneurship in the U.S. House of Representatives*

David Austen-Smith and Jeffrey S. Banks
*Positive Political Theory II: Strategy and Structure*

# Positive Political Theory I
## Collective Preference

*David Austen-Smith and Jeffrey S. Banks*

*Ann Arbor*

THE UNIVERSITY OF MICHIGAN PRESS

First paperback edition 2000
Copyright © by the University of Michigan 1999
All rights reserved
Published in the United States of America by
The University of Michigan Press
Manufactured in the United States of America
⊚ Printed on acid-free paper

2010   2009   2008   2007        7   6   5   4

*A CIP catalog record for this book is available from the British Library.*

Library of Congress Cataloging-in-Publication Data

Austen-Smith, David.
    Positive political theory I : collective preference / David
Austen-Smith, Jeffrey S. Banks.
        p.   cm.— (Michigan studies in political analysis)
    Includes bibliographical references and index.
    ISBN 0-472-10480-2 (cloth : alk. paper)
    1. Political science—Methodology.   2. Political science—Decision
making.   3. Rational choice theory.   4. Social choice.   I. Banks,
Jeffrey S.   II. Title.   III. Series.
JA71.A76   1999.
320′.01′1-dc21                                           98-42902
                                                          CIP

ISBN 0-472-08721-5 (pbk. : alk. paper)

ISBN 978-0-472-10480-2 (cloth : alk. paper)
ISBN 978-0-472-08721-1 (pbk. : alk. paper)

ISBN13 978-0-472-02246-5 (electronic)

*Dedicated to the memory of*

*William H. Riker*
*1921–1993*

*Teacher, Colleague, Friend*

# Contents

# Acknowledgments

The genesis of this book lies in graduate classes we taught at the University of Rochester, roughly through the decade 1986-1996. Many people have contributed to it in one way or another. We are very grateful to all of the students who have suffered through our classes at Rochester, offering constructive criticism, insight, and commentary on both the material itself and on our presentation thereof. Among these students we are particularly indebted to Daniel Diermeier, Tim Feddersen, Tarik Kara, Eichi Miyagawa, Alastair Smith and Tayfun Sonmez. Special thanks are due to John Duggan (who, among other things, proposed using the diagrams in Section 3.5), David Epstein (who suggested Example 3.4) and Tim Groseclose, all of whom were kind enough to use earlier drafts of the manuscript in classes they taught and to offer valuable feedback for improving the text based on their experiences. In addition, conversations over the years with Randy Calvert, John Ferejohn, Richard McKelvey, Bill Riker, Norman Schofield, and doubtless many others have influenced our appreciation of preference aggregation theory and its role in understanding politics. We thank them all.

We are also grateful to Bob Turring who drew the figures, deciphering our handwritten scrawls and accomodating our changes with considerable patience. Some of the material used in the Preface and Chapter 7 is taken from our paper [4] and appears with permission from the *Annual Review of Political Science, Volume 1,* copyright 1998, by *Annual Reviews.* The final draft of the manuscript was completed while the second author was a Fellow at the Center for Advanced Study in the Behavioral Sciences at Stanford University. He gratefully acknowledges financial support from the National Science Foundation under grant SBR-9601236. Both authors are similarly grateful to the National Science Foundation for financial support under grant SBR-9510877.

Finally, we should like to thank our wives, Maggie Weiss and Shannon Banks, and children, Clare and Luke Austen-Smith, and Bryan and Danny

Banks, for putting up with us both separately and together while we worked on the manuscript and beyond. Any value in the book (and pretty much everything else) would be considerably diminished without their continued love and support.

# Preface

Positive political theory is concerned with understanding political phenomena through analytical models which, it is hoped, yield insight into why political outcomes look the way they do and not some other way. Examples of such outcomes include the parties or candidates elected at various times, the bills adopted by legislatures, and decisions on going to war or designing a constitution. The models typically begin with the presumption that political outcomes are the consequence, intended or otherwise, of decisions made by the relevant individuals, be they voters and candidates in the first example, elected representatives and appointed ministers in the second, or heads of state and citizens in the third.

Most models within positive political theory are members of one of two families, although the demarcation line between the two is at times opaque. One family is motivated by the canonic rational choice theory of individual decision-making. In its simplest form, this theory assumes an individual has well-defined preferences over a given set of alternatives and chooses any alternative with the property that no other alternative in the set is strictly preferred by the individual, that is, the individual chooses a best alternative. In politics, however, it is rarely the case that only one individual's preferences are relevant for any collective choice; even dictators are sensitive to at least some others in the polity. Consequently, the first family of models in positive political theory examines the possibility that individual preferences are directly aggregated into a collective, or social, preference relation which, as in the theory of individual decision-making, is then maximized to yield a set of best alternatives (where "best" is here defined as being most preferred with respect to the collective preference relation). If a set of best alternatives for a given method of aggregation necessarily exists, then we have a model of observed collective choices as being elements from this set, analogous to the model of individual choice, and it is in principle possible to ascertain whether the model does or does not provide a good explanation for what is observed in the real world of politics.

One missing piece of the direct aggregation story is the appropriate method by which the aggregation of individuals' preferences into social preference is made, for example by majority rule, unanimity, or dictatorship. Although this is typically dictated by explicit features inherent in the political phenomena in question (e.g. plurality rule elections), there are occasionally more amorphous situations in which the choice might best be considered in terms of classes of rules, all of which satisfy some critical properties of the situation. The idea here is to think of the aggregation rule as a particular feature of the model itself and so appropriately left to the analyst to decide depending on what exactly she is attempting to explain. But whatever rule is appropriate for any given model, the model itself is well-specified as an explanatory model of political outcomes only to the extent that the rule yields best alternatives. So for the direct preference aggregation approach to work as a general theory of politics, we need to determine the extent to which different aggregation methods insure the existence of best alternatives and to characterize these alternatives where possible. These issues are the subject of the current volume.

It is important to emphasize that direct aggregation of individual preferences is not equivalent to indirect aggregation of preferences through the aggregation of individual actions. For example, an individual may have well-defined preferences over a set of candidates but choose to abstain in an election, or to vote strategically. Consequently, there is no *a priori* reason to suppose that elections lead to the same outcome that would occur if aggregation were directly over given preferences rather than indirectly over recorded votes. Of course, we expect the actions of purposive individuals to be intimately connected to their respective preferences and such connections are the subject of the second principal family of models within positive political theory (and also the subject of our second volume).

In the second family of models individuals are no longer modeled as passive participants in the collective decision making, but rather make individual choices of behavior that jointly determine the collective choice of outcome. These models fall naturally into the methodology of game theory. Here the fundamental moving parts of the model include the set of possible behaviors or strategies available to each of the participants, as well as a description of how any list of strategies relates to the set of outcomes. As with the preference aggregation rules in the first family of models, the appropriate choice by the analyst of the important features is at times influenced by explicit features of the political phenomenon in question (e.g. the closed rule in parliamentary decision-making, presidential veto power, germaneness rules for amendments and party primaries for selecting electoral candidates), while at other times (e.g. when trying to understand the consequences of intra-committee bargaining) there may not exist such explicit features to provide a roadmap to the correct model and there are more degrees of freedom with respect to modeling choices.

Unlike with direct preference aggregation models, there is no presumption in game theory models that collective outcomes are best elements relative to some underlying social preference relation. Rather, they are the consequences of a set of mutually consistent individual decisions within a given set of behavioral constraints. It is thus the composition of preferences and constraints that explains collective choices in this family of models and not, as in the first family, the application of an aggregation rule to preferences *per se*. These two approaches are contrasted explicitly in our concluding chapter. Here a simple example suffices to illustrate their differences.

There are three individuals, 1, 2, and 3, who must come to some collective choice from a set of three mutually exclusive alternatives, $x, y$, and $z$. Let $z$ be a given status quo policy and assume $x$ and $y$ are the only feasible alternatives to $z$ (for instance, $z$ might be the current minimum wage level and alternatives $x$ and $y$ might be two proposals to adjust this level). Individual 1 is assumed to prefer $x$ the most, followed by $y$, and finally to consider $z$ the worst option; individual 2 strictly prefers $z$ to $x$ and strictly prefers $x$ to $y$; finally, individual 3 prefers alternative $y$ best, ranks $x$ next best, and considers $z$ to be the worst outcome. Then under simple majority rule, a direct preference aggregation model predicts a collective choice of $x$ (since $x$ is pairwise majority preferred to both $y$ and $z$) and the explanation for such a prediction is in terms of $x$ being uniquely best relative to the underlying aggregation rule.

Now suppose instead of direct preference aggregation by majority rule, the choice of an alternative from the list $x, y$, and $z$ is determined according to the following set of rules. Individual 3 has the sole right to propose a take-it-or-leave-it change in policy away from the status quo, $z$. So individual 3 can either make no proposal, in which case $z$ remains the collective choice, or can propose alternative $x$ or $y$ as the new policy; if individual 3 does offer a proposal then the collective decision is reached via majority vote between $z$ and the proposal. Under this institutional arrangement, it is clear that individual 3 offers alternative $y$, $y$ defeats $z$, and $y$ becomes the collective choice. Thus in this example, the model of indirect preference aggregation offers a distinct prediction of a collective choice and this is supported by reference not only to individuals' preferences and the aggregation rule, but also to the behavioral constraints governing the choice process and the particular choices individuals make.

*Prima facie*, it seems reasonable to infer that results from the direct collective preference models have little, if any, relevance for those from the indirect game theory models. We consider such an inference inappropriate. Our argument to this effect, however, must wait until Chapter 7 when the salient theory of direct preference aggregation has been laid out.

As remarked earlier, the central themes of the book concern the extent to which different ways of aggregating individuals' preferences insure the existence of best alternatives. The first four chapters consider situations in which the number of feasible choices is finite. Chapter 1 develops the theory of choice and preference in the abstract. The goal here is to identify properties, termed rationality conditions, on preferences that insure well-defined best choices under all circumstances, and properties on observed choices that legitimate treating such choices *as if* they are generated by preferences satisfying particular rationality conditions. In subsequent chapters we assume there is a given society of individuals, each of whom has preferences satisfying sufficient rationality conditions for well-defined (individual) choices. Chapter 2 then explores the extent to which various methods of aggregating the individual preferences yield some sort of collective preference that itself exhibits sufficient rationality properties to support well-defined (collective) choices. In particular, the focus of Chapter 2 is on the relationship between these rationality conditions and the concentration of decision making power within society. The results are not encouraging and suggest that, without some restrictions on either the number of alternatives that can be considered for collective choice or on the detailed structure of individuals' preferences, there is no hope of finding acceptable aggregation methods that are guaranteed to generate best alternatives. Consequently, Chapters 3 and 4, respectively, look at what happens when we restrict the feasible set of alternatives and the admissible lists of preferences. Chapter 3 provides an axiomatic characterization of three empirically important classes of aggregation method and identifies exactly when any such method is sure to yield a nonempty set of best alternatives in terms of the number of available alternatives, irrespective of the list of individual preferences. Chapter 4 complements Chapter 3 in that it imposes no restrictions on the number of feasible alternatives, but instead looks for restrictions on the admissible lists of individual preferences that are sure to aggregate into a collective preference for which best alternatives are well defined. Furthermore, the best elements here are readily identified in terms of the primitive properties of individual preferences.

For many problems, assuming that the number of alternatives is finite is unduly restrictive; for example, the political choice of tax and expenditure levels is usefully modeled as choosing from an infinite set. Chapter 5 introduces the spatial model, the model that constitutes the foundation of much applied theoretical work in political science. It turns out here that the rationality conditions on preferences sufficient to insure choices from a finite set are not generally sufficient to insure choices from an infinite set of alternatives. Consequently, the first task addressed in Chapter 5 is to provide an analogous theory of individual and collective choice suitable for the spatial model. This in turn leads to a series of results on the existence and characterization of best alternatives in infinite sets under a very wide class of empirically important preference aggregation rules. Here, we find analogies to results in Chapters 3 and 4: an aggregation method is sure to yield a nonempty set of best alternatives if the number of dimensions of the policy space is suitably restricted and we provide a multidimensional version of the characterization of best elements identified in Chapter 4. This leaves open what happens with larger dimensional policy spaces. Chapter 6, therefore, pursues this question, first studying the stability of best alternatives when they exist and, second, characterizing exactly what is true of collective preferences when no best alternative exists. Finally, Chapter 7 draws the threads together and, *inter alia*, juxtaposes the theory of direct preference aggregation with the more indirect preference aggregation approach of game theory.

Throughout the book the development of the theory is cumulative and although most (but not all) of the results reported were originally derived by others, in the interests of continuity we have chosen to leave the relevant credits to a "further reading" section at the end of each chapter. If we have missed anyone in this regard, we apologize. With very few exceptions, all of the results are proved explicitly in the text and we have tried to make the formal arguments as transparent and self-contained as possible. Consequently, some of the proofs are less succinct than they might otherwise be and some of the results are not proved in their most general form.

# Chapter 1

# Choice and Preference

It is natural to think of individuals choosing what they prefer and it is precisely this intuition that supports, for instance, empirical work in which legislators' policy preferences are inferred from their observed voting behavior. Indeed, individual preference is occasionally defined in terms of choice. But there is no logical reason why this should be so. Individuals might make choices in the absence of any well-defined preference, or on the basis of the preferences of others. Moreover, many of the choices of interest in political science are the "choices" of groups; electorates' choices of presidents, governments and legislatures, and governments' choices of policy, being important examples. In such cases, it is not at all clear what it means to say that choices reflect preferences, or whether it is meaningful to speak of preferences at all. This chapter, then, is concerned with the primitive concepts of preference and choice. In particular, we are interested in three questions. First, given that choice in any situation is motivated by some underlying set of preferences, what must be true of these preferences to insure that such choice is invariably well-defined? Second, assuming that choices are made in any situation, under what conditions can we infer that such choices are made consistently with some set of more fundamental preferences over alternatives? And third, when choices are indeed consistent with some set of preferences, what can we say about the structure of these preferences given information only about how choices are made?

## 1.1  Preference-driven choice

The primitives of the model are as follows: there exists a finite set of outcomes, denoted $X$, with common elements $x, y, a, b$, etc. For the first four chapters no structure will be placed on $X$, other than to assume all elements of $X$ are mutually exclusive, in the sense that the choice of any one necessarily implies rejection of the others. For example, an individual voting for one candidate in a presidential election precludes that individual from voting for any other candidate in that election; and choosing to be a pacifist precludes fighting for one's country.

A *binary relation* on the set $X$ describes the relative merits of any two outcomes in $X$ with respect to some criterion. Familiar examples of binary relations include the weak inequality relation, "$\geq$", defined on a set of integers, where the expression $x \geq y$ is interpreted as "integer $x$ is at least as big as the integer $y$"; the relation "is more egalitarian than" defined on a set of policies; and the relations "is older than" or "is more tolerant than" defined on a set of individuals.

In what follows binary relations on $X$ will be related to the views of either individuals separately, or else the views of a group of individuals collectively, regarding alternatives in $X$. In this sense, then, we will refer to such relations as *preference relations* associated with either an individual or a group. Letting $R$ denote this relation, the expression "$xRy$" represents the statement "the outcome $x$ is at least as good as the outcome $y$". Hence if $R$ refers to a particular individual, say individual $j$, then $xRy$ is interpreted as, "outcome $x$ is at least as good as outcome $y$ from individual $j$'s perspective"; and if $R$ refers to a group of individuals, then $xRy$ is interpreted as, "outcome $x$ is at least as good as outcome $y$ from the group's perspective." It should be emphasized, however, that there is no suggestion here that $x$ being ranked "at least as good as" $y$ for some individual or group necessarily means that $x$ is in any sense normatively desirable.

Given any binary relation $R$, we can construct two associated binary relations, $P$ and $I$, which characterize *strict preference* and *indifference*, respectively:

$$xPy \quad \Leftrightarrow \quad xRy \,\&\, \sim [yRx]$$
$$xIy \quad \Leftrightarrow \quad xRy \,\&\, yRx$$

(where, for any statement "$s$", "$\sim [s]$" means "*not s*"). Thus, $xPy$ means outcome $x$ is strictly preferred to outcome $y$, while $xIy$ means each is at least as good as the other; the analogies for the weak inequality $\geq$ would thus be the strict inequality $>$ and equality $=$, respectively. Note that the strict preference relation $P$ is *asymmetric*, in that if $xPy$ then necessarily $\sim [yPx]$, whereas $I$ is *symmetric*: $xIy$ implies $yIx$. So at times we will refer to $P$ and $I$ as the asymmetric and symmetric parts of $R$, respectively.

Now let $\mathcal{X}$ denote the set of all nonempty subsets of $X$, i.e. $\mathcal{X} = \{S : S \in 2^X \setminus \{\emptyset\}\}$. We can think of $X$ as the universal set of outcomes, whereas a particular situation, or agenda, involves a subset of $X$. Given a preference relation $R$, and a subset of alternatives $S \in \mathcal{X}$, define the *maximal set* associated with $(R, S)$ as

$$M(R, S) = \{x \in S : \forall y \in S, \ xRy\}.$$

That is, $M(R, S)$ gives those alternatives that are top-ranked in $S$ with respect to the preference relation $R$ (note that if both $x$ and $y$ are in $M(R, S)$, then it must be the case that $xIy$). The set $M(R, S)$ is often referred to as the *choice set* from $S$ given $R$. However, since no choice is involved and elements of $M(R, S)$ need not be in any normative sense "good", we prefer the neutral terminology of the maximal set. Of course, any substantive interest in the set $M(R, S)$ depends on identifying $M(R, S)$ with explicit choices or claiming that $M(R, S)$ reflects some set of normative criteria. But for now, the additional structure on the relation $R$ or the set $S$ required to make specific such interpretations is unneccesary.

Our first question, then, is this: what conditions on the binary relation are required for $M(R, S)$ to be nonempty for all subsets of alternatives $S$?

**Definition 1.1** *A binary relation $R$ on $X$ is* → each alternative is at least as good as itself
  *(1) Reflexive if for all $x \in X$, $xRx$.*
  *(2) Complete if for all $x, y \in X$, $x \neq y$, either $xRy$ or $yRx$ (or both).*

Because the relation $R$ carries the interpretation, "at least as good as", requiring $R$ to be reflexive is to rule out trivially self-contradictory sentences concerning preferences (so from this perspective, it is evident that the asymmetric part of $R$, $P$, is *not* reflexive). Completeness says that any two alternatives can be meaningfully compared via the relation $R$. When we think of an individual $i$'s preferences, insisting on completeness is to insist that $i$ is always capable of ranking any pair of alternatives and this may seem overly restrictive. For instance, it might be implausible that any individual is capable of evaluating a life of pain but free from material concern, against a life free from pain but lived in poverty. However, such examples typically rely on some informational imperfection: the reason it is hard to compare the preceding alternatives is because it is hard to know what either life would be like – in other words, the alternatives are incompletely specified. So the example points to the importance of fully specifying the alternatives under consideration, rather than to the implausibility of completeness.

Clearly, reflexivity and completeness are necessary for the set $M(R, S)$ to be nonempty for all $S$ (if $\sim [xRx]$, then $M(R, \{x\}) = \emptyset$; if $\sim [xRy]$ & $\sim [yRx]$ then $M(R, \{x, y\}) = \emptyset$), so in all of what follows we will assume these properties hold.

Next we consider properties of $R$ concerning sets of pairwise comparisons:

**Definition 1.2** *A binary relation $R$ on $X$ is*

(1) *Transitive if for all $x, y, z \in X$, $xRy$ & $yRz$ implies $xRz$*

(2) *Quasi-transitive if for all $x, y, z \in X$, $xPy$ & $yPz$ implies $xPz$*

(3) *Acyclic if for all $\{x, y, z, \ldots, u, v\} \in X$, $xPy$ & $yPz \ldots$ & $uPv$ implies $xRv$*

A transitive relation is such that if outcome $x$ is at least as good as outcome $y$, and $y$ is at least as good as $z$, then $x$ must also be at least as good as $z$. If $R$ is transitive, we also have the following [Exercise]:

(a) $xPy$ & $yPz$ imply $xPz$ (i.e. the asymmetric part of $R$ is transitive)

(b) $xIy$ & $yIz$ imply $xIz$ (i.e. the symmetric part of $R$ is transitive)

(c) $xRy$ & $yPz$ imply $xPz$, and $xPy$ & $yRz$ imply $xPz$

Thus, if $R$ is transitive and $x, y$ are both in $M(R, S)$, then from (c) we have that for all $z \in S$, $xPz$ if and only if $yPz$, i.e. when $R$ is transitive any two alternatives in the maximal set are in the same relation to any third alternative.

Quasi-transitivity, on the other hand, only requires the asymmetric part of $R$ to be transitive. Thus if $R$ is transitive, it is necessarily quasi-transitive as well; however the converse need not hold. To see this, consider the following:

**Example 1.1** Let $X = \{x, y, z\}$ with $xPy$, $yIz$, $zIx$. Then $R$ is quasi-transitive, but not transitive: $yRz$ & $zRx$ but $\sim [yRx]$. $\square$

Similarly, quasi-transitivity implies acyclicity, but not conversely:

**Example 1.2** Let $X = \{x, y, z\}$ with $xPy$, $yPz$, $xIz$. Then $R$ is acyclic, but not quasi-transitive. $\square$

Finally note that, since $R$ is complete, an implication of quasi-transitivity is that $xRy$ and $yPz$ implies $xRz$.

A weak order is a reflexive, complete and transitive binary relation. If $R$ is a weak order then $M(R, S)$ is nonempty for all $S \in \mathcal{X}$. To see this, select any $x \in S$, and compare $x$ to all other alternatives in $S$. If $xRy$ for all $y \in S$, then $x$ is in $M(R,S)$ and we are done. Otherwise there must exist an alternative $y \in S$ such that $\sim [xRy]$; since $R$ is complete, this implies $yRx$ (in fact, $yPx$), so now compare $y$ to all alternatives in $S \backslash \{x\}$. If $yRz$ for all such alternatives then, since $yRx$ as well, we have that $y \in M(R,S)$. Otherwise, there must exist an alternative $z \in S \backslash \{x\}$ such that $\sim [yRz]$, implying (again by completeness) $zRy$ (in fact, $zPy$). Since $R$ is transitive, then, $zRx$ as well (in fact, $zPx$). Now compare $z$ to all alternatives in $S \backslash \{x,y\}$; etc. Since the universal set of alternatives $X$ is assumed finite, any subset $S$ must be finite as well, implying such a process must end at some point. Thus there must exist some alternative which is at least as good as all other alternatives if $R$ is reflexive, complete, and transitive, which proves the nonemptiness of $M(R,S)$. Finally, since the set $S$ was chosen arbitrarily, this argument proves the nonemptiness of $M(R,S)$ for all $S \in \mathcal{X}$.

Although transitivity is a sufficient condition (along with reflexiveness and completeness) for $M(R, \cdot)$ to be nonempty, it is not a necessary condition: in Example 1.1 above, $R$ was not transitive, and yet $M(R,X) = \{x,z\}$. Similarly, the argument above shows quasi-transitivity as sufficient for $M(R, \cdot)$ to be nonempty; indeed, this argument demonstrates that if $R$ is quasi-transitive, then for any alternative $z$ in $S$ but not in $M(R,S)$, there must exist an alternative $y \in M(R,S)$ such that $yPz$. However, as with transitivity, quasi-transitivity is not necessary for $M(R,S)$ to be nonempty (Example 1.2).

**Theorem 1.1** *Let $R$ be reflexive and complete; then $M(R,S) \neq \emptyset$ for all $S \in \mathcal{X}$ if and only if $R$ is acyclic.*

**Proof.** (Sufficiency) For any $S \subseteq X$ choose $x \in S$. If, for all $s \in S$, $xRs$ then we are done; otherwise (since $R$ is reflexive and complete) there must exist $y \in S \backslash \{x\}$ such that $yPx$. If for all $s \in S$, $yRs$, then again we are done; otherwise there exists $z \in S \backslash \{x,y\}$ such that $zPy$ and, by acyclicity, it must be that $zRx$ as well. If for all $s \in S$, $zRs$, we are done; otherwise there exists $w \in S \backslash \{x,y,z\}$ such that $wPz$ whence, by acyclicity, $wRy$ and $wRx$ as well. Because $X$ (and hence $S$) is finite, we can continue this logic to conclude that there must exist an alternative weakly preferred to all other alternatives in $S$.

(Necessity) Assume $x_1 P x_2, x_2 P x_3, \ldots, x_{n-1} P x_n$; we wish to show that $x_1 R x_n$. Let $S = \{x_1, \ldots, x_n\} \in \mathcal{X}$ and suppose $M(R,S) \neq \emptyset$. Because $x_{i-1} P x_i$, $i = 2, \ldots, n$, we have $x_i \notin M(R,S)$, $i = 2, \ldots, n$. Therefore,

$R$
reflexive
complete
acyclic
$\overset{\text{iff}}{\longleftrightarrow} M(R,S) \neq \emptyset$

since $M(R, S) \neq \emptyset$, it must be that $x_1 \in M(R, S)$ and this implies $x_1 R x_i$, $i = 2, \ldots, n$; in particular, $x_1 R x_n$, as required.□

We can think of transitivity, quasi-transitivity, and acyclicity as requiring more-or-less amounts of "rationality" in a preference relation $R$. The above result shows that acyclicity of $R$ is the minimal requirement consistent with the general existence of a nonempty maximal set.

Of course, it is possible that choices are made in the absence of any acyclic preference relation over $X$. However, Theorem 1.1. says that if this is the case then there must exist circumstances in which there is no logical connection between choice and preference. In other words, if choices are presumed to be preference-driven (i.e. chosen elements lie in $\overline{M(R, S)}$ for a given preference relation $R$), then necessarily those preferences are acyclic on $X$. So, for example, if an analyst presumes a legislator's voting decisions are necessarily driven by the legislator's policy preferences, then the analyst must be assuming that the legislator in question can be modeled as an individual with acyclic preferences over the set of all bills that might appear on the agenda; i.e. that the legislator is (minimally) rational. But the analyst's presumption here may not be justified and, since we at most observe choices and not preferences, the only way to validate an assumption of preference-driven decisionmaking is through these choices. To do this requires identifying observable properties of choice behavior which are at least sufficient to support an inference that, in the current example, legislator voting decisions reflect (acyclic) preference-driven choices. The rest of the chapter is therefore devoted to finding such properties.

## 1.2 Rationalizable choice

In the preceding section we considered the problem of the existence of maximal outcomes with respect to some underlying preference relation $R$ over the set of outcomes $X$. And for preference-driven choice, chosen elements are maximal with respect to the preference relation. An alternative perspective is to examine the outcomes actually chosen, and then ask whether these choices are "rational", in the following sense: does there exist a binary relation $R$ which would generate the chosen outcomes as the maximal outcomes according to $R$? If so, then we can think of these choices as being consistent with maximization relative to an underlying preference relation.

**Definition 1.3** *A choice function is a map* $C : \mathcal{X} \to \mathcal{X}$ *such that for all* $S \in \mathcal{X}$, $C(S) \subseteq S$.

① individual level, we can assume acyclicity

† we are assuming preference driven choice

Recall that $\mathcal{X}$ is defined to be the family of all nonempty subsets of $X$. Therefore, if $C(\cdot)$ is a choice function and $S \in \mathcal{X}$ then necessarily $C(S)$ is nonempty.

In contrast to the maximal set $M(R, S)$, which we might think of as the outcomes that "should" be chosen given the preference relation $R$, a choice function $C(\cdot)$ simply reports the selected alternatives from any feasible set, or agenda, taken from $X$. As such, there is no presumption that choices generated through $C(\cdot)$ reflect any preference or other criterion whatsoever.

Notice that, as with a maximal set $M(R, S)$, there is no insistence that the set $C(S)$ contains only one element. If in fact $C(S)$ does contain exactly one alternative for all subsets $S$, then we say that the choice function $C(\cdot)$ is *resolute*. The interpretation of $M(R, S)$ containing several elements is straightforward; if $x, y \in M(R, S)$ then $x$ is indifferent to $y$ under the given preference relation $R$. However, since the choice function $C(\cdot)$ is defined independently of any underlying preference relation, this interpretation in terms of indifference is not entirely satisfactory when $C(\cdot)$ is not resolute. Instead, if both $x$ and $y$ are in $C(S)$ for some $S$, this simply means that both $x$ and $y$ have been observed as selected alternatives when the agenda is $S$. In other words, because the only data available are the agenda and the choices themselves, if there are any salient differences motivating the choice of $x$ in one instance and that of $y$ in another, they are unobservable. Of course, there is no such problem of interpretation if in fact choices can be treated *as if* they are generated by some underlying, or implicit, preference relation. The following definition makes precise the relevant idea here.

**Definition 1.4** *A choice function $C(\cdot)$ is rationalizable if there exists a binary relation $R$ on $X$ such that for all $S \in \mathcal{X}$, $C(S) = M(R, S)$; in which case, we say $C(\cdot)$ is rationalized by $R$.*

Not every choice function is rationalizable. For example, the choice function $C$ on $\{x, y, z\}$ such that

$$C(\{x, y, z\}) = C(\{y, z\}) = \{y\}$$

and

$$C(\{x, y\}) = C(\{x, z\}) = \{x\}$$

is not rationalizable: for some preference relation $R$ to rationalize $C$, $R$ must (by the first row) declare $yPx$ and likewise (by the second row) declare $xPy$, which is impossible. Thus the issue for this section concerns what conditions on a choice function imply, and are implied by, rationalizability.

*reconcilable iff not every best element is chosen, but no not best element is chosen*

Before proceeding, however, it is worth noting that a choice function may not be rationalizable in the sense of Definition 1.4, yet may nevertheless be preference-driven in a weaker sense. Consider the following criterion of "reconcilability": for all $S \in \mathcal{X}$, $C(S) \subseteq M(R, S)$. Thus, under reconcilability, not all maximal elements are required to be chosen but all chosen elements are required to be maximal. So, for instance, the choice function of the preceding paragraph, although not rationalizable, is reconcilable by $xIy$, $xPz$ and $yPz$. However, while appealing, this weakening of rationalizability is not discriminating: by setting $R$ equal to universal indifference over all alternatives, *all* choice functions are reconcilable.

It turns out that in answering the question of which choice functions are rationalizable we can, without loss of generality, restrict attention to a particular binary relation derived from the choice function itself. Given a choice function $C(\cdot)$, define the *base relation* associated with $C(\cdot)$, denoted $R_C$, by

$$\forall x, y \in X, \ xR_Cy \Leftrightarrow x \in C(\{x, y\}).$$

Because $C(\{x, y\}) \neq \emptyset$ for all $x, y \in X$, $R_C$ is necessarily reflexive and complete.

**Lemma 1.1** $C(\cdot)$ *is rationalizable if and only if it is rationalized by its base relation* $R_C$, *i.e. if and only if for all* $S \in \mathcal{X}$, $C(S) = M(R_C, S)$.

**Proof.** Sufficiency is obvious (if $R_C$ rationalizes $C(\cdot)$ then by definition $C(\cdot)$ is rationalizable), so let $R$ rationalize $C(\cdot)$; we will show that in fact any such $R$ must be equal to $R_C$. For all $x, y \in X$ we have by definition of $M(R, \cdot)$ that $xRy \Leftrightarrow x \in M(R, \{x, y\})$, and, since $R$ rationalizes $C(\cdot)$, $x \in M(R, \{x, y\}) \Leftrightarrow x \in C(\{x, y\})$. But by the definition of $R_C$, we have that $x \in C(\{x, y\}) \Leftrightarrow xR_Cy$. Therefore, for all $x, y \in X$, $xRy \Leftrightarrow xR_Cy$, implying $R = R_C$. $\square$

So in what follows we can without loss of generality focus on the base relation as that which does or does not rationalize a given choice function.

Next, we turn to a set of consistency conditions for choice functions. These conditions take the form of restrictions on how a choice function $C(\cdot)$ behaves as we vary the situation (i.e. the subset of feasible alternatives) to which it is applied.

**Definition 1.5** *A choice function* $C(\cdot)$ *satisfies condition* $\alpha$ *if and only if for all* $S, T \in \mathcal{X}$, $S \subseteq T$ *implies* $C(T) \cap S \subseteq C(S)$.

*the preference relation we can derive w/o assuming rationality by just seeing which of 2 option gets chosen* α = "contraction - consistency"

Condition $\alpha$ requires that if $x$ is chosen from $T$ and we remove alternatives (not including $x$) from $T$, then $x$ should still be chosen. But notice that the condition does not preclude alternatives rejected from $T$ being chosen from $S$. This is reasonable because an alternative rejected from $T$ may have been rejected due to the presence of a superior alternative available in $T$ but not in $S$. The definition is depicted graphically in Figure 1.1.

*alternatives chosen from the big set but not chosen from the smaller set; doesn't make sense*

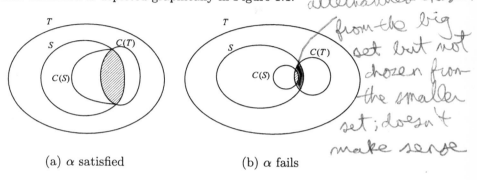

(a) $\alpha$ satisfied         (b) $\alpha$ fails

Figure 1.1: Condition $\alpha$

Condition $\alpha$ formalizes the intuitive property of choice behavior that if some alternative ($x$) is chosen in a large contest ($T$), then it should still be chosen in any smaller contest ($S$) that involves only some of the originally available alternatives (including $x$) but no new possibilities. Although apparently reasonable, not all choice functions used in the political world satisfy the property. For example, a common electoral rule in multi-candidate contests is the *runoff rule*. In essence this rule chooses candidates from any given set that are top-ranked in that set by the most number of individuals. If the set of candidates chosen, say $S$, from all those running, say $T$, contains more than a single individual, then the rule is applied a second time to the set $S$ itself. In principle, this iteration could continue; in practice, only two rounds are typically used with a tie-breaker whenever the second iteration fails to identify a single individual (for example, under the French system ties are broken in favor of the oldest candidate). The runoff rule fails condition $\alpha$.

*eg. where $C(T)$ is primary winners $\nu C(S)$ is general election winner*

To see that runoff violates $\alpha$, suppose each of five individuals has transitive strict preferences over a finite set of alternatives $T = \{x, y, z\}$ and, for any nonempty subset $S \subseteq T$, for all $b \in S$, let $v_S(b)$ denote the number of individuals with $b$ top-ranked in $S$. Define the choice function $C$ by:

$$\forall S \subseteq 2^T \setminus \{\emptyset\}, \; C(S) = \{a \in S : \forall b \in S, \; v_S(a) \geq v_S(b)\}.$$

Now let individuals 1 and 2 rank $x$ better than $y$ and $y$ better than $z$; let individuals 3 and 4 rank $y$ better than $z$ and $z$ better than $x$; and let individual 5 rank $z$ better than $x$ and $x$ better than $y$. Let $S = \{x, y\}$. Then $C(T) = \{x, y\} = S$, but $C(S) = \{x\}$.

The importance of condition $\alpha$, an example of a "contraction-consistency" property, is apparent from the following result.

**Lemma 1.2** *If $C(\cdot)$ satisfies $\alpha$, then $R_C$ is acyclic.*

**Proof.** Let $T = \{x_1, \ldots, x_n\}$ and suppose $x_1 P_C x_2$, $x_2 P_C x_3, \ldots, x_{n-1} P_C x_n$; we wish to show that if $C(\cdot)$ satisfies $\alpha$, then $x_1 R_C x_n$. For any $i = 2, \ldots, n$, suppose $x_i \in C(T)$; then $\alpha$ implies $x_i \in C(\{x_{i-1}, x_i\})$ which, by definition of the base relation, contradicts $x_{i-1} P_C x_i$. Hence, $x_i \notin C(T)$, $i = 2, \ldots, n$. Therefore since $C(T) \neq \emptyset$, it must be that $x_1 \in C(T)$. Applying $\alpha$ again, then, it must be that $x_1 \in C(\{x_1, x_n\})$, implying $x_1 R_C x_n$. $\square$

Therefore, if $C(\cdot)$ satisfies $\alpha$ then, by Lemma 1.2 and Theorem 1.1, the maximal set $M(R_C, S)$ will be nonempty for all $S$. Yet it may be that $C(\cdot)$ is not rationalizable, as the following example shows:

**Example 1.3** Let $X = \{x, y, z\}$ with $C(\{x, y\}) = \{x, y\}$, $C(\{x, z\}) = \{x\}$, $C(\{y, z\}) = \{y\}$, $C(X) = \{x\}$. Then $C(\cdot)$ satisfies $\alpha$, and hence the base relation is acyclic: $x I_C y$, $x P_C z$, $y P_C z$. But $M(R_C, X) = \{x, y\} \neq C(X)$. $\square$

The wedge between the maximal set and the choice set in Example 1.3 is not due to choice behavior as the set of available alternatives is reduced, but to choice behavior as the set is expanded. This suggests that along with a contraction-consistency property on choices, rationalizability of a choice function also requires some sort of "expansion-consistency" condition. Such a property is the following.

**Definition 1.6** *A choice function $C(\cdot)$ satisfies condition $\gamma$ if and only if for all $S, T \in \mathcal{X}$, $C(S) \cap C(T) \subseteq C(S \cup T)$.*

In words, condition $\gamma$ asks that if $x$ is chosen from $S$ and from $T$, then $x$ should be among those chosen when considering all of $S$ and $T$. Analogous to condition $\alpha$, condition $\gamma$ does not preclude alternatives rejected in both choices from $S$ and $T$ being chosen when all alternatives from $S$ and $T$ are considered together. Figure 1.2 illustrates the condition.

γ = "expansion consistency"

elements chosen in both S+T, but not chosen when all elements of both are considered together") doesn't make sense

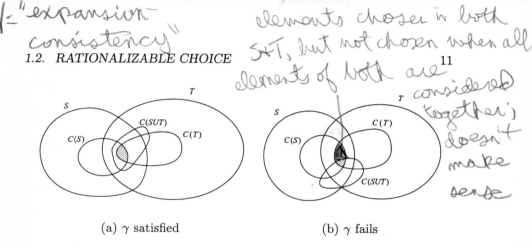

(a) γ satisfied  (b) γ fails

Figure 1.2: Condition γ

Condition $\gamma$ is sensible: if an alternative is chosen in several small contests, then that alternative should be chosen in a large contest involving all of the alternatives from the smaller ones. But as with condition $\alpha$, not all political choice rules satisfy the property. For example, *plurality rule* (whereby an alternative $x$ is chosen over an alternative $y$ if the number of individuals strictly preferring $x$ to $y$ exceeds the number strictly preferring $y$ to $x$) with more than two candidates fails to satisfy condition $\gamma$. To see this, assume the set of all candidates is $X = \{x, y, z\}$ and the choice function is the same as that for the runoff example above; *viz.*:

$$\forall S \in \mathcal{X}, \ C(S) = \{a \in S : \forall b \in S, \ v_S(a) \geq v_S(b)\}.$$

$$\begin{array}{ccc} 45 & 35 & 20 \\ x & z & y \\ y & y & x \\ z & x & z \end{array}$$

Assume there is a large electorate, each member of which has transitive strict preferences over $X$. Let 45% of the electorate rank $x$ better than $y$ and $y$ better than $z$; 35% of the electorate ranks $z$ better than $y$ and $y$ better than $x$; and the remaining 20% of the electorate ranks $y$ better than $x$ and $x$ better than $z$. Then $C(\{x, y\}) = C(\{y, z\}) = \{y\}$ but $C(X) = \{x\}$.

**Theorem 1.2** $C(\cdot)$ *is rationalizable if and only if it satisfies $\alpha$ and $\gamma$.*

**Proof.** (Sufficiency) By Lemma 1.2, $R_C$ is acyclic; hence, by Theorem 1.1, for all $T \in \mathcal{X}$, $M(R_C, T) \neq \emptyset$. Now let $\{x, y\} \subseteq T$. By $\alpha$, $\{x, y\} \cap C(T) \subseteq C(\{x, y\})$. So by definition of $R_C$, $x \in C(T)$ and $y \in T$ imply $xR_Cy$. Therefore, $C(T) \subseteq M(R_C, T)$. Let $x \in M(R_C, T)$; then for all $y \in T$, $x \in C(\{x, y\})$. By $\gamma$, therefore, $x \in C(\{x, y\}) \cap C(\{x, z\})$ implies $x \in C(\{x, y, z\})$. Hence, for any $w \in T \backslash \{x, y, z\}$, $\gamma$ implies $x \in C(\{x, y, z\}) \cap C(\{x, w\})$ and therefore $x \in C(\{x, y, z, w\})$; etc. Since $T$ is finite, repeated applications of $\gamma$ eventually yield $x \in C(T)$. And because $x$

is an arbitrary element of $M(R_C, T)$, therefore, we have $M(R_C, T) \subseteq C(T)$. Thus $M(R_C, T) = C(T)$ and the result follows from Lemma 1.1.

(Necessity) To see that $\alpha$ is necessary, let $x \in C(T) \cap S$, where $S \subseteq T$; then since $R_C$ rationalizes $C(\cdot)$ (by Lemma 1.1), it must be that for all $y \in T$, $xR_Cy$ and, therefore, for all $y \in S$ $xR_Cy$. Thus $x \in M(R_C, S)$ and, since $R_C$ rationalizes $C(\cdot)$, we have $x \in C(S)$, as required. To see that $\gamma$ is necessary, let $x \in C(S) \cap C(T)$; then since $R_C$ rationalizes $C(\cdot)$ we have for all $y \in S$, $xR_Cy$ and for all $z \in T$, $xR_Cz$. Hence, for all $y \in S \cup T$, $xR_Cy$. Therefore $x \in M(R_C, S \cup T)$ and, since $R_C$ rationalizes $C(\cdot)$, we have $x \in C(S \cup T)$.$\square$

## 1.3    Application: The unitary actor assumption

It is immediate from Theorem 1.2 and the examples used above to illustrate conditions $\alpha$ and $\gamma$ that, in general, the choices of electorates using either the runoff choice rule or simple plurality rule for multi-candidate contests cannot be interpreted analytically as if driven by some underlying "social preference" relation.

For a somewhat different illustration of the value of the axiomatization given in Theorem 1.2, consider the common assumption in international relations theory that countries can be treated as rational unitary actors. Suppose in fact that foreign policy in some country, say the USA, is the outcome of bargaining between the President and the Congress in which the former influences policy choice in part by the threat of using his or her veto power. Then removing this threat is equivalent to removing an unchosen alternative from the set of possible outcomes. But since, by hypothesis, the threat supported the actual policy selected, removing the threat alters the policy choice. Thus observed USA foreign policy choices will violate condition $\alpha$, in which case such choices are not rationalizable; i.e. it is illegitimate to treat the foreign policy of the USA as if it were the choice a unitary actor with acyclic preferences.

## 1.4    Transitive rationalizability

Since by definition a choice function $C(\cdot)$ is such that $C(S)$ is nonempty for all $S \in \mathcal{X}$, Theorem 1.1 implies that if a binary relation $R$ rationalizes $C(\cdot)$, $R$ must be acyclic (as well as reflexive and complete). Theorem 1.2 then characterizes rationalizable choice functions; i.e. provides conditions on choices under which such choices are consistent with an underlying acyclic preference relation on $X$. As remarked earlier, acyclicity is in a real sense a minimal rationality condition on preferences. It is therefore of some interest to look for conditions on rationalizable choices under which the implicit preference relation on $X$ exhibits rationality properties stronger than acyclicity. In particular, when is $C(\cdot)$ rationalized by a quasi-transitive or a transitive relation $R$?

Example 1.3 showed how the base relation is acyclic, but not necessarily quasi-transitive, when $C(\cdot)$ satisfies $\alpha$; in addition the base relation did not rationalize $C(\cdot)$. The next example shows the same lack of quasi-transitivity when $C(\cdot)$ satisfies $\alpha$ and $\gamma$ (i.e. when $R_C$ *does* rationalize $C(\cdot)$).

**Example 1.4** Let $X = \{x, y, z\}$ with $\{x\} = C(\{x, y\})$, $\{y\} = C(\{y, z\})$, $\{x, z\} = C(\{x, z\})$, $\{x\} = C(\{x, y, z\})$; then $C(\cdot)$ satisfies $\alpha$ and $\gamma$, so $R_C$ rationalizes $C(\cdot)$, but $R_C$ is not quasi-transitive: $x P_C y$, $y P_C z$, and $x I_C z$.□

So $\alpha$ and $\gamma$ are not sufficient to insure any rationality beyond acyclicity. In view of the common parliamentary practice of selecting from a set of alternatives by dividing the set into smaller subsets, choosing some alternative(s) from each subset, and finally making the final decision from the choices so made, the following condition has considerable empirical relevance.

**Definition 1.7** *A choice function $C(\cdot)$ satisfies path independence (PI) if and only if for all $S, T \in \mathcal{X}$, $C(S \cup T) = C(C(S) \cup C(T))$.*

Path independence says the following: if $S \cup T = V$, then the choices from $V$ are the same as those arrived at by "decentralizing" the problem and first choosing from $S$ and from $T$, and then choosing from among these chosen alternatives. In other words, what is eventually chosen via decentralizing the problem should not depend on the details of the decentralization.

**Lemma 1.3** *If $C(\cdot)$ satisfies PI then*
   *(1) $C(\cdot)$ satisfies $\alpha$; and*
   *(2) the base relation $R_C$ is quasi-transitive.*

**Proof.** To see (1), let $S \subseteq T$ and let $x \in S \cap C(T)$; then by PI we have that $x \in C(C(S) \cup C(T \backslash S))$, which can only occur if $x \in C(S)$. To see (2), let $x P_C y$ and $y P_C z$. By the definition of $R_C$ we have $C(\{x, y\}) = \{x\}$ and $C(\{y, z\}) = \{y\}$; therefore by PI $C(\{x, y, z\}) = C(C(\{x\}) \cup C(\{y, z\})) = C(\{x\} \cup \{y\}) = \{x\}$. But also $C(\{x, y, z\}) = C(C(\{x, y\}) \cup C(\{z\})) = C(\{x\} \cup \{z\})$, so that $\{x\} = C(\{x, z\})$. Hence, $x P_C z$ as required.□

As with condition $\alpha$, while path independence implies a certain degree of consistency in the base relation $R_C$, it does not characterize rationalizable choice functions by itself:

**Example 1.5** Let $X = \{x, y, z\}$ with $C(\{x, y\}) = \{x, y\}$, $C(\{y, z\}) = \{y, z\}$, $C(\{x, z\}) = \{x, z\}$, and $C(X) = \{x, y\}$; then $C(\cdot)$ satisfies PI, and so $R_C$ is quasi-transitive ($xI_Cy$, $yI_Cz$, $xI_Cz$), but $C(\cdot)$ is not rationalized by $R_C$ (and hence is not rationalizable): $M(R_C, X) = X \neq \{x, y\} = C(X)$.□

**Theorem 1.3** $C(\cdot)$ *is rationalized by a quasi-transitive relation if and only if it satisfies PI and* $\gamma$.

**Proof.** (Sufficiency) By Lemma 1.3(1) PI implies $\alpha$; therefore by Theorem 1.2 $C(\cdot)$ is rationalizable by $R_C$. And by Lemma 1.3(2), $R_C$ is quasi-transitive.

(Necessity) That $\gamma$ is necessary follows from Theorem 1.2 as well. To see that PI is necessary, we have by Lemma 1.1 that, for all $S, T \in \mathcal{X}$,

$$C(C(S) \cup C(T)) = M(R_C, C(S) \cup C(T)) = M(R_C, M(R_C, S) \cup M(R_C, T)).$$

We wish to show that $M(R_C, M(R_C, S) \cup M(R_C, T))$ equals $M(R_C, S \cup T)$, and hence equals $C(S \cup T)$. Since

$$M(R_C, S \cup T) \subseteq M(R_C, M(R_C, S) \cup M(R_C, T))$$

is immediate from the definition of $M(R_C, \cdot)$, we need only show that

$$M(R_C, M(R_C, S) \cup M(R_C, T)) \subseteq M(R_C, S \cup T).$$

Let $x \in M(R_C, M(R_C, S) \cup M(R_C, T))$ and, without loss of generality, assume $x \in S$. Then $x$ must be in $M(R_C, S)$ and so, for all $y \in S$, $xR_Cy$. Further, for all $z \in M(R_C, T)$, $xR_Cz$. Next, since $R_C$ is assumed quasi-transitive, for all $w \notin M(R_C, T)$ there exists some $v \in M(R_C, T)$ such that $vP_Cw$ (recall the implication of quasi-transitivity when $R$ is complete). Therefore, since $xR_Cv$ for any such $v$ and $R_C$ is quasi-transitive, for all $w \notin M(R_C, T)$, $xR_Cw$ as well. Hence, for all $s \in S \cup T$, $xR_Cs$ implying $x \in M(R_C, S \cup T)$, as desired.□

Comparing Theorems 1.3 and 1.4, we see that in moving from rationalizability by an acyclic preference relation to the more demanding rationalizability by a quasi-transitive relation, it is the contraction-consistency property of the choice function that is strengthened. For both characterization results, the expansion-consistency property, condition $\gamma$, suffices. Is this feature of the characterizations fundamental? That is, for any rationalizable choice function $C(\cdot)$, do the consistency properties of the underlying base relation $R_C$ depend critically on contraction-consistency, rather than expansion-consistency, properties of $C(\cdot)$? The answer is No, as is apparent from Theorem 1.4 below that deals with the issue of when a choice function can be rationalized by a transitive (and therefore by a quasi-transitive or acyclic) binary relation.

**Definition 1.8** *A choice function $C(\cdot)$ satisfies condition $\beta$ if and only if for all $S, T \in \mathcal{X}$, $S \subseteq T$ and $C(S) \cap C(T) \neq \emptyset$ imply $C(S) \subseteq C(T)$.*

That is, if $x$ is chosen from a set $(S)$, the set expands $(T)$, and $x$ is still chosen, then all previously chosen alternatives must again be chosen. Note that any resolute choice function automatically satisfies $\beta$ (since then $C(S) \cap C(T) \neq \emptyset$ automatically implies $C(S) = C(T)$).

While $\beta$ is an expansion-consistency condition like $\gamma$, there is no logical relation between the two. Example 1.4 above gives an instance of a choice function satisfying $\gamma$ but not $\beta$, and the following example shows the converse.

**Example 1.6** Let $X = \{x, y, z\}$ with $\{x\} = C(\{x,y\})$, $\{y\} = C(\{y,z\})$, $\{x\} = C(\{x,z\})$, $\{y\} = C(\{x,y,z\})$; then $C(\cdot)$ satisfies $\beta$ (since $C(\cdot)$ is resolute) but does not satisfy $\gamma$ (which would require $x$ to be in $C(\{x,y,z\})$ as well).□

However, in the presence of $\alpha$ we have that $\beta$ implies $\gamma$ and, further, that the base relation $R_C$ is transitive.

$$\alpha + \beta \rightarrow \gamma \ \& \ R_c \ \text{trans}$$

**Lemma 1.4** *If $C(\cdot)$ satisfies $\alpha$ and $\beta$ then*
  *(1) $C(\cdot)$ satisfies $\gamma$; and*
  *(2) the base relation $R_C$ is transitive.*

**Proof.** (1) Let $x \in C(S) \cap C(V)$ and let $T = S \cup V$; we wish to show $x \in C(T)$. Let $z \in S \cap C(T)$; then by $\alpha$, $z \in C(S)$ as well. But then $C(S) \cap C(T) \neq \emptyset$ so that, by $\beta$, $C(S) \subseteq C(T)$. Thus since $x \in C(S)$, we have $x \in C(T)$, as desired.
  (2) Suppose $xR_Cy$ & $yR_Cz$; we wish to show $x \in C(\{x,z\})$. (i) If $x \in C(\{x,y,z\})$, then by $\alpha$ it must be that $x \in C(\{x,z\})$, as desired. (ii) If $y \in C(\{x,y,z\})$, then $\alpha$ implies $y \in C(\{x,y\})$, and so by $\beta$ it must be that

$x \in C(\{x, y, z\})$ as well; thus by (i) we are done. (iii) If $z \in C(\{x, y, z\})$ then $\alpha$ implies $z \in C(\{y, z\})$, and so by $\beta$ it must be that $y \in C(\{x, y, z\})$ as well; thus by (ii) we are done. Since $C(\{x, y, z\}) \neq \emptyset$, then, these three cases are exhaustive. Therefore, $\alpha$ plus $\beta$ imply $R_C$ is transitive.$\square$

**Theorem 1.4** $C(\cdot)$ *is rationalized by a transitive relation if and only if it satisfies $\alpha$ and $\beta$.*

**Proof.** (Sufficiency) Follows from Lemma 1.4 and Theorem 1.2.

(Necessity) Necessity of $\alpha$ is a consequence of Theorem 1.2 showing $\alpha$ to be necessary if $C(\cdot)$ is rationalizable at all. To see that $\beta$ is necessary, let $S \subseteq T$, $x \in C(S) \cap C(T)$, and $y \in C(S)$. We wish to check that $y \in C(T)$. Since $y \in C(S)$ and $R_C$ rationalizes $C(\cdot)$, it must be that $yR_Cx$. Further, since $x \in C(T)$ we have that for all $z \in T$, $xR_Cz$. Since $R_C$ is assumed transitive, then, for all $z \in T$, $yR_Cz$ as well implying $y \in C(T)$.$\square$

Since condition $\beta$ automatically holds when a choice function is resolute, we have an immediate corollary.

**Corollary 1.1** *If a choice function $C(\cdot)$ is resolute, then it is rationalized by a transitive relation if and only if it satisfies $\alpha$.*

An alternative logic for Corollary 1.1 (specifically, one that is independent of condition $\beta$) is the following: if $C(\cdot)$ is resolute, then the base relation $R_C$ admits no indifference between distinct alternatives. In this case, transitivity, quasi-transitivity, and acyclicity are all equivalent (since $R_C$ is complete) and therefore any rationalizable resolute choice function is transitively rationalizable. Next, if $C(\cdot)$ satisfies $\alpha$ then by Lemma 1.2 $R_C$ is acyclic and, therefore, transitive if $C(\cdot)$ is resolute. Finally, $C(\cdot)$ resolute and satisfying $\alpha$ implies $C(\cdot)$ satisfies $\gamma$ as well, thereby establishing rationalizability (in fact, all that is needed for this result is that $C(\cdot)$ be pairwise resolute, i.e. for all $x, y \in X$, $C(\{x, y\})$ is singleton).

So far we have characterized rationalizable choice functions (of varying degrees of "rationality") by the intersection of one contraction-consistency property and one expansion-consistency property. This suggests that, by focusing on the properties of such intersections, we should be able to formulate conditions that individually characterize rationalizable choice functions. We close this section by introducing two such conditions, each of which identifies choice functions admitting transitive rationalizations.

**Definition 1.9** *A choice function $C(\cdot)$ satisfies the Arrow axiom if and only if for all $S \subseteq T$, $S \cap C(T) = \emptyset$ or $S \cap C(T) = C(S)$.*

This is a natural strengthening of $\alpha$, from $S \cap C(T) \subseteq C(S)$ to $S \cap C(T) = C(S)$ (or else $S \cap C(T) = \emptyset$). The condition then states that if $S$ is a subset of $T$ and if there exist alternatives in $S$ that are chosen from $T$, then it is precisely these alternatives that must be chosen from $S$.

The final condition we consider differs from the previous criteria in that it is not exclusively concerned with choice consistency between subsets and supersets. In particular, it says that if an alternative $x$ is revealed "better" than another, $y$, in that $x$ is chosen when $y$ is rejected, then if ever $y$ is chosen $x$ must not be available.

**Definition 1.10** *A choice function $C(\cdot)$ satisfies the weak axiom of revealed preference (WARP) if and only if for all $S, T \in \mathcal{X}$, $x \in C(S)$, $y \in S \backslash C(S)$ and $y \in C(T)$ imply $x \notin T$.*

Figure 1.3 illustrates WARP.

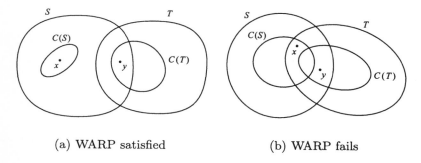

(a) WARP satisfied                        (b) WARP fails

Figure 1.3: Weak Axiom of Revealed Preference

The final result of the chapter demonstrates just how each of these two conditions on choice capture the intersection of the relevant contraction-consistency and expansion-consistency properties on a choice function necessary for rationalizability by a transitive relation. Perhaps more surprisingly the result also shows, from a purely formal perspective, that the Arrow axiom and WARP are in fact identical conditions.

**Theorem 1.5** *The following are equivalent:*
  *(1) $C(\cdot)$ satisfies $\alpha$ and $\beta$*
  *(2) $C(\cdot)$ satisfies Arrow*
  *(3) $C(\cdot)$ satisfies WARP.*

**Proof.** We show $(1) \Rightarrow (2) \Rightarrow (3) \Rightarrow (1)$.

$(1) \Rightarrow (2)$: Let $S \subseteq T$. By $\alpha$, $S \cap C(T) \subseteq C(S)$. What remains to be shown is that if $S \cap C(T) \neq \emptyset$, then $C(S) \subseteq S \cap C(T)$. Let $x \in S \cap C(T)$; then, by $\alpha$, $x \in C(S)$ as well. Therefore $C(S) \cap C(T) \neq \emptyset$, and so by $\beta$ $C(S) \subseteq C(T)$. But then, since $C(S) \subseteq S$, it must be that $C(S) \subseteq S \cap C(T)$.

$(2) \Rightarrow (3)$: Let $V$ and $T$ be any two sets in $\mathcal{X}$. Let $x \in C(V)$, $y \in V \backslash C(V)$, and $y \in C(T)$; we want to show that if $C(\cdot)$ satisfies Arrow, then $x \notin T$. Define $S = V \cap T$, which is nonempty since $y \in V$ and $y \in T$. Because $y \in C(T)$, $S \cap C(T) \neq \emptyset$; and since $S \subseteq T$ we have by Arrow that $S \cap C(T) = C(S)$. Therefore $y \in C(S)$. But since $y \notin S \cap C(V)$, $S \cap C(V) \neq C(S)$ and, since $S \subseteq V$, we have by Arrow that $S \cap C(V) = \emptyset$. But then $x \in C(V)$ implies $x \notin S$, which implies $x \notin T$.

$(3) \Rightarrow (1)$: Let $S \subseteq T$. WARP implies that if $y \in S \backslash C(S)$ then $y \notin C(T)$, which is the contrapositive of $\alpha$. To see that WARP implies $\beta$, suppose $x \in C(S) \cap C(T)$ and $y \in C(S)$; we need to show $y \in C(T)$. But if $y \notin C(T)$, then we would have $x \in C(T)$, $y \in T \backslash C(T)$, $y \in C(S)$, and $x \in S$, which contradicts WARP.$\Box$

Therefore, by Theorem 1.4, $C(\cdot)$ satisfying WARP is equivalent to $C(\cdot)$ being rationalizable by a transitive relation, and similarly for Arrow.

## 1.5  Application: Choice of coalitional partners

In Section 1.3, we illustrated the rationalizability theorem (Theorem 1.2) by observing that some institutional feature of the policy-making process, in the example the Presidential veto in the USA, could invalidate an assumption that a collective (in the example, the USA) might plausibly be considered a unitary rational actor when building models of foreign policy determination. This of course does not imply that either the President or members of Congress themselves are not rational actors. A similar observation can be made when considering parliamentary parties.

Post-WWII politics in West Germany has essentially involved three major political parties: the Social Democrats (SPD), the Free Democrats (FPD), and the Christian Democrats (CDU). Typically, no party wins an outright majority in the general election and government is by coalition. For instance, in both 1965 and 1969 the family of possible governing coalitions included any pair of parties from the set {SPD,CDU,FDP}; the 1965 governing coalition was {CDU,FDP} and the 1969 coalition was {SPD,FDP}.

If we wish to treat the FDP as a given rational actor over the period then, in view of its choices in 1965 and 1969, its preferences over the set

$$X = \{\{\text{CDU,SPD}\}, \{\text{CDU,FDP}\}, \{\text{SPD,FDP}\}\}$$

have to be given by the transitive relation $R^{FDP}$ such that

$$\{\text{CDU,FDP}\} I^{FDP} \{\text{SPD,FDP}\} P^{FDP} \{\text{CDU,SPD}\}.$$

Given these preferences the FDP's implied choice function is not resolute. In particular,

$$M(R^{FDP}, \{\{\text{CDU,FDP}\}, \{\text{SPD,FDP}\}\}) = \{\{\text{CDU,FDP}\}, \{\text{SPD,FDP}\}\}$$

and so both the 1965 and the 1969 choices are consistent with $R^{FDP}$. On the other hand, if we instead insist the FDP has a resolute choice function, then its choice behavior violates WARP: in 1965 the FDP agreed to form a coalition with the CDU rather than with the SPD, and in 1969 it rejected the CDU in favor of a coalition with the SPD. Therefore, under the assumption of resoluteness, Theorem 1.5 implies that the choice behavior of the FDP has no transitive rationalization and, moreover, must violate condition $\alpha$ or condition $\beta$. However, there is nothing in the theory or the data given here that tells us which of the two alternative interpretations - nonresolute choice function with a transitive rationalization, or resolute choice function without a transitive rationalization – is correct.

## 1.6  Discussion

Explanations of political outcomes within positive political theory typically begin with the presumption that such outcomes are the results of purposive decisions made by relevant individuals (e.g. voters, legislators, bureaucrats, or revolutionaries) or groups of individuals (e.g. political parties, interest groups, or nation states). Since purposive decisions are held to reflect active choices and appropriately considered evaluations of relative merit, concepts of "choice" and "preference" for individuals and groups are fundamental to the theory. In this chapter, therefore, we formalize these two concepts and study some important relationships between them. Specifically, for any set $X$ of alternatives, preferences over the set are modeled as a binary relation on $X$, where a natural substantive interpretation of the relation, say $R$, is "at least as good as"; and choices from $X$ are modeled as a mapping, say $C$, from the family of all nonempty subsets of $X$ into itself that identifies which alternatives are selected.

While tightly defined, the theory developed here is extremely flexible. For example, the given set of alternatives could be a set of final outcomes such as the list of candidates for the presidency of the USA, or it might be a set of actions such as whether a country is to threaten a foreign nation with military intervention or to impose economic sanctions. In the first example, an individual's preferences over presidential candidates might be taken as primitive and exogenous whereas, in the second example, his or her preferences might be derived from beliefs about the likely consequences of each action. Similarly, a choice in the first example might refer to the choice of an electorate or a single voter and, in the second example, the choice could be that of a legislative committee or a head of state. With these remarks in mind, we address three issues about choice and preference in the given sense.

The first issue concerns what must be true of preferences to insure well-defined choice. Since choice is defined in terms of selecting a nonempty subset of alternatives from those available and preference is defined in terms of a binary relation "at least as good as", this issue amounts to finding conditions on this relation $R$ under which the set of $R$-maximal elements from those available is always nonempty (where an alternative $x$ is $R$-maximal in a set if, for all alternatives $y$ in the set, $xRy$). Theorem 1.1 identifies an appropriate set of conditions when any set of available alternatives is finite. The most important condition is that $R$ is *acyclic* on $X$. Acyclicity is called a rationality condition on $R$; it is not the strongest such condition (transitivity is the strongest) and neither is it the weakest (Exercise 1.2). However, Theorem 1.1 tells us that acyclicity is the weakest rationality condition consistent with preferences supporting a well-defined choice from every (finite) set of alternatives. Consequently, if we wish to model decision-makers, be they individuals or collectivities, as having preferences and making choices that reflect these preferences (i.e. as choosing $R$-maximal alternatives), then necessarily we must assume that decision-makers are rational at least to the extent that their preferences are acyclic.

Perhaps regrettably, preferences are not directly observable; at most choices are observable. The second issue addressed, then, concerns the rationalizability of choices; that is, the properties of choice behavior that legitimize any inference that choices reflect consistent preferences. Thus we wish to identify conditions on $C$ that lead to observed choices which always coincide with the $R$-maximal alternatives for a given preference relation $R$. In view of Theorem 1.1, therefore, such properties must also imply that $R$ is acyclic (Lemma 1.2 and Theorem 1.2). As remarked earlier, care must be taken when interpreting the results here, especially when observed choices violate the identified properties for rationalizability. Such violations do not necessarily imply that the observed choices fail to reflect rational, preference-driven, decision-making; only that the pattern of observed choices is not sufficient for an analyst to conclude surely that it reflects such decision-making (Section 1.5 illustrates this point).

The final issue considered in Chapter 1 is largely an elaboration of the second: given that a choice behavior is rationalizable, what more can we say about the extent to which the implicit preferences are rational than that they must be acyclic? Theorems 1.3, 1.4, and 1.5 describe the most important answers to this question and provide logical connections between the theoretical construct of transitive or quasi-transitive preferences and the observable choice behavior consistent with such a construct.

For the remainder of this book, we take individual preferences over final outcomes as primitives to any model, assuming moreover that such preferences are at least transitive. This assumption should not be interpreted as an empirical claim about people. Rather it is a conservative methodological presumption: if individuals are as rational as conceivable yet, as a group, their collective decisions are subject to irrationality, then this is an important finding. In contrast, deriving collective inconsistency from a model in which individuals are subject to no rationality constraints is without interest. Given a list of (transitive) individual preferences the fundamental problem in collective choice, that is, in moving from these individual preferences to social decisions, is to determine whether the concept of "collective preference" has any meaning. In other words, when is it the case that a collective preference relation derived from individual preferences supports collective choices that are maximal with respect to that relation? The preceding results elucidating the formal connections between choice and preference, although apparently abstract, prove important when exploring this problem.

## 1.7 Exercises

**1.1** (a) Prove that a binary relation $R$ is transitive on $X$ if and only if the following three conditions hold for all $\{x, y, z\} \subseteq X$:

(1) $xPy$ & $yPz \Rightarrow xPz$

(2) $xIy$ & $yIz \Rightarrow xIz$

(3) $xIy$ & $yPz \Rightarrow xPz$, and $xPy$ & $yIz \Rightarrow xPz$.

(b) Prove that if $R$ is complete (but not necessarily transitive), then (1) and (2) imply (3).

**1.2** A binary relation $R$ is *triple-acyclic* on $X$ if and only if, for all triples $\{x,y,z\} \subseteq X$, $R$ is acyclic on $\{x,y,z\}$. Prove that if $R$ is acyclic on $X$ then $R$ is triple-acyclic on $X$, but not the converse.

**1.3** A choice function $C(\cdot)$ satisfies *condition* $\alpha 2$ iff, $\forall S \in \mathcal{X}$, $x \in C(S)$ implies $x \in C(\{x,y\})$, $\forall y \in S \backslash \{x\}$; and $C(\cdot)$ satisfies *condition* $\gamma 2$ iff, $\forall S \in \mathcal{X}$, $x \in S$ & $x \in C(\{x,y\})$, $\forall y \in S \backslash \{x\}$ imply $x \in C(S)$. Prove or provide counterexamples to each of the following claims.
   (a) Condition $\alpha$ implies $\alpha 2$ but not the converse.
   (b) Condition $\gamma$ implies $\gamma 2$ but not the converse.
   (c) A choice function $C(\cdot)$ satisfies both $\alpha$ and $\gamma$ if and only if it satisfies both $\alpha 2$ and $\gamma 2$.
   (d) If $C(\cdot)$ satisfies $\alpha 2$ then $R_C$ is acyclic.

**1.4** Discuss the implications of your answers to Exercise 1.3 for the results in Chapter 1 on rationalizable choice functions.

**1.5** In the definition of path independence, $S$ and $T$ need not partition $V$, i.e. $S \cap T$ may be nonempty. A weaker demand is that a choice function $C(\cdot)$ satisfies *partition path independence* (PPI): $\forall S, T \in \mathcal{X}$ such that $S \cap T = \emptyset$, $C(S \cup T) = C(C(S) \cup C(T))$.
   (a) Construct a choice function $C(\cdot)$ that satisfies PPI but not PI.
   (b) Which of the results in Chapter 1 involving PI, if any, fail when PI is replaced by PPI? (Be sure to prove your answer where necessary.)

**1.6** Prove, or provide counterexamples to, the following claims:
   (a) if $C(\cdot)$ satisfies PPI, then $C(\cdot)$ satisfies $\alpha$
   (b) if $C(\cdot)$ is resolute, then $\alpha 2$ and $\gamma 2$ are equivalent.

**1.7** Prove that if $\forall S \in \mathcal{X}$, $M(R,S) \neq \emptyset$, then $R$ is transitive iff $M(R, \cdot)$ satisfies $\beta$.

**1.8** A choice function $C(\cdot)$ satisfies *condition* $\epsilon$ iff $S \subset T$ implies $\sim [C(T) \subset C(S)]$. Prove or disprove the following claims:
   (a) $C(\cdot)$ satisfies PI if and only if it satisfies $\alpha$ and $\epsilon$.
   (b) $C(\cdot)$ satisfies PPI if and only if it satisfies $\alpha$ and $\epsilon$.
   (c) If $C(\cdot)$ satisfies $\beta$ then it satisfies $\epsilon$.

**1.9** A choice function $C(\cdot)$ satisfies *condition* $\beta +$ iff $\forall S \subseteq T$, either $S \cap C(T) = \emptyset$ or $C(S) \subseteq S \cap C(T)$. [Note that $\alpha$ plus $\beta +$ give Arrow] Prove, or provide counterexamples to, the following claims:

(a) if $C(\cdot)$ satisfies $\beta+$ then it satisfies $\gamma2$;

(b) if $C(\cdot)$ satisfies $\beta+$ then it satisfies $\beta$;

(c) if $C(\cdot)$ satisfies $\beta+$ then the base relation $R_C$ is acyclic;

(d) $C(\cdot)$ is transitively rationalizable if and only if it satisfies $\beta+$ and $\alpha2$.

**1.10** Given a choice function $C(\cdot)$, define the *revealed preference relation*, $\bar{R}_C$, as: $\forall x, y \in X$, $x\bar{R}_C y \Leftrightarrow \exists S \in \mathcal{X}$ such that $x \in C(S)$ and $y \in S$.

(a) Give an example of a choice function for which the revealed preference relation $\bar{R}_C$ is not the same as the base relation $R_C$.

(b) Prove, or provide counterexamples to, the following claims:

(i) if $C(\cdot)$ satisfies $\gamma2$, then $\bar{R}_C = R_C$;

(ii) if $C(\cdot)$ satisfies $\alpha2$, then $\bar{R}_C = R_C$;

(iii) if $C(\cdot)$ satisfies $\beta+$, then $\bar{R}_C$ must be transitive.

## 1.8   Further reading

Samuelson [68], Houthakker [39], Chernoff [17] and Arrow [2] provide early results relating choices and preferences; important subsequent papers include Richter [59], Herzberger [38] and Sen [78]. Theorem 1.1 was first proved by von Neumann and Morgenstern [89], but Sen [77] is the standard reference for social choice theory. Plott [57] first formalized path independence and his analysis is pursued by Parks [55] and by Ferejohn and Grether [30]. Sen [77, chs. 1,1*] provides a classic overview of the theory, comprehensively updated in Suzumura [88, chs. 1,2,3]. See also Moulin [53].

# Chapter 2

# Power and Collective Rationality

Chapter 1 was concerned with the logical structure of concepts of preference and choice. This concern is motivated largely by the fact that whereas the choices of given individuals or societies are directly observable, preferences – even if they are known to exist – are not so apparent. Nevertheless, individuals are typically assumed to make choices based on some deeper notion of preference, and social choices are derived through some aggregation of these individual preferences (for instance, via majority rule or dictatorship). As such, it is important to understand the properties of the preference aggregation schemes that are used and that could be used. Further, we should like to know when social choices can legitimately be treated analogously to individual choices as reflecting some underlying "as if" social preference.

Prior to the 1950s, the approach to the issues above was largely piece-meal. Typically, someone would observe that a rule for aggregating votes exhibited some sort of undesirable property (for instance, the rule might yield intransitivities or be capable of choosing an alternative that was preferred only by a minority), and so propose an alternative scheme immune from the identified flaw. However, the alternative would sooner or later be found to violate a distinct criterion of acceptability, leading to yet another proposal; and so forth. Because the universe of conceivable methods for aggregating individuals' preferences into a social decision is huge, the piece-meal approach is not very promising. An alternative line of attack is to begin by stating a list of properties deemed necessary for any aggregation scheme to be considered acceptable and then to investigate the structure of the class of rules (if any) satisfying the properties. By varying the list,

25

we can then explore the trade-offs across rules in terms of the properties that they satisfy. This analytical perspective, and the fundamental result it reveals, is due to Kenneth Arrow and it is here that we begin. Specifically, in what follows we use the analytical apparatus and results of Chapter 1 to address the following substantive question: Given a group of individuals each of whom has preferences over some finite set of mutually exclusive alternatives (e.g. presidential candidates or levels of federal taxation), how might we aggregate these individual preferences to derive social preferences over, or social choices from, this set?

## 2.1   Aggregation and Arrow's Theorem

Let $N = \{1, \ldots, n\}$ be a finite set of individuals, $n \geq 2$, and let $X$ be a finite set of alternatives with $\mathcal{X}$ the set of all nonempty subsets of $X$. Throughout this chapter, assume $|X| \geq 3$ (where, for any finite set $Y$, $|Y|$ denotes the cardinality of $Y$). We assume throughout that each individual possesses a weak order on $X$, where we let $R_i$ denote the order for $i \in N$ and let $\mathcal{R}$ denote the set of all weak orders on $X$. When there is no indifference, individual $i$'s preferences $P_i$ are said to be *strict*, or *linear*, and $\mathcal{P}$ denotes the set of all strict orders on $X$. A *preference profile* is then an $n$-tuple of weak orders $\rho = (R_1, \ldots, R_n)$ describing the preferences of all individuals. Let $\mathcal{R}^n$ denote the set of all preference profiles, and for any $\rho \in \mathcal{R}^n$ and $S \in \mathcal{X}$ let $\rho|_S = (R_1|_S, \ldots, R_n|_S)$ denote the restriction of $\rho$ to the set $S$, i.e. $\rho|_S$ describes the individuals' preferences only over those alternatives in $S$. For any profile $\rho \in \mathcal{R}^n$ and any $x, y \in X$, let $P(x, y; \rho) \equiv \{i \in N : x P_i y\}$; the sets $R(x, y; \rho)$ and $I(x, y; \rho)$ are defined similarly. Finally, let $\mathcal{B}$ denote the set of all reflexive and complete binary relations on $X$.

**Definition 2.1** *A preference aggregation rule is a map, $f : \mathcal{R}^n \to \mathcal{B}$.*

Thus a preference aggregation rule assigns to every possible preference profile a reflexive and complete binary relation, which we can think of as the *social* preference relation $f(\rho)$. That the domain of an aggregation rule is equal to $\mathcal{R}^n$ is often referred to as a condition of *unrestricted domain*: an aggregation rule is required to give a binary relation for all logically possible preference orderings by the individuals. For notational ease, in most of the discussion below we will suppress the underlying preference profile and write $xRy$ for $x f(\rho) y$, $xPy$ for $(x f(\rho) y$ & $\sim [y f(\rho) x])$, and $xIy$ for $(x f(\rho) y$ & $y f(\rho) x)$. As well, we will at times characterize an aggregation rule by its asymmetric part only, e.g. $xPy$ under rule $f$ if and only if condition $A$

occurs, where (by the presumed completeness of $f(\cdot)$) it is understood that if $A$ does *not* occur then $yRx$.

**Example 2.1** Three examples of preference aggregation rules are:

(1) *Simple majority rule:* $\forall x, y \in X$, $xPy$ if and only if $|P(x, y; \rho)| > n/2$.

(2) *Pareto extension rule:* $\forall x, y \in X$, $xPy$ if and only if $R(x, y; \rho) = N$ and $P(x, y; \rho) \neq \emptyset$.

(3) *Borda rule:* $\forall x, y \in X$, $xPy$ if and only if $\sum_N r_i(x) < \sum_N r_i(y)$, where $r_i(x)$ is the ordinal rank of $x$ in $i$'s preference ordering on $X$ (where, for convenience, we assume all individuals have strict preferences).□

Next, consider the following three criteria an aggregation rule might satisfy:

**Definition 2.2** *An aggregation rule $f$ is:*

*(1) nondictatorial if there does not exist $i \in N$ such that, for every $\rho \in \mathcal{R}^n$ and for any $x, y \in X$, $xP_iy$ implies $xPy$.*

*(2) weakly Paretian if, for every $\rho \in \mathcal{R}^n$ and for any $x, y \in X$, and all $i \in N$, $xP_iy$ implies $xPy$.*

*(3) independent of irrelevant alternatives if, for every $\rho, \rho' \in \mathcal{R}^n$ and for any $x, y \in X$, $\rho|_{\{x,y\}} = \rho'|_{\{x,y\}}$ implies $f(\rho)|_{\{x,y\}} = f(\rho')|_{\{x,y\}}$.*

Thus, a nondictatorial aggregation rule says that no one individual has sufficient influence to have $x$ be socially preferred to $y$ whenever he or she prefers $x$ to $y$ regardless of the others' preferences; a weakly Paretian aggregation rule requires $x$ to be socially preferred to $y$ whenever all individuals strictly prefer $x$ to $y$; and an independent of irrelevant alternatives aggregation rule requires the social preference between $x$ and $y$ to depend only on the individual preferences between $x$ and $y$. Clearly, any dictatorial rule satisfies (2) and (3), yet fails to satisfy (1); a constant rule (i.e. a rule $f$ such that for some complete binary relation $T \in \mathcal{B}$ and for all $\rho \in \mathcal{R}^n$, $f(\rho) = T$) satisfies (1) and (3) but not (2); and the Borda rule satisfies (1) and (2) but not (3), as the following example demonstrates:

**Example 2.2** Let $N = \{1, 2, 3\}$, $X = \{w, x, y, z\}$, $f$ be the Borda rule, and consider the profile $\rho$ :

$$wP_1xP_1yP_1z$$

$$yP_2zP_2xP_2w$$

$$zP_3yP_3wP_3x$$

Then $wPx$, since $\sum_N r_i(w) = 8 < \sum_N r_i(x) = 9$. Now consider the profile $\rho'$ :

$$yP_1'zP_1'wP_1'x$$
$$xP_2'yP_2'zP_2'w$$
$$zP_3'yP_3'wP_3'x$$

Then $xP'w$ since $\sum_N r_i'(x) = 9 < \sum_N r_i'(w) = 10$. Yet the relative ranking of $w$ against $x$ is the same in both $\rho$ and $\rho'$.$\Box$

On the other hand, majority rule and the Pareto extension rule satisfy all of (1), (2), and (3) of Definition 2.2.

As properties of an aggregation rule, the three conditions of weak Pareto, non-dictatorship and independence of irrelevant alternatives, taken individually, are very appealing. The notion of a dictator implicit in the definition above is extreme, implying that to exclude such a dictator is mild. To see just how mild a condition non-dictatorship really is, note that a dictator as defined here differs from the colloquial use of the term in two important respects. First, it embodies considerably more power: for example, suppose there were one million pairwise decisions to be made. Then a given individual $i$ is *not* a dictator as defined here if, out of a million decisions, $i$'s strict preferences over 999,999 decisions are invariably respected by the aggregation rule under every profile but there exists *one* decision, say over $x$ and $y$, and *one* profile, say $\rho$, such that $i$ strictly prefers $x$ to $y$ under $\rho$ yet the aggregation rule declares $x$ indifferent to $y$ given $\rho$ (and only $\rho$). And second, a "dictator" may never appreciate her power. One way of understanding this is to think of a preference aggregation rule as a computer program that takes preference profiles as data input and generates a social preference ranking as output. If $f$ is dictatorial, it ignores all the data input except for a single individual $i$'s particular preference ordering and, to all intents and purposes, reproduces $i$'s ordering as the output.

Similarly, it is hard to argue against the normative requirement of weak Pareto: if everyone in a community strictly prefers one alternative to another, then the preference aggregation rule must respect this unanimous preference. And, consonant with the condition of non-dictatorship, the unanimity requirement embodied in weak Paretianism is indeed weak since it does not apply when at least one individual is indifferent over some pair of alternatives. For example if, in a society of a million individuals, 999,999 of them strictly prefer $x$ to $y$ but one individual is indifferent between $x$ and $y$, then the weak Pareto condition fails to bite and there is no requirement for the aggregation rule even to declare $x$ at least as good as $y$, let alone $x$ strictly preferred to $y$.

The independence condition is somewhat more subtle. It in fact imposes two conditions on pairwise social rankings: when arriving at a social ranking of a given pair of alternatives, an aggregation rule satisfying independence of irrelevant alternatives can use only information on individuals' *ordinal preferences* over *that pair* as inputs into the ranking of the alternatives. Thus information on preference intensity (e.g. the value individual $i$ places on alternative $x$ is three times as much as $i$ places on alternative $y$, whereas individual $j$ values $y$ only twice as much as $j$ values $x$) and information on individuals' relative evaluations of alternatives other than the pair under consideration (e.g. individual $i$ has $x$ top-ranked and $y$ bottom-ranked in $X$, whereas individual $j$ ranks all alternatives in $X$ except $x$ as better than $y$), are deemed irrelevant data for determining the social preference between $x$ and $y$. Requiring ordinality is more a practical than a normative demand: as yet there is no satisfactory general method for unequivocally quantifying individuals' evaluations of particular alternatives let alone for comparing any such quantifications across people. The same is not true of the restriction to information on a pair when evaluating that pair. In thinking about this part of the independence condition, it is important to recall that elements of the set $X$ are defined to be exhaustive and mutually exclusive descriptions of the relevant alternatives. Thus conditional preferences of the form, "$h$ would be better president than $i$ if there is peace, but not if there is war" can be defined over $X$ only if "$h$" and "$i$" are *not* alternatives in $X$; rather, for the statement to make sense it must be that the alternatives are "$h$ and war", "$i$ and war", "$h$ and peace", and "$i$ and peace". Independence then says that if everyone's preferences over, say, "$h$ and peace" and "$i$ and war" coincide under two different profiles on $X$, then the collective preference of this pair must likewise coincide; independence *per se* does not require that if "$h$ and peace" is ranked above "$i$ and war", then necessarily "$h$ and war" must be ranked above "$i$ and peace". Given such a comprehensive notion of the set of alternatives, the independence condition seems very natural: why should individuals' evaluations of mutually exclusive alternatives other than the pair under consideration influence the relative social ranking of that pair?

None of the three conditions above say anything about the consistency properties of a preference aggregation rule. As with the consistency properties of any binary relation introduced in Definition 1.2, consider the following three degrees of "collective rationality" an aggregation rule might exhibit:

**Definition 2.3** *An aggregation rule $f$ is*
  *(1) transitive if for all $\rho \in \mathcal{R}^n$, $f(\rho)$ is transitive;*
  *(2) quasi-transitive if for all $\rho \in \mathcal{R}^n$, $f(\rho)$ is quasi-transitive;*
  *(3) acyclic if for all $\rho \in \mathcal{R}^n$, $f(\rho)$ is acyclic.*

A transitive aggregation rule is often called a *social welfare function*; an acyclic aggregation rule is called *social decision function*, while a quasi-transitive aggregation rule is called a *quasi-transitive social decision function*.

In subsequent sections we examine quasi-transitive and acyclic aggregation rules; here, however, we consider only transitive rules. Note that the Borda rule is necessarily transitive, since it assigns a number to each alternative and hence alternatives are ordered according to their number; further a constant rule can be transitive, as can a dictatorial rule (if the dictator, in addition, determines social indifference: $xI_iy$ implies $xIy$). On the other hand, majority rule and the Pareto extension rule fail to satisfy transitivity:

**Example 2.3** Let $N = \{1,2\}$ so majority rule and the Pareto extension rule are equivalent, let $X = \{x,y,z\}$ and let the preferences be given by $xP_1zP_1y$ and $yP_2xP_2z$. Then $zIy$ and $yIx$, but $xPz$.□

Therefore, each of the aggregation rules described in Example 2.1 fails to be either transitive, or nondictatorial, or weakly Paretian, or independent of irrelevant alternatives.

Are there any aggregation rules satisfying all four of these criteria? What is perhaps the most important result in the theory of preference aggregation says the answer is "no".

**Theorem 2.1 (Arrow's General Possibility Theorem)** *If an aggregation rule is transitive, weakly Paretian and independent of irrelevant alternatives, then it is dictatorial.*

Alternatively, any transitive aggregation rule must necessarily fail to be either nondictatorial, or weakly Paretian, or independent of irrelevant alternatives.

Although there clearly exist dictatorial rules that are transitive, weakly Paretian, and independent of irrelevant alternatives (simply fix some $i \in N$ and choose $f(\rho) \equiv R_i$ for all $\rho \in \mathcal{R}^n$), the converse of Theorem 2.1 is not true; that is, there exist dictatorial aggregation rules that violate transitivity for some profile or fail to be independent of irrelevant alternatives. For example, suppose there are exactly three alternatives, $X = \{x,y,z\}$, and let

$B$ be an asymmetric binary relation on $X$ such that $xBy$, $yBz$, and $zBx$. Now consider the aggregation rule $f$ defined by:

$$\forall a, b \in X, \ \forall \rho \in \mathcal{R}^n, \begin{cases} aP_1b & \Rightarrow & aP_{f(\rho)}b \\ aI_1b & \Rightarrow & [aP_{f(\rho)}b \ \Leftrightarrow \ aBb] \end{cases}$$

Then $f$ is certainly dictatorial since individual 1's strict preferences are always respected, but $f$ is not transitive on profiles such that individual 1 is indifferent over all alternatives.

Before proving the theorem in general, the role of the various criteria defined above and the structure of the general argument are illustrated for a simple 2-person example with 3-alternatives in which both individuals have strict preferences only.

**Example 2.4** Let $N = \{1, 2\}$, $X = \{x, y, z\}$, and suppose no individual is ever indifferent between any two alternatives: for all $a, b \in X$, either $aP_ib$ or $bP_ia$, $i \in N$. Then there are 36 possible profiles $\rho = (R_1, R_2)$ on $X$, and all of the possible scenarios can be summarized in a $6 \times 6$ table:

|       | xyz | xzy | yxz | yzx | zxy | zyx |
|-------|-----|-----|-----|-----|-----|-----|
| xyz   |     |     |     |     |     |     |
| xzy   |     |     |     |     |     |     |
| yxz   |     |     | $f(\rho_{34})$ |     |     |     |
| yzx   |     |     |     |     |     |     |
| zxy   |     |     |     |     |     |     |
| zyx   |     |     |     |     |     |     |

Table 2.1: domain of the preference aggregation rule, $f$

The rows of Table 2.1 describe the possible preferences individual 1 could have, and similarly the columns describe the possible preferences individual 2 could have. In every case, **xyz** denotes $xP_iyP_iz$, etc. Thus each of the 36 cells of the table corresponds to a possible profile; for instance, (row 3, column 4) gives the profile $\rho_{34} = (\mathbf{yxz}, \mathbf{yzx})$. An entry in the table then describes the associated social preference relation on $X$ generated by $f$; e.g. $f(\rho_{34})$. Hereafter, we refer to "cell $(i, j)$" to indicate a situation in which the profile is given from Table 2.1 by row $i$ and column $j$.

The requirement that an aggregation rule $f$ satisfy unrestricted domain states that, given $f$, we should be able to fill each of the 36 cells with a ranking of $\{x, y, z\}$. In other words, $f$ must always be capable of producing a social preference.

Requiring that $f$ be transitive is a *"within cell"* or *"intra-profile"* consistency condition. It insists that in each of the 36 cases, the ranking be complete, reflexive, and transitive. The remaining conditions of Theorem 2.1 are additional consistency restrictions on what sorts of ranking are permissible. Weak Paretianism, like transitivity, is a "within cell" condition: it says that $f$ must respect pairwise unanimity. So invoking this condition alone, several parts of the ranking of $X$ for each profile can immediately be written into Table 2.1; these are entered in italics in Table 2.2, where $xy, xz$ means $xPy$, $xPz$ etc.

|       | xyz      | xzy      | yxz      | yzx      | zxy      | zyx      |
|-------|----------|----------|----------|----------|----------|----------|
| xyz   | $xyz$    | $xy,xz$  | $xz,yz$  | $yz$     | $xy$     |          |
| xzy   | $xz,xy$  | $xzy$    | $xz$     |          | $xy,zy$  | $zy$     |
| yxz   | $xz,yz$  | $xz$     | $yxz$    | $yz,yx$  |          | $yx$     |
| yzx   | $yz$     |          | $yz,yx$  | $yzx$    | $zx$     | $yx,zx$  |
| zxy   | $xy$     | $xy,zy$  |          | $zx$     | $zxy$    | $zx,zy$  |
| zyx   |          | $zy$     | $yx$     | $yx,zx$  | $zx,zy$  | $zyx$    |

Table 2.2: $f$ satisfies weak Pareto

Unlike the weak Pareto condition, independence of irrelevant alternatives is an *"across cell"* or *"inter-profile"* consistency condition: it says that if ever $f$ declares $xRy$ in one cell, say $(i,j)$, then in *all* other cells in which both 1's preferences over $\{x,y\}$ and 2's preferences over $\{x,y\}$ are identical to those of cell $(i,j)$, $f$ *must* declare the same ranking of $x$ and $y$. For instance, suppose that in cell (1,4) of Table 2.2, $f$ ranks $xPy$; then independence of irrelevant alternatives says $f$ *must* rank $x$ strictly better than $y$ in cells (1,3), (1,6), (2,3), (2,4), (2,6), (5,3), (5,4), and (5,6). The consequence of this implication for Table 2.2 is illustrated in Table 2.3.

|       | xyz      | xzy      | yxz      | yzx      | zxy      | zyx      |
|-------|----------|----------|----------|----------|----------|----------|
| xyz   | $xyz$    | $xy,xz$  | $xyz$    | $xyz$    | $xy$     | $xy$     |
| xzy   | $xz,xy$  | $xzy$    | $xz,xy$  | $xy$     | $xy,zy$  | $xy,zy$  |
| yxz   | $xz,yz$  | $xz$     | $yxz$    | $yz,yx$  |          | $yx$     |
| yzx   | $yz$     |          | $yz,yx$  | $yzx$    | $zx$     | $yx,zx$  |
| zxy   | $xy$     | $xy,zy$  | $xy$     | $zxy$    | $zxy$    | $zxy$    |
| zyx   |          | $zy$     | $yx$     | $yx,zx$  | $zx,zy$  | $zyx$    |

Table 2.3: assume $xPy$ in (1,4) and apply independence to $(x,y)$

As discussed earlier, the independence condition really has two parts: first, to rank any pair of alternatives $\{a,b\}$, $f$ can only use the information given by the individuals' ordinal preferences; and second, only individuals' rankings of $a$ and $b$ matter – the relative location of the remaining alternative, $z$, is deemed utterly irrelevant.

Given Table 2.3, observe that in cell (1,4), the transitive rationality of $f$ yields $xPz$; i.e. $f$ decides once again in favor of 1's preferences when there is conflict. Applying the independence restriction, this fact implies that *whenever* 1 prefers $x$ over $z$ and 2 prefers $z$ over $x$, then $f$ must rank $x$ better than $z$. Such a situation also occurs in cells (1,5), (1,6), (2,4), (2,5), (2,6), (3,4), (3,5), and (3,6). And similarly, in cell (5,4) of Table 2.3, by transitivity $f$ ranks $zPy$, once more favoring 1 over 2 in the presence of conflict; such conflict also occurs in cells (2,1), (2,3), (2,4), (5,1), (5,3), (6,1), (6,3), and (6,4), and so $f$ is required to rank $z$ and $y$ consistently here. In sum, independence applied to $(x,z)$ and $(z,y)$ in Table 2.3 yields Table 2.4.

| | **xyz** | **xzy** | **yxz** | **yzx** | **zxy** | **zyx** |
|---|---|---|---|---|---|---|
| **xyz** | $xyz$ | $xy,xz$ | $xyz$ | $xyz$ | $xy,xz$ | $xy,xz$ |
| **xzy** | $xzy$ | $xzy$ | $xzy$ | $xzy$ | $xzy$ | $xzy$ |
| **yxz** | $xz,yz$ | $xz$ | $yxz$ | $yxz$ | $xz$ | $yxz$ |
| **yzx** | $yz$ | | $yz,yx$ | $yzx$ | $zx$ | $yx,zx$ |
| **zxy** | $xy,zy$ | $xy,zy$ | $xy,zy$ | $zxy$ | $zxy$ | $zxy$ |
| **zyx** | $zy$ | $zy$ | $zyx$ | $zyx$ | $zx,zy$ | $zyx$ |

Table 2.4: independence applied to $(x,z)$ and $(z,y)$

Now note, again by transitivity, that $f$ declares $yPz$ in cell (3,6) and $zPx$ in cell (6,3). In both cases, $f$ decides in favor of 1's preferences against 2's opposition. Arguing as above, we can then apply independence to generate Table 2.5 from Table 2.4.

| | **xyz** | **xzy** | **yxz** | **yzx** | **zxy** | **zyx** |
|---|---|---|---|---|---|---|
| **xyz** | $xyz$ | $xyz$ | $xyz$ | $xyz$ | $xyz$ | $xyz$ |
| **xzy** | $xzy$ | $xzy$ | $xzy$ | $xzy$ | $xzy$ | $xzy$ |
| **yxz** | $xz,yz$ | $xz,yz$ | $yxz$ | $yxz$ | $xz,yz$ | $yxz$ |
| **yzx** | $yzx$ | $yzx$ | $yzx$ | $yzx$ | $yzx$ | $yzx$ |
| **zxy** | $zxy$ | $zxy$ | $zxy$ | $zxy$ | $zxy$ | $zxy$ |
| **zyx** | $zy,zx$ | $zy,zx$ | $zyx$ | $zyx$ | $zx,zy$ | $zyx$ |

Table 2.5: independence applied to $(y,z)$ and $(z,x)$

Finally, observe from cell (4,5) of Table 2.5 that transitive rationality of $f$ demands $yPx$. Applying independence one final time, therefore, yields Table 2.6 in which all pairs are ranked in all cells. As Table 2.6 makes clear, the consequence of assuming $xPy$ in cell (1,4) of Table 2.1 and requiring $f$ to be transitive, weakly Paretian, and independent of irrelevant alternatives is to make individual 1 a "dictator".

|       | **xyz** | **xzy** | **yxz** | **yzx** | **zxy** | **zyx** |
|-------|---------|---------|---------|---------|---------|---------|
| **xyz** | $xyz$ | $xyz$ | $xyz$ | $xyz$ | $xyz$ | $xyz$ |
| **xzy** | $xzy$ | $xzy$ | $xzy$ | $xzy$ | $xzy$ | $xzy$ |
| **yxz** | $yxz$ | $yxz$ | $yxz$ | $yxz$ | $yxz$ | $yxz$ |
| **yzx** | $yzx$ | $yzx$ | $yzx$ | $yzx$ | $yzx$ | $yzx$ |
| **zxy** | $zxy$ | $zxy$ | $zxy$ | $zxy$ | $zxy$ | $zxy$ |
| **zyx** | $zyx$ | $zyx$ | $zyx$ | $zyx$ | $zyx$ | $zyx$ |

Table 2.6: independence applied to $(y, x)$

Had we assumed $yPx$ initially in cell (1,4), then (by symmetry of the example) individual 2 would have turned out to be the "dictator". The only remaining possibility is for $f$ to declare indifference when 1 and 2 have conflicting preferences over $\{x, y\}$; but as is readily checked, this is impossible. To see this suppose, in cell (1,4) of Table 2.1, $f$ ranks $x$ socially indifferent to $y$: $xIy$. Then transitive rationality yields $xPz$. In sum, the social ranking of $X$ under $f$ for the profile $\rho_{14} = (\textbf{xyz}, \textbf{yzx})$ is $xIy$, $yPz$, $xPz$. Now consider cell (2,6) with profile $\rho_{26} = (\textbf{xzy}, \textbf{zyx})$. $f$ weakly Paretian gives $zPy$. And because both 1's and 2's preferences over $\{x, z\}$ are as in cell (1,4), independence of irrelevant alternatives requires $xPz$. Hence, by transitive rationality, $xPy$. But both 1's and 2's preferences over $\{x, y\}$ in cell (2,6) are exactly as they are in cell (1,4). Therefore, independence of irrelevant alternatives demands $f$ to rank $\{x, y\}$ identically in cells (2,6) and (1,4): contradiction. Consequently, in cell (1,4), $f$ must decide in favor either of 1 or of 2, leading to a "dictatorship". And this is exactly what Theorem 2.1 says must be true in general.□

We now turn the above illustration into a general argument for the theorem. In the following definitions, the preference aggregation rule is understood as fixed.

**Definition 2.4** *A set $L \subseteq N$ is semidecisive for $x$ against $y$ (written, $x\tilde{D}_Ly$) if for every $\rho \in \mathcal{R}^n$, $[xP_iy$, all $i \in L$ and $yP_jx$, all $j \notin L]$ implies $xPy$. A set $L$ is decisive for $x$ against $y$ (written, $xD_Ly$) if for every $\rho \in \mathcal{R}^n$, $[xP_iy$, all $i \in L]$ implies $xPy$.*

In words, if a set of individuals $L$ is semidecisive for $x$ against $y$ then, whenever all members of $L$ share a strict preference for $x$ over $y$ and are totally opposed by all those not in $L$, the aggregation rule strictly decides in favor of $L$. Notice that should there exist even one individual (either in $L$ or not in $L$) who has, say, $x$ indifferent to $y$, then knowing that $L$ is semidecisive for $x$ against $y$ does *not* allow us to conclude that $x$ is ranked higher than $y$ under the aggregation rule. On the other hand, if $L$ is decisive for $x$ against $y$ then, whenever all members of $L$ share a strict preference for $x$ over $y$, the aggregation rule ranks $x$ strictly preferred to $y$, *irrespective* of the preferences of members not in $L$. Thus if $L$ is decisive for $x$ against $y$ then $L$ is semidecisive for $x$ against $y$, but the converse is false.

**Definition 2.5** *A set $L \subseteq N$ is decisive if, for all ordered pairs $(x, y)$, $L$ is decisive for $x$ against $y$.*

**Example 2.5** Some examples of decisive sets are:
 (1) If $f$ is dictatorial with $i$ the dictator, then a coalition $L \subseteq N$ is decisive if and only if $i \in L$.
 (2) If $f$ is majority rule, then a set of individuals $L \subseteq N$ is decisive if and only if $|L| > n/2$.
 (3) If $f$ is the Pareto extension rule, then the only decisive set is $N$ itself [Exercise].

**Lemma 2.1** *Let $f$ be a quasi-transitive preference aggregation rule that is independent of irrelevant alternatives and weakly Paretian. If $L$ is semidecisive for $x$ against $y$ then, for all ordered pairs $(v, w)$ in $X \times X$, $L$ is decisive for $v$ against $w$.*

**Proof.** Let $L$ be semidecisive for $x$ against $y$ and consider any profile $\rho$ such that $x P_i z$ all $i$ in $L$. Now consider a profile $\rho'|_{\{x,y,z\}}$ such that:

$$\forall i \; \in \; L, \; x P_i' y P_i' z$$
$$\forall j \; \notin \; L, \; y P_j' x, \; y P_j' z$$

where $z$ is distinct from $x$ and $y$ (recall $X$ contains at least three alternatives). Since $x \tilde{D}_L y$ by assumption, $x P' y$; by $f$ weakly Paretian, $y P' z$; so by the quasi-transitivity of $f$, $x P' z$. But since only the preferences of $i \in L$ over $x$ and $z$ have been specified in $\rho'$ and $R_i'|_{\{x,z\}} = R_i|_{\{x,z\}}$ all $i$ in $L$, $f$ independent of irrelevant alternatives implies $x P z$ and $x D_L z$. Hence, because $z$ is arbitrary save for $z \notin \{x, y\}$,

$$(*) \; \forall z \notin \{x, y\}, \; x \tilde{D}_L y \Rightarrow x D_L z.$$

And since $L$ is decisive for $x$ against $z$ implies $L$ is semidecisive for $x$ against $z$, interchanging $y$ and $z$ in the above argument implies $L$ is decisive for $x$ against $y$.

Now let $\rho^\circ$ be any profile with $yP_i^\circ z$ all $i$ in $L$, and let $\rho^+$ be such that:

$$\forall i \in L, \ yP_i^+ xP_i^+ z$$
$$\forall j \notin L, \ zP_j^+ x, \ yP_j^+ x.$$

From the previous step, we have $x\tilde{D}_L z$; hence $xP^+ z$. By $f$ weakly Paretian $yP^+ x$; and by the quasi-transitivity of $f$, $yP^+ z$ follows. Since only the preferences of $i$ in $L$ over $\{y, z\}$ are specified and $R_i^+|_{\{y,z\}} = R_i^\circ|_{\{y,z\}}$ all $i$ in $L$, independence of irrelevant alternatives implies $yP^\circ z$ and $yD_L z$. Hence, by $z$ arbitrary save for $z \notin \{x, y\}$, the preceding two steps yield,

$$(**) \ \forall z \notin \{x, y\}, \ x\tilde{D}_L y \Rightarrow yD_L z.$$

Now, because $L$ is decisive for $y$ against $z$, $L$ is semidecisive for $y$ against $z$. By (*), therefore, $L$ is decisive for $y$ against $x$. Finally, combining (*) and (**) yields that for *any* pair of distinct alternatives $\{v, w\} \subseteq X \backslash \{x, y\}$,

$$x\tilde{D}_L y \ \Rightarrow \ xD_L v, \text{ by (*)}$$
$$\Rightarrow \ vD_L w, \text{ by (**) with } v \text{ replacing } y. \square$$

**Proof of Theorem 2.1** By Lemma 2.1 and the fact that if $f$ is transitive it must be quasitransitive, it suffices to show there exists some individual $i$ and some pair of alternatives $x, y \in X$ such that $i$ is semidecisive for $x$ against $y$. Since $f$ is weakly Paretian, there surely exists a decisive, and so semidecisive, group for any pair of alternatives; i.e. $N$ itself. For each ordered pair $(a, b) \in X^2$, let $\lambda(ab)$ denote the size of the smallest semidecisive group for $a$ against $b$, and define $\lambda \equiv \min[\lambda(ab) : (a, b) \in X^2]$. Without loss of generality, suppose $L$ is semidecisive for $x$ against $y$ with $|L| = \lambda$. If $\lambda = 1$ the proof is complete. So assume $\lambda > 1$ and consider any profile $\rho \in \mathcal{R}^n$ with $\rho|_{\{x,y,z\}}$ such that:

$$i \in L, \qquad\ \ xP_i yP_i z$$
$$\forall j \in L\backslash\{i\}, \ \ zP_j xP_j y$$
$$\forall k \notin L, \qquad yP_k zP_k x.$$

By $L$ semidecisive for $x$ against $y$, $xPy$. Because $|L| = \lambda$, $\sim[zPy]$ (otherwise, $L\backslash\{i\}$ is semidecisive for $z$ against $y$ and $|L\backslash\{i\}| = \lambda - 1$); hence, $yRz$

by the completeness of $f(\rho)$. Applying transitivity yields $xPz$. But then independence of irrelevant alternatives implies that $i$ is semidecisive for $x$ against $z$, contradicting $\lambda > 1$.□

Theorem 2.1 shows that rules such as majority rule and the Pareto extension rule, which as noted above are nondictatorial, weakly Paretian, and independent of irrelevant alternatives, must fail to be transitive *even when there are only two individuals.* And it is worth observing that the result goes through if the independence condition is relaxed to permit *intra*-personal cardinal preferences. That is, suppose individuals' preferences all have cardinal representations such that statements of the form, "$x$ is worth 2.5 times more to $i$ than is $y$", are empirically valid but *inter*-personal statements of the form, "$x$ is worth 2.5 times more to $i$ than to $j$", remain illegitimate; then allowing cardinal intra-personal data to be used by a preference aggregation rule does not affect the (suitably revised) Arrow General Possibility Theorem. Thus it is the exclusion of interpersonal comparability by the independence condition that matters and not the insistence on ordinality *per se.*

It is difficult to overstate the importance and subtlety of Arrow's General Possibility Theorem. Mathematically, the result is straightforward, requiring little more than a rudimentary understanding of set theory to understand the argument. Conceptually, the result is far reaching: when there are at least three alternatives, *every* method of aggregating individual preferences into some kind of social preference *must* violate at least one of the conditions of unrestricted domain, transitivity, weak Paretianism, nondictatorship, and independence of irrelevant alternatives. Thus the choice of any particular aggregation rule necessarily involves trading off at least one of the conditions against the remainder.

The normative appeal of each of the last three criteria listed above, those Arrow suggested as necessary properties of any generally acceptable aggregation rule, has already been discussed. And while in some particular instances, certain classes of preference profile may well not be empirically germane, insisting on a general domain restriction *a priori* is typically hard to justify. This is largely because the normative force of such restrictions must rely on the substantive interpretation of the alternatives under consideration rather than on the fact that they lead to inconsistencies or difficulties in achieving reasonable aggregations. For instance, a preference ordering that ranks a world in which acts of child abuse are legal to a world in which they are not may well be deemed a preference that an aggregation rule might ignore. However, as Example 2.4 illustrates, there is no reason to presume the set of alternatives to be one on which any profile of preferences can be *prima facie* excluded as somehow illegitimate; problematic profiles, that is, can readily occur on quite mundane sets of alternatives. In this regard, it is important to recognize that Arrow's Theorem does not assert that preference aggregation rules yield unstable or objectionable aggregate decisions for all profiles, only that there exist sets of profiles under which such decisions necessarily occur. Given the desirability of having aggregation rules defined on the full domain $\mathcal{R}^n$, therefore, only the transitivity requirement remains to be considered.

Imposing some intra-profile consistency condition on preference aggregation rules is essential if collective decisions are not to generate mutually contradictory prescriptions. However, Theorem 1.1 shows that transitivity is far from necessary to generate consistent choices; acyclicity of the relevant preference relation is enough. So demanding the preference aggregation rule be transitive is arguably demanding too much. Consequently, it is important to study just what can be done if the rationality condition is weakened away from full transitivity. In particular, since the full force of transitivity is used only in the very last step of the proof to Theorem 2.1 (i.e. concluding from $xPy$ & $\sim[zPy]$ that $xPz$), relaxing transitivity to quasi-transitivity suggests that there exist nondictatorial rules satisfying all the remaining conditions. Before exploring this suggestion, the value of Theorem 2.1 is further illustrated with a substantive application.

## 2.2   Application: Choosing a representative

As an application of Arrow's Theorem, consider the following problem: the collective $N$ must select a member to be its representative with regard to certain decisions and wants to know whether there is any "reasonable" means of doing so. The collective can make this selection as a function of their preferences over the universal set of alternatives $X$, and so a *representation rule* is a function $g : \mathcal{R}^n \to N$ assigning to each preference profile an individual from the group. Note that, since each member of the collective possesses a weak ordering on $X$, any representation rule assigns a weak order $R_{g(\rho)}$ to every preference profile and, furthermore, such a weak order must necessarily be weakly Paretian: if, for all $i$ in $N$, $xP_iy$ then necessarily $xP_{g(\rho)}y$ since $g(\rho)$ is a member of $N$.

Suppose now that each individual has a strong ordering on $X$, i.e. indifference does not occur (this makes the following definition of a dictator more transparent). We say that a representation rule $g$ is *dictatorial* if for all $\rho, \rho' \in \mathcal{P}^n$, $g(\rho) = g(\rho')$; and is *independent of irrelevant alternatives* if for all $\rho, \rho' \in \mathcal{P}^n$, $\rho|_{\{x,y\}} = \rho'|_{\{x,y\}}$ implies $R_{g(\rho)}|_{\{x,y\}} = R_{g(\rho')}|_{\{x,y\}}$. Thus, if $g$ is dictatorial then the same individual is selected by the collective for any preference profile, and if $g$ satisfies independence then if two preference profiles agree on a pair of alternatives, the selected individuals' preferences on this pair must agree as well (that is, different individuals may be selected, but they must have a common preference over the pair). Then we have the following consequence of Arrow's Theorem:

**Theorem 2.2** *A representation rule is independent of irrelevant alternatives if and only if it is dictatorial.*

Therefore any nondictatorial representation rule must be such that for some pair of profiles $\rho, \rho' \in \mathcal{P}^n$ and some pair of alternatives $\{x, y\} \in X$ individual preferences are the same in $\rho$ and $\rho'$ and yet the collective selects different individuals under $\rho$ and $\rho'$ with different preferences concerning $x$ and $y$.

## 2.3 Quasi-transitive and acyclic rules

Arrow's Theorem demonstrates the impossibility of aggregating individual preferences into a transitive collective preference relation in any reasonable manner. However, from Theorem 1.1 in Chapter 1 we know that transitivity of a complete binary relation is sufficient, but not necessary, for the set of "best" alternatives according to this relation to be nonempty; rather, acyclicity is necessary and sufficient for this to be so. Therefore if one is merely interested in aggregating preferences so as to determine a social choice, Arrow's Theorem might not seem a bother. Indeed, there in fact exist preference aggregation rules that are weakly Paretian, nondictatorial, independent, and quasi-transitive, the simplest example of which is the Pareto extension rule. As noted above, this rule is nondictatorial, weakly Paretian, and independent. To see that it is quasi-transitive, let $xPy$ and $yPz$; then it must be the case that for every individual $i \in N$, $xR_iy$ and $yR_iz$ with at least one (not necessarily fixed) individual having strict preferences in each case; therefore by the transitivity of individual preferences it must be that for every $i \in N$, $xR_iz$ with $xP_jz$ for at least some $j$ as well, thereby implying $xPz$. Hence the Pareto extension rule is quasi-transitive.

Although this aggregation rule evades the pitfalls of Arrow's Theorem while still generating a nonempty choice set, it does so by being particularly undiscriminating. For example, suppose there are at least as many individuals as alternatives and that each alternative is most preferred by some individual; then the Pareto extension rule declares *every* alternative to be as good as every other. In effect, under the Pareto extension rule every individual has a *veto* over every pair of alternatives in that, if some individual strictly prefers $x$ to $y$ then $y$ *cannot* be ranked strictly higher than $x$ by the rule, irrespective of others' preferences over $x$ and $y$. As the result below shows, this feature is endemic to any "reasonable" quasi-transitive aggregation rule.

**Definition 2.6** *An individual $i \in N$ has a veto for $x$ against $y$ if for every $\rho \in \mathcal{R}^n$, $xP_iy$ implies $\sim [yPx]$; $i \in N$ has a veto if, for all ordered pairs $(x, y)$, $i$ has a veto for $x$ against $y$.*

**Definition 2.7** *An aggregation rule is oligarchic if there exists $L \subseteq N$ (called an oligarchy) such that*
   *(1) every member of $L$ has a veto; and*
   *(2) $L$ is decisive.*

A dictator is an oligarchy of size one and the oligarchy under the Pareto extension rule is $N$.

**Theorem 2.3** *If an aggregation rule is quasi-transitive, weakly Paretian and independent of irrelevant alternatives, then it is oligarchic.*

**Proof.** Say that $i \in N$ has a *semiveto for $x$ against $y$* if, whenever $xP_iy$ and, $\forall j \neq i$, $yP_jx$, $\sim [yPx]$. Consider any profile $\rho$ such that $\rho|_{\{x,y,z\}}$ is given by:

$$xP_iyP_iz$$
$$\forall j \neq i, \quad yP_jx, yP_jz.$$

Suppose $i$ has a semiveto for $x$ against $y$; then $\sim [yPx]$ or, since $f(\cdot)$ is complete, $xRy$. By $f$ weakly Paretian, $yPz$. Therefore, $f(\cdot)$ quasi-transitive implies $xRz$ (else $zPx$ in which case quasi-transitivity implies $yPx$, a contradiction). By independence of irrelevant alternatives, $i$ has a veto for $x$ against $z$. Proceeding as in the proof for Lemma 2.1, *mutatis mutandis*, we can conclude that if $i$ has a semiveto for some $x$ against some $y$, $i$ must have a veto over all ordered pairs $(a, b) \in X^2$. Now, by $f$ weakly Paretian there exists a smallest semidecisive group. As in the proof of Theorem 2.1, let $\lambda$ be the size of a smallest such set and, without loss of generality, suppose $L$ is semidecisive for $x$ against $y$ with $|L| = \lambda$. By Lemma 2.1, $L$ is decisive over all ordered pairs $(a, b) \in X^2$. If $\lambda = 1$, the proof is complete (a dictator is an oligarchy of size one). So assume $\lambda > 1$ and consider any profile $\rho$ such that $\rho|_{\{x,y,z\}}$ is,

$$
\begin{array}{ll}
i \in L, & xP_iyP_iz \\
\forall j \in L\backslash\{i\}, & zP_jxP_jy \\
\forall k \notin L, & yP_kzP_kx.
\end{array}
$$

Arguing exactly as in the proof of Theorem 2.1, we conclude that $xPy$ and $yRz$. By $f$ quasi-transitive, it must be that $xRz$. Hence $i$ has a semiveto for $x$ against $z$ and, therefore, $i$ has a veto over all ordered pairs $(a, b) \in X^2$. Finally, since $i \in L$ was chosen arbitrarily, this implies that $L$ is an oligarchy.□

Thus relaxing the consistency property of transitivity to quasi-transitivity disperses effective decision making power in the collective from a dictator to an oligarchy. However, oligarchies can be small (indeed, they can be dictatorships) and the larger they become the less discriminating is the rule. Of course, quasi-transitivity is still stronger than necessary if one is merely interested in the existence of reasonable social decisions. So, next we consider aggregation rules that are acyclic. To see that there exist aggregation rules that are acyclic but not oligarchic, consider the rule employed by the United Nations Security Council prior to 1965. The Council then consisted of five permanent members (China, France, Great Britain, Soviet Union, United States) and six other members, for a total of eleven at any one time. The passage of a motion requires seven "yes" votes, as well as the concurring votes of all five permanent members. If we interpret a "yes" vote as strictly preferring adoption of the motion, interpret a "concurring" vote as weakly preferring the motion and let individuals' 1,...,5 denote the permanent members, the aggregation rule of the Security Council is then

$$
\forall x, y \in X, \; xPy \Leftrightarrow |P(x, y; \rho)| \geq 7 \; and \; xR_iy \; i = 1, \ldots, 5.
$$

This rule is evidently weakly Paretian and independent of irrelevant alternatives; in addition, each of the permanent members has a veto. However, in contrast to an oligarchy, even if *all* permanent members favor an alternative, they still require the assent of at least two other members. That is, the set of decisive coalitions are those coalitions that include all the permanent members and have at least seven members total; hence the permanent members themselves do not constitute a decisive coalition.

On the other hand the Security Council rule *is* acyclic. To see this, suppose we have alternatives $\{x_1, \ldots, x_r\}$ such that $x_1Px_2$, $x_2Px_3$, ..., and

$x_{r-1}Px_r$. Since at least seven individuals must strictly prefer $x_1$ to $x_2$ for this to be so and the permanent members make up five of the eleven individuals, at least one permanent member must strictly prefer $x_1$ to $x_2$, say individual 1. Further, since 1 must weakly prefer $x_j$ to $x_{j+1}$ for $x_j$ to be strictly preferred to $x_{j+1}$, for $j = 2, \ldots, r-1$, it must be that $x_2R_1x_3$, $x_3R_1x_4$, ..., and $x_{r-1}R_1x_r$ as well. But then by the transitivity of $R_1$, $x_1P_1x_r$ and, since 1 is a permanent member of the Council, it cannot be the case that $x_rPx_1$, implying the rule is acyclic.

It turns out that the feature shared by the pre-1965 UN Security Council rule and all other acyclic rules is not that there exist individuals with a veto, but rather that there exists a set of individuals who are in *all* decisive coalitions (the permanent members in the above example). So for any aggregation rule $f$, let $\mathcal{L}(f)$ denote the set of decisive coalitions associated with $f$. It is useful to note two properties of the family $\mathcal{L}(f)$.

**Definition 2.8** *A family of coalitions $\mathcal{L} \subseteq 2^N$ is*
*(1) monotonic if $L \in \mathcal{L}$ and $N \supseteq L' \supset L$ imply $L' \in \mathcal{L}$;*
*(2) proper if $L \in \mathcal{L}$ implies $N \backslash L \notin \mathcal{L}$.*

In words, if $\mathcal{L} = \mathcal{L}(f)$ for some rule $f$, then monotonicity says that adding people to a decisive set yields another decisive set. And properness says that two decisive sets must include at least one individual in common.

**Lemma 2.2** *For any aggregation rule $f$, $\mathcal{L}(f)$ is monotonic and proper.*

**Proof.** Properness of $\mathcal{L}(f)$ follows from the fact that $f$, as a preference aggregation rule, maps into complete binary relations; hence it cannot be the case that $xPy$ and $yPx$. Monotonicity follows since if, for all $i \in L'$, $xP_iy$ then for all coalitions $L \subset L'$, for all $i \in L$, $xP_iy$. Therefore, if $L \in \mathcal{L}(f)$ then $xPy$. Thus $[\forall i \in L', \ xP_iy]$ implies $xPy$ and, since this holds for all $x, y \in X$, $L' \in \mathcal{L}(f)$ by definition of a decisive set.$\Box$

**Definition 2.9** *An aggregation rule $f$ is collegial if and only if*

$$K(\mathcal{L}(f)) \equiv \bigcap_{L \in \mathcal{L}(f)} L$$

*is nonempty. The set $K(\mathcal{L}(f))$ is called the collegium.*

If $f$ is oligarchic then it is collegial, and the collegium itself constitutes a decisive set. As we show later, unlike the definition of a dictator or an oligarchy, the definition of a collegium says nothing about the veto or decisive power of its members, individually or collectively. On the other hand, if there exists an individual with a veto, then that individual must be a member of the collegium. The extent to which collegial rules concentrate decisionmaking power, therefore, is less clear than with dictatorial and oligarchic rules. We consider this issue further, below.

**Theorem 2.4** *Suppose $|X| \geq n$. Then any aggregation rule that is acyclic and weakly Paretian is collegial.*

**Proof.** First note that since $f$ is weakly Paretian there exists a decisive set; hence $\mathcal{L}(f) \neq \emptyset$. Now suppose that $f$ is non-collegial. Then for all $i \in N$ there exists some $L \in \mathcal{L}(f)$ such that $i \notin L$; in particular, since $\mathcal{L}(f)$ is monotonic by Lemma 2.2, for every $i \in N$, $N\backslash\{i\} \in \mathcal{L}(f)$. Noting that $|X| \geq n$ by assumption, let the outcomes in $X$ be ordered as $\{x_1, \ldots, x_n, \ldots\}$ and assume $\rho|_{\{x_1,\ldots,x_n\}}$ is:

$$x_1 P_1 x_2 P_1 \ldots P_1 x_n$$
$$x_2 P_2 x_3 P_2 \ldots P_2 x_n P_2 x_1$$
$$x_3 P_3 x_4 \ldots P_3 x_n P_3 x_1 P_3 x_2.$$
$$\ldots$$
$$x_n P_n x_1 P_n \ldots P_n x_{n-2} P_n x_{n-1}.$$

Then, for all $j = 2, \ldots, n$, $P(x_{j-1}, x_j; \rho) = N\backslash\{j\}$, implying (since $N\backslash\{j\} \in \mathcal{L}(f)$) $x_{j-1} P x_j$. Also, $P(x_n, x_1; \rho) = N\backslash\{1\}$, implying (since $N\backslash\{1\} \in \mathcal{L}(f)$) $x_n P x_1$. Therefore we have a cycle on $\{x_1, \ldots, x_n\}$ : $x_n P x_1 P x_2 P \ldots P x_n$. $\square$

That $f$ is weakly Paretian is used in the proof to Theorem 2.4 only to insure that $\mathcal{L}(f)$ is nonempty; and, in contrast to previous results, the result does not require $f$ to satisfy independence of irrelevant alternatives (but note that some degree of independence is implicit in the definition of a decisive coalition). Furthermore, the result requires that there exist enough distinct alternatives to permit construction of a suitable profile. Because in general we wish to place no constraints on the size of $X$, such an assumption is legitimate. However, this feature of the argument raises a question – deferred to Chapter 3 – about what happens when the number of alternatives is less than the number of individuals. Finally, as with previous results, the converse of Theorem 2.4 is not true; that is there exist weakly Paretian and collegial aggregation rules that are not acyclic. Indeed, as we show in Chapter 3, the post-1965 UN Security Council rule is an example.

As indicated earlier, it is not true that if $i$ is a member of the collegium under an aggregation rule satisfying the conditions of Theorem 2.4, then $i$

has a veto over all ordered pairs, $(a, b) \in X^2$. This is shown by the following example.

**Example 2.6** Define the aggregation rule $f$ by: $\forall x, y \in X$, $\forall \rho \in \mathcal{R}^n$, $xPy$ iff:

$$\textit{either } [\forall i \in N, \ xP_iy] \ \textit{ or } \ [x = a, \ y = b \text{ and } \exists j \in N \text{ with } aR_jb].$$

Then $f$ is weakly Paretian and independent of irrelevant alternatives by construction. Similarly, $\mathcal{L}(f) = \{N\}$ so $K(\mathcal{L}(f)) \neq \emptyset$, but no individual has a veto over all alternatives, since in particular no individual has a veto for $b$ against $a$. To see that $f$ is acyclic, consider an arbitrary set of alternatives $\{x_1, \ldots, x_r\}$ such that for all $t = 1, \ldots, r-1$, $x_tPx_{t+1}$. There are two cases:

(1) $x_t = a$ and $x_{t+1} = b$ for no $t = 1, \ldots, r-1$. Then by definition of $f$,

$$\forall t = 1, \ldots, x_{r-1}, \ x_tPx_{t+1} \Rightarrow \forall i \in N, \ x_tP_ix_{t+1}.$$

Therefore, since, $\forall i \in N$, $R_i \in \mathcal{R}$, we have $x_1P_ix_r$. Hence, $x_1Px_r$.

(2) $x_{t'} = a$ and $x_{t'+1} = b$ for some $t' \in \{1, \ldots, r-1\}$. Then by definition of $f$, $\exists j \in N$ such that

$$x_1P_jx_2P_jx_3 \ldots P_jx_{t'}R_jx_{t'+1}P_jx_{t'+2} \ldots P_jx_r.$$

Hence, $x_1P_jx_r$ since $R_j \in \mathcal{R}$. By definition of $f$, therefore, $x_1Rx_r$. Therefore $f$ is acyclic.$\square$

Although in the above example no individual has a veto over all (ordered) pairs of alternatives, it is the case that some individuals have a veto over some pairs of alternatives. The next result generalizes the example.

**Lemma 2.3** *Let $|X| > n$. If an aggregation rule is acyclic, weakly Paretian, and independent of irrelevant alternatives, then there exists $i \in N$ and a pair of alternatives $\{x, y\}$ such that $i$ has a veto for $x$ over $y$.*

**Proof.** Suppose the claim is false and let $X = \{x_1, \ldots, x_n, x_{n+1}, \ldots\}$; in what follows we ignore alternatives $\{x_{n+2}, \ldots\}$ (if they exist), which is legitimate by independence of irrelevant alternatives. By the supposition, for every $i \in N$, $i$ has no veto for $x_{i+1}$ against $x_i$; by independence, the social preference ranking of $\{x_i, x_{i+1}\}$ depends exclusively on individuals' preferences over this pair; hence there exists a restricted profile $\rho^{(i)}|_{\{x_i, x_{i+1}\}}$ such that $x_{i+1}P_i^{(i)}x_i$ and $x_iP^{(i)}x_{i+1}$. Now let $\rho^{(0)}|_{\{x_1, x_{n+1}\}}$ be such that, for all

$i \in N$, $x_{n+1}P_i^{(0)}x_1$, and pick any profile $\rho \in \mathcal{R}^n$ such that $\rho|_{\{x_1,\ldots,x_{n+1}\}}$ is given by piecing together the pairwise restricted profiles, $\rho^{(i)}|_{\{x_i,x_{i+1}\}}$ and $\rho^{(0)}|_{\{x_1,x_{n+1}\}}$, along with the relevant transitive completions: *viz.*

$$\forall i = 1, \ldots, n, \ \rho|_{\{x_i,x_{i+1}\}} = \rho^{(i)}|_{\{x_i,x_{i+1}\}}; \text{ and } \rho|_{\{x_1,x_{n+1}\}} = \rho^{(0)}|_{\{x_1,x_{n+1}\}}.$$

Since there are more alternatives than individuals, such a profile $\rho$ exists. By independence and construction of the profile $\rho$, we have:

$$x_1 P x_2 P \ldots P x_{n-1} P x_n P x_{n+1}.$$

And by $f$ weakly Paretian, we have $x_{n+1}Px_1$; but this contradicts $f$ acyclic.□

Consider now the following strengthening of the independence of irrelevant alternatives condition.

**Definition 2.10** *An aggregation rule $f$ is neutral if and only if for all $\rho, \rho' \in \mathcal{R}^n$, all $x, y, a, b \in X$, $P(x,y;\rho) = P(a,b;\rho')$ & $P(y,x;\rho) = P(b,a;\rho')$ imply $xRy$ if and only if $aR'b$.*

In words, a neutral aggregation rule treats all pairwise comparisons the same: the labeling of the alternatives is immaterial, all that matters is the individuals' preferences. To see that neutrality is stronger than independence of irrelevant alternatives, set $a = x$ and $b = y$ in the above definition; then the definition is precisely that of independence of irrelevant alternatives. The following example further illustrates the difference between the two conditions.

**Example 2.7** Let $X = \{w, x, y, z\}$, $N = \{1, 2\}$ and consider the profiles $\rho$ and $\rho'$ :

$$wP_1xP_1yP_1z$$
$$zP_2yP_2xP_2w$$

$$wP_1'zP_1'xP_1'y$$
$$yP_2'xP_2'zP_2'w$$

Suppose we are told that the preference aggregation rule $f$ is independent of irrelevant alternatives and ranks, $wPx$. Then we can infer *at most* that $f$ must also rank $wP'x$ and that $xRy \Leftrightarrow xR'y$, $wRz \Leftrightarrow wR'z$ and $wRy \Leftrightarrow$

$wR'y$. On the other hand, if $f$ is neutral and ranks $wPx$, then we can infer that $f$ must also rank $wP'x$, $yPz$, $zP'y$, $xPy$, $xP'y$, $wPy$, $wP'y$, $xPz$, $zP'x$, $wPz$, and $wP'z$. In other words, we can infer *every* pairwise ranking under *both* profiles from the information that $f$ is neutral and that $wPx$.□

Now if $i \in N$ has a veto for the ordered pair $(x, y)$ under the aggregation rule $f$ and $f$ is neutral, then clearly $i$ will have a veto for *all* ordered pairs. Therefore we have the following immediate corollary to Theorem 2.4 and Lemma 2.3:

**Theorem 2.5** *Let $|X| > n$. If an aggregation rule is acyclic, weakly Paretian and neutral, then some individual has a veto.*

If it is also assumed that the aggregation rule satisfies a certain "monotonicity" property, then this result holds for $|X| = n$ as well [Exercise].

## 2.4   Decisive sets and filters

The proofs given for Theorems 2.1, 2.3, and 2.4 above are classical and clearly demonstrate the role played by each of the maintained conditions. However, there is an alternative approach to establishing the results, focussing directly on decisive sets, that exposes a deep common structure underlying each of the theorems. Before going on to ask what happens if we eschew any notion of preference-driven collective choice, therefore, we first explore the relationships between the families of decisive sets induced by transitive, quasi-transitive and acylic preference aggregation rules that are independent of irrelevant alternatives and weakly Paretian.

For notational ease let $\mathcal{Q}$ denote the subset of $\mathcal{B}$ such that $R$ is quasitransitive, $\mathcal{A}$ the subset of $\mathcal{B}$ such that $R$ is acyclic, and recall $\mathcal{R}$ is the subset of $\mathcal{B}$ such that $R$ is transitive.

For any set $T$, let $\mathcal{T}$ denote a family of subsets of $T$. $\mathcal{T}$ may have certain properties; five possibilities are:

$$(P1) \quad T \in \mathcal{T}, \ \emptyset \notin \mathcal{T}$$
$$(P2) \quad T_1 \in \mathcal{T} \ \& \ T_1 \subset T_2 \Rightarrow T_2 \in \mathcal{T}$$
$$(P3) \quad T_1, T_2 \in \mathcal{T} \Rightarrow T_1 \cap T_2 \in \mathcal{T}$$
$$(P4) \quad T_1, T_2, \ldots, T_t \in \mathcal{T} \Rightarrow \cap_{s=1}^{t} T_s \neq \emptyset$$
$$(P5) \quad T_1 \notin \mathcal{T} \Rightarrow T \backslash T_1 \in \mathcal{T}.$$

Note that, together, (P1) and (P3) imply (P4).

**Definition 2.11** *A family of subsets $\mathcal{T}$ is*
*(1) a filter iff $\mathcal{T}$ satisfies (P1), (P2) and (P3);*
*(2) a prefilter iff $\mathcal{T}$ satisfies (P1), (P2) and (P4);*
*(3) an ultrafilter iff $\mathcal{T}$ satisfies (P1), (P2), (P3) and (P5).*

An immediate implication of the preceding definitions and Theorem 2.4 is that if $|X| \geq n$ and if $f$ is weakly Paretian, then $\mathcal{L}(f)$ is a prefilter. Less immediate results are given in the following theorem.

**Theorem 2.6** *Let a preference aggregation rule $f$ be weakly Paretian and independent of irrelevant alternatives. Then,*
*(1) $f : \mathcal{R}^n \to \mathcal{R}$ implies $\mathcal{L}(f)$ is an ultrafilter;*
*(2) $f : \mathcal{R}^n \to \mathcal{Q}$ implies $\mathcal{L}(f)$ is a filter.*

**Proof.** By definition, $f$ weakly Paretian implies $N \in \mathcal{L}(f)$. Similarly, for any profile such that, $\forall i \in N$, $xP_iy$, $f$ weakly Paretian implies $\sim [yPx]$; hence, $\emptyset \notin \mathcal{L}(f)$. So (P1) holds in each case. Next, note that (P2) holds by definition of a decisive set.

Now suppose $f : \mathcal{R}^n \to \mathcal{Q}$ and consider two decisive sets, $L, M \in \mathcal{L}(f)$. Let $\rho$ be any profile such that,

$$i \in L \cap M, \quad xP_izP_iy$$
$$\forall j \in L \backslash M, \quad xP_jz, \, yP_jz$$
$$\forall k \in N \backslash L, \quad zP_kx, \, zP_ky.$$

Since $\forall i \in L \in \mathcal{L}(f)$, $xP_iz$, we have $xPz$. Since $\forall i \in M \in \mathcal{L}(f)$, $zP_iy$, we have $zPy$. By $f(\cdot) \in \mathcal{Q}$, therefore, $xPy$. Hence, by $f$ independent of irrelevant alternatives, $L \cap M$ is decisive for $x$ against $y$. Because $x$ and $y$ are arbitrary, we must have $L \cap M \in \mathcal{L}(f)$; i.e. (P3) holds here. This proves claim (2) of the theorem.

Because $\mathcal{Q} \supset \mathcal{R}$, the preceding argument shows (P3) holds for $f : \mathcal{R}^n \to \mathcal{R}$. To complete the proof of claim (1), consider a set $L \subseteq N$, a triple $\{x, y, z\} \subseteq X$, and a profile $\rho$ such that $\forall i \in L$, $xP_iz$. Assume $N \backslash L$ is *not* decisive for $y$ against $x$; $\sim [yD_{N \backslash L}x]$. Since $\sim [yD_{N \backslash L}x]$, there must exist a profile $\rho^1$ such that, $\forall j \in N \backslash L$, $yP_j^1x$ yet $xR^1y$. Now consider $\rho^2$ with $\rho^2|_{\{x,y\}} = \rho^1|_{\{x,y\}}$ and $\rho^2|_{\{x,z\}} = \rho|_{\{x,z\}}$:

$$\forall i \in L, \quad xP_i^2z, \, yP_i^2z$$
$$\forall j \in N \backslash L, \quad yP_j^2x, \, yP_j^2z.$$

By $f$ independent of irrelevant alternatives, $xR^2y$. By $f$ weakly Paretian, $yP^2z$. So by $f(\cdot) \in \mathcal{R}$, $xP^2z$. Whence $f$ independent of irrelevant alternatives gives $L$ decisive for $x$ against $z$; $xD_Lz$. Now let $\rho'$ be such that, $\forall i \in L$, $zP_i'y$ and consider the profile $\rho^3$ with $\rho^3|_{\{x,y\}} = \rho^1|_{\{x,y\}}$ and $\rho^3|_{\{y,z\}} = \rho'|_{\{y,z\}}$:

$$\forall i \in L, \qquad zP_i^3 y,\; zP_i^3 x$$
$$\forall j \in N\backslash L, \quad yP_j^3 x,\; zP_j^3 x.$$

By $f$ independent of irrelevant alternatives, $xR^3y$. By $f$ weakly Paretian, $zP^3x$. So by $f(\cdot) \in \mathcal{R}$, $zP^3y$. Whence $f$ independent of irrelevant alternatives gives $L$ decisive for $z$ against $y$; $zD_Ly$. Therefore, since $z$ is arbitrary up to $z \notin \{x,y\}$, we can, *mutatis mutandis*, repeat the preceding argument to yield:

$$
\begin{aligned}
\sim [yD_{N\backslash L}x] &\Rightarrow [\forall z \notin \{x,y\},\, xD_Lz \;\&\; zD_Ly] \\
&\Rightarrow \;\sim [zD_{N\backslash L}x] \\
&\Rightarrow [\forall w \notin \{x,z\},\, xD_Lw \;\&\; wD_Lz] \\
&\Rightarrow \;\sim [zD_{N\backslash L}w] \\
&\Rightarrow [\forall v \notin \{w,z\},\, wD_Lv \;\&\; vD_Lz] \\
&\Rightarrow \;\sim [vD_{N\backslash L}w] \\
&\Rightarrow [\forall s \notin \{v,w\},\, wD_Ls \;\&\; sD_Lv].
\end{aligned}
$$

In other words, if $N\backslash L$ is not decisive for some ordered pair of alternatives $(y,x) \in X^2$, then $L$ must be decisive for all ordered pairs of alternatives $(a,b) \in X^2$. Therefore, given $f$ weakly Paretian and independent of irrelevant alternatives, $f : \mathcal{R}^n \to \mathcal{R}$ implies (P5). This proves claim (1).□

**Corollary 2.1** *Arrow's General Possibility Theorem.*

**Proof.** By Theorem 2.6(1), if $f$ is transitive, weakly Paretian, and independent of irrelevant alternatives, then $\mathcal{L}(f)$ is an ultrafilter. Let $L^* \equiv \bigcap_{L \in \mathcal{L}(f)} L$. By (P3), $L^* \in \mathcal{L}(f)$; and by (P1), $L^* \neq \emptyset$. Let $i \in L^*$ and suppose $\{i\} \notin \mathcal{L}(f)$. Then, by (P5), $N\backslash\{i\} \in \mathcal{L}(f)$. But this contradicts $i \in L^*$. Hence $L^* = \{i\} \in \mathcal{L}(f)$ and $f$ is dictatorial.□

Theorem 2.6 and the preceding remark reveal clearly the trade-off between the concentration of power in a society and the extent to which social preferences are "rational": the set $\bigcap_{L\in\mathcal{L}(f)} L$ is a dictator when $f(\cdot) \in \mathcal{R}$, an oligarchy when $f(\cdot) \in \mathcal{Q}$, and a collegium when $f(\cdot) \in \mathcal{A}$. The converse statements to the result, however, are not true.

**Example 2.8** Let $N = \{1,2\}$ and $X = \{x,y,z\}$. Let $B \in \mathcal{B}$ be asymmetric with $xBy$, $yBz$, $zBx$. Define the aggregation rule $f$ by,

$$\forall a,b \in X, \; aPb \Leftrightarrow aP_1b \text{ or } (aI_1b \;\&\; aBb).$$

Then $\mathcal{L}(f) = \{\{1\}, \{1,2\}\}$ is an ultrafilter (hence a filter and a prefilter). But for any $\rho \in \mathcal{R}^2$ with $xI_1yI_1z$, $f(\rho) \notin \mathcal{A} \supset \mathcal{Q} \supset \mathcal{R}.\square$

For any proper set of decisive coalitions, $\mathcal{L}$, define the aggregation rule induced by $\mathcal{L}$, denoted, $f_{\mathcal{L}}$ as:

$$\forall x, y \in X, \; xP_{\mathcal{L}}y \Leftrightarrow [\exists L \in \mathcal{L} : \forall i \in L, \; xP_iy].$$

Then the following is immediate from the relevant definitions.

**Theorem 2.7** *Let $\mathcal{L}$ be a proper family of decisive coalitions. If $\mathcal{L}$ is,*
*(1) an ultrafilter, then $f_{\mathcal{L}} : \mathcal{R}^n \to \mathcal{R}$;*
*(2) a filter, then $f_{\mathcal{L}} : \mathcal{R}^n \to \mathcal{Q}$;*
*(3) a prefilter, then $f_{\mathcal{L}} : \mathcal{R}^n \to \mathcal{A}$.*
*In each case, $f_{\mathcal{L}}$ is weakly Paretian and independent of irrelevant alternatives.*

## 2.5 Collective choice rules

Insisting on rationality of social preferences requires some concentration of power within the society; as demonstrated in the above theorems, the degree of rationality required determines the degree of concentration. Often, however, all that is required is for an "acceptable" social choice to be made, which in principle is considerably less demanding than requiring any rationality property for social preferences. For instance, suppose there are four alternatives, $X = \{w, x, y, z\}$; suppose under some profile there exists a majority preference cycle over the triple $\{x, y, z\}$; and suppose that for each alternative $b$ in the triple there is a majority of individuals that strictly prefers the alternative $w$. Then there is an unequivocally "best" alternative relative to majority rule (i.e. $w$) although the majority preference relation under the profile is evidently cyclic. So can we do better without any collective rationality conditions at all? To address this question, we shift attention away from preference aggregation rules to collective choice rules, i.e. to aggregation rules that map preference profiles directly into choices rather than into binary relations over alternatives.

**Definition 2.12** *A collective choice rule is a map, $\varphi : \mathcal{R}^n \times \mathcal{X} \to \mathcal{X}$, such that $\varphi(\rho, \cdot)$ is a choice function; i.e. for all $(\rho, S) \in \mathcal{R}^n \times \mathcal{X}$, $\varphi(\rho, S) \subseteq S$.*

Thus a collective choice rule associates with every preference profile and set of alternatives a nonempty subset of those alternatives (recall that $\mathcal{X}$ is defined to be the family of all nonempty subsets of $X$).

Consider now the following conditions on choices from two-alternative sets:

**Definition 2.13** *A collective choice rule $\varphi$ is:*

*(1) nondictatorial if there does not exist $i \in N$ such that for all $\rho \in \mathcal{R}^n$ and all $x, y \in X$, $xP_iy$ implies $\{x\} = \varphi(\rho, \{x,y\})$.*

*(2) veto-proof if there does not exist $i \in N$ such that for all $\rho \in \mathcal{R}^n$ and all $x, y \in X$, $xP_iy$ implies $x \in \varphi(\rho, \{x,y\})$.*

*(3) weakly Paretian if for all $\rho \in \mathcal{R}^n$ and all $x, y \in X$, $xP_iy$ $\forall i \in N$ implies $\varphi(\rho, \{x,y\}) = \{x\}$.*

*(4) independent of irrelevant alternatives if for all $\rho \in \mathcal{R}^n$ and any $x, y \in X$, $\rho|_{\{x,y\}} = \rho'|_{\{x,y\}}$ implies $\varphi(\rho, \{x,y\}) = \varphi(\rho', \{x,y\})$.*

These conditions are simply the natural analogues to properties of preference aggregation rules introduced earlier, and similar remarks apply equally here. Similarly, the following definitions are self-explanatory in the light of the discussion of choice functions in Chapter 1.

**Definition 2.14** *A collective choice rule $\varphi$ satisfies:*

*(1) weak axiom of revealed preference if for all $\rho \in \mathcal{R}^n$, $\varphi(\rho, \cdot)$ satisfies the weak axiom of revealed preference.*

*(2) path independence if for all $\rho \in \mathcal{R}^n$, $\varphi(\rho, \cdot)$ satisfies path independence.*

*(3) condition $\alpha$ if for all $\rho \in \mathcal{R}^n$, $\varphi(\rho, \cdot)$ satisfies condition $\alpha$.*

**Theorem 2.8** *If a collective choice rule $\varphi$ is weakly Paretian, independent of irrelevant alternatives and nondictatorial, then $\varphi$ fails to satisfy the weak axiom of revealed preference.*

**Proof.** Suppose $\varphi$ satisfies the hypotheses of the claim and also satisfies the weak axiom of revealed preference (WARP). By Theorems 1.4 and 1.5 and the fact that $\varphi(\rho, \cdot)$ is a choice function, we know that WARP implies the base relation $R_\varphi(\rho)$ is transitive for all $\rho$. Since $R_\varphi(\rho)$ is by definition reflexive and complete for all $\rho \in \mathcal{R}^n$, $R_\varphi(\rho)$ is thus a transitive aggregation rule. Further, since $\varphi$ satisfies independence of irrelevant alternatives we know that $R_\varphi(\cdot)$ satisfies the definition of independence in terms of an aggregation rule; and $\varphi$ being weakly Paretian implies $R_\varphi(\cdot)$ is a weakly Paretian aggregation rule. Therefore, applying Theorem 2.1 we have that the aggregation $R_\varphi(\cdot)$ must be dictatorial; hence $\varphi$ is dictatorial, contradicting the supposition.$\square$

This result, a collective choice rule analogue to Arrow's Theorem, suggests that so long as we insist on social choices being based on reasonable criteria, relaxing the requirement that $X$ be ranked by an aggregation rule is not going to lead to any more normatively attractive results than with demanding some degree of collective rationality. The following two results, providing choice rule analogues to Theorems 2.3 and 2.5, affirm the suggestion.

**Theorem 2.9** *If a collective choice rule $\varphi$ is weakly Paretian, independent of irrelevant alternatives and veto-proof, then $\varphi$ fails to satisfy path independence.*

**Proof.**  Suppose $\varphi$ satisfies the hypotheses of the claim and also satisfies path independence. By Lemma 1.3(2) and the fact that, for all profiles $\rho \in \mathcal{R}^n$, $\varphi(\rho, \cdot)$ is a choice function, we know that path independence implies the base relation associated with $\varphi(\rho, \cdot)$, denoted $R_\varphi(\rho)$, is quasi-transitive for all $\rho$. And since $R_\varphi(\rho)$ is by definition reflexive and complete for all $\rho \in \mathcal{R}^n$, $R_\varphi(\cdot)$ is a quasi-transitive aggregation rule. Further, since $\varphi$ satisfies independence of irrelevant alternatives we know that $R_\varphi(\cdot)$ satisfies the definition of independence in terms of an aggregation rule; and $\varphi$ being weakly Paretian implies $R_\varphi(\cdot)$ is a weakly Paretian aggregation rule. Therefore, applying Theorem 2.3 we have that the aggregation $R_\varphi(\cdot)$ must be oligarchic, implying some individuals have a veto with respect to pairwise comparisons. Hence $\varphi$ cannot be veto-proof; a contradiction.□

As Theorem 2.9 is the analogue to Theorem 2.3 with respect to collective choice rules, so too we can identify an analogue to Theorem 2.5.

**Definition 2.15** *A collective choice rule $\varphi$ is neutral if for all $\rho, \rho' \in \mathcal{R}^n$ and all $x, y, a, b \in X$, $[P(x, y; \rho) = P(a, b; \rho')$ & $P(y, x; \rho) = P(b, a; \rho')]$ imply $[x \in \varphi(\rho, \{x, y\})$ if and only if $a \in \varphi(\rho', \{a, b\})]$.*

As before, if $\varphi$ is neutral then $\varphi$ is independent of irrelevant alternatives.

**Theorem 2.10** *Let $|X| > n$; if a collective choice rule $\varphi$ is weakly Paretian, neutral, and veto-proof, then $\varphi$ fails to satisfy condition $\alpha$.*

**Proof.**  Suppose $\varphi$ satisfies the hypotheses of the claim and also satisfies condition $\alpha$. By Lemma 1.1 and $\varphi(\rho, \cdot)$ a choice function, the base relation associated with $\varphi(\rho, \cdot)$, $R_\varphi(\rho)$, is acyclic for all $\rho \in \mathcal{R}^n$ And since by definition $R_\varphi(\rho)$ is reflexive and complete for all $\rho \in \mathcal{R}^n$, $R_\varphi(\cdot)$ is an acyclic aggregation rule. Further, if $\varphi$ is a neutral and weakly Paretian collective choice rule then $R_\varphi(\cdot)$ will be a neutral and weakly Paretian aggregation rule. Therefore by Theorem 2.5 there exists an individual with a veto with respect to $R_\varphi(\cdot)$. Hence $\varphi$ is not veto-proof; a contradiction.□

In this sense the aggregation theorems are even more powerful when one considers collective choice rules: arguably reasonable restrictions imposed only on pairwise choices guarantee a lack of contraction-consistency with respect to collective choice. Another way to look at these results is as follows. Suppose majority rule is the agreed-upon method for selecting alternatives in pairwise comparisons (in Section 3.6 below we will see a normative justification of this); let $\varphi_m$ denote any collective choice rule that employs majority rule on pairwise choice sets. Now since the majority method as a collective choice rule is veto-proof, independent of irrelevant alternatives, and nondictatorial, Theorem 2.9 implies $\varphi_m$ must fail to be path independent. Therefore, however choices are made from sets larger than two, such choices are sensitive to the path through which they come about. But then this says that when there are at least three alternatives in $X$, *any* collective choice rule which uses majority rule on pairwise subsets is subject to manipulation by those in charge of choosing the sequence in which alternatives are considered.

## 2.6   Discussion

In moving from Chapter 1 to this chapter, the locus of concern shifts from the notions of preference and choice in the abstract to that of aggregating individual preferences into some collective preference relation. In Chapter 1, we investigated the conditions required of any given preference relation over a set to insure that preference-based choices are well-defined for any agenda (subset of feasible alternatives). The essential condition turned out to be acyclicity of preferences. In this chapter, we begin with an arbitrary collection of transitive preference relations over the set, and investigate conditions under which this set of transitive preferences can be aggregated into a single preference relation capable of inducing well-defined choices (i.e. elements of the maximal set) from any agenda. The focal interpretation here is that it is individual members of society who hold the transitive preference relations and the aggregation is up to a "social" preference relation.

The results are fairly dramatic. There turns out to be a fundamental trade-off between what one might loosely call "collective rationality" and the extent to which decision-making power is concentrated in the hands of a subset of individuals. Suppose any aggregation procedure is required to satisfy *weak Pareto* (if everyone agrees $x$ is strictly better than $y$, then the aggregate preference relation should also rank $x$ strictly better than $y$) and *independence of irrelevant alternatives* (when aggregating individuals' preferences over a given pair of alternatives $x$ and $y$, the aggregation procedure should only use the ordinal information contained in individuals' preferences over this pair). Then Theorem 2.1 (Arrow's Theorem) states that the only logically possible procedure that can lead to a transitive aggregate preference relation for any arbitrary set of individual preferences is the procedure that selects a given individual by name and simply replicates that individual's preference ordering (save possibly for cases in which the individual is indifferent); Theorem 2.3 states that the only logically possible procedure that can lead to a quasi-transitive aggregate preference relation is one in which each member of an identified set of individuals is given a veto over all decisions and, should all members of the set agree on a ranking, then the procedure reflects their choice; and Theorem 2.4, together with Lemma 2.3, states that the only logically possible procedures that can lead to an acyclic aggregate preference relation on all sets of alternatives, are those in which at least one individual is given a veto over some decisions. In general, there is a close connection between the rationality properties of a preference aggregation rule and the structure of the family of decisive coalitions it induces, where a coalition is decisive if, whenever all members of the coalition share a common strict preference, the aggregation rule records this preference as the social preference (Theorems 2.6 and 2.7).

One response to the preceding results is to look for aggregation procedures that take individual preferences directly into social choices, finessing any demand for a social preference. However, there is, as we argue in Chapter 1, an intimate relationship between consistent choice (however defined) and the existence of an implicit acyclic preference relation. Consequently, as Theorems 2.8, 2.9, and 2.10 make clear, this approach offers no escape from the trade-off between consistent aggregate choice and concentration of power.

It is worth reiterating here that the use of the term "power" is not entirely the colloquial one. For instance, an individual whose preferences determine all but one decision – however many or however important – is *not* a "dictator" in the sense of Theorem 2.1; so to say that an aggregation rule is dictatorial is to say that it concentrates power to a far greater extent than any historical dictator has ever experienced. On the other hand, such a "dictator" may never appreciate her power – preference aggregation rules are analogous to computer programs: the input is the list of individual preference relations over the set of alternatives; the output is an aggregate preference relation; and a preference aggregation rule is the software used to map input into output. Thus, in and of themselves, the results of this chapter do not say anything directly about how particular electoral rules, voting procedures, or markets, say, work in practice. When such rules are applied, the inputs are individuals' reports of (parts of) their preference relations rather than the preference relations *per se* and there is no logically necesssary reason to presume that such reports will always be offered (people abstain) or reflect true preferences (people are strategic). So claims of the sort, "Arrow's Theorem shows that social choices must be cyclic" are simply *nonsequiturs*. However, the results do have deep empirical and normative import. For example, since no extant or proposed collective decision making procedure embodies the sort of concentration of power reflected in Arrow's Theorem, the result implies that *no* such procedure can both insure well-defined decisions and satisfy two (individually) weak normative desiderata of respecting pairwise unanimity and independence.

Although aggregating individual preferences directly into social choices is not a promising approach to avoiding the trade-off between collective rationality and the concentration of decision-making power, Theorem 2.4 suggests that acyclic aggregate preference relations might be derived on restricted sets of alternatives. Similarly, the results leave open the possibility of successfully aggregating more restricted classes of individual preferences than the class of all transitive relations. The next two chapters take up these issues.

## 2.7 Exercises

**2.1** (a) Discuss the extent to which independence of irrelevant alternatives is implicit in the definition of a decisive set.
(b) Prove that the only decisive set under the Pareto extension rule is $N$.

**2.2** (a) Develop an example to show that the construction used in the proof to Lemma 2.3, where $|X| > n$, fails when $|X| = n$.
(b) An aggregation rule is *weakly monotonic* if, $\forall x, y \in X$, $\forall \rho, \rho' \in \mathcal{R}^n$,

$$[\rho|_{X \setminus \{x\}} = \rho'|_{X \setminus \{x\}}, \ P(x,y;\rho) \subseteq P(x,y;\rho'), \ R(x,y;\rho) \subseteq R(x,y;\rho') \ \& \ xPy]$$

imply $xP'y$. Show: If $f$ is acyclic, neutral, and weakly monotonic, then there exists an individual with a veto when $|X| \geq n$. Briefly compare this result to Theorem 2.5.

**2.3** A preference aggregation rule $f$ satisfies *citizens' sovereignty* if, $\forall x, y \in X$ ($x \neq y$), $\exists \rho \in \mathcal{R}^n$ such that $xPy$. Prove that if $f$ is independent of irrelevant alternatives, weakly monotonic and satisfies citizens' sovereignty then $f$ is weakly Paretian. What if anything can you say if $f$ is not presumed independent of irrelevant alternatives?

**2.4** A preference aggregation rule $f$ satisfies *minimal liberalism* if there exist two distinct individuals $i, j \in N$ and two (not necessarily distinct) pairs of alternatives $\{w, x\}$, $\{y, z\}$ in $X$ such that $i$ is decisive both ways over $\{w, x\}$ and $j$ is decisive both ways over $\{y, z\}$. Prove that there exists no weakly Paretian and acyclic preference aggregation rule $f$ satisfying minimal liberalism. Briefly discuss the import of this result.

**2.5** Let $\varphi : \mathcal{R}^n \times X \to \mathcal{X}$ be a collective choice rule, and (since $X$ is fixed) write $\varphi(\rho, X) \equiv \varphi(\rho)$. Consider the following conditions and result (Denicolo [24]):

(1) $\forall x, y \in X, \ yP_i x \ \forall i \in N \Rightarrow x \notin \varphi(\rho)$.

(2) $\forall x, y \in X, \ \forall \rho, \rho' \in \mathcal{R}^n, \ [x \in \varphi(\rho), \ y \notin \varphi(\rho), \ \& \ \rho|_{\{x,y\}} \equiv \rho'|_{\{x,y\}}] \Rightarrow y \notin \varphi(\rho')$.

(3) $\exists i \in N$ such that, $\forall x, y \in X, \ \forall \rho \in \mathcal{R}^n, \ xP_i y \Rightarrow y \notin \varphi(\rho)$.

**Theorem** If $\varphi$ satisfies (1) and (2), then $\varphi$ satisfies (3).

Explain the relationship between this result and Arrow's General Possibility Theorem. [HINT: look for a formal connection between the two by constructing a preference aggregation rule, say $f_\varphi$, from the collective choice rule $\varphi$ as follows: for any profile $\rho$ and any pair of alternatives, $x, y$, let $\rho(xy)$ be the profile constructed from $\rho$ by moving $\{x, y\}$ to the top of every individuals' ranking under $\rho$, and preserving the orderings between $x$ and $y$ and between all other alternatives; now say $xf_\varphi(\rho)y$ iff $x \in \varphi(\rho(xy))$.]

## 2.8 Further reading

The literature on the axiomatic theory of preference aggregation is vast. McLean [47] reviews some very early (i.e. medieval) formal analysis of voting procedures; Sen [79][80][81] are outstanding surveys of the more contemporary literature that cover a great deal more than is in Chapter 2. See also Plott [58] and Riker [60] for explicit interpretations of the theory for politics and public policy analysis. Arrow [1][3] is the seminal reference for the modern theory; Blau [11] corrected the original Arrow [1] proof of Theorem

2.1, and Sen [77] showed that admitting intra-personal cardinalities left the result intact. Theorem 2.3 is due to Gibbard [32]; Guha [36] and Mas-Colell and Sonnenschein [44] also explore the trade-off between power and collective rationality by looking only for quasi-transitive preference aggregation rules. Theorem 2.4 is due to Brown [15][16]; Blau and Deb [13], and Blair and Pollak [10] continue the study of acyclic rules. See also Ferejohn [27] for a discussion of the relationship between the collegium and individuals with veto power. Blair, Bordes, Kelly, and Suzumura [9] is the key paper for aggregation results that eschew any explicit imposition of rationality conditions on preference aggregation rules. Sen [82] goes further: he shows that we can replace all explicit consistency conditions on choice functions with a stronger independence condition than Arrow's and still find that the power/rationality trade-off persists. Much of the literature generated by Arrow's Theorem explores the consequences of relaxing conditions other than collective rationality and non-dictatorship: Hansson [37] and Kirman and Sonderman [41] look at Arrow's Theorem with an infinite number of individuals (arguably the appropriate assumption when considering intergenerational social choice or very large societies); Wilson [90] is the first to prove a version of the result without assuming $f$ weakly Paretian; Blau [12] relaxes the rationality assumptions on individual preferences; and Sen [80] surveys much of what can occur without the independence condition. In particular, relaxing the Arrovian independence condition in principle allows preference aggregation rules to use information on interpersonal comparisons of welfare, thus permitting a wider-ranging normative analysis of social choice than that offered here.

# Chapter 3

# Restricting Outcomes

In Chapter 2, the domain of a preference aggregation rule is explicitly written as the set of all profiles of weak preference orders on $X$, $\mathcal{R}^n$. Thus the domain condition used in the results derived so far involves only two substantive restrictions: that individual preferences be weak orders and that the set of alternatives be finite. With these restrictions, we saw in Chapter 2 how the set of decisive coalitions associated with a preference aggregation rule is intimately related to the possibility of "rationally" aggregating individual preferences. For example, Theorem 2.1 (Arrow's Theorem) states that any transitive and weakly Paretian aggregation rule satisfying independence of irrelevant alternatives must have a unique minimal decisive set and this set is singleton (the "dictator"), while Theorem 2.4 shows that any acyclic and weakly Paretian rule must have some individuals in *all* decisive coalitions (the "collegium") if the number of alternatives is sufficiently large. An open issue, therefore, concerns how these and related theorems depend upon the apparently mild domain restrictions imposed on preference aggregation rules. In particular, Theorem 2.4 left the door open for rules to be acyclic if the number of alternatives is not some arbitrary finite integer, but suitably restricted. After all, for many practical problems there are relatively few alternatives to be considered: for example, there is typically only a small number of candidates or parties in any general election; there are only a few feasible locations for the safe confinement of nuclear waste; and there are only two available choices once an alternative to the status quo is proposed by a committee under legislative closed rule. In this chapter, therefore, we maintain the assumption that any logically possible profile of weak preference orders is admissible and explore in detail the structure of three (related) classes of empirically important rules, focusing on the extent to which rules in these classes can be expected to be acyclic over restricted sets of alternatives. Such a focus is justified by Theorem 1.1, which states that without acyclicity there is always the possibility that a rule will fail to yield a well-defined selection from every agenda and that, if a preference aggregation rule $f$ is acyclic, then for every agenda $S \subseteq X$ the maximal set $M(f(\cdot), S)$ is nonempty. In the next chapter, we leave the sets of alternatives unconstrained and examine instead the properties of the identified classes of rule under restrictions on admissible preference profiles.

The relationship between the three classes of rule – *simple rules*, *voting rules*, and *counting rules* – turns out to be as illustrated in Figure 3.1.

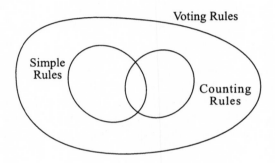

Figure 3.1: Three classes of preference aggregation rules

Thus all simple rules and all counting rules are voting rules, but the converse is not true; and while some counting rules are simple, there are simple rules that are not counting rules and there are counting rules that are not simple. In what follows, we first define and characterize each class of rule and then provide results on their acyclicity. And although the broadest class is that of voting rules, it is pedagogically convenient to begin with analyzing simple rules. This we now do.

## 3.1   Decisive coalitions and simple rules

We begin by attempting to discover when it is sufficient to examine an aggregation rule's set of decisive coalitions, or, put another way, when it is the case that the information about social preference contained in a set of decisive coalitions is the same as that in the underlying aggregation rule.

Recall that the set of decisive coalitions associated with an aggregation rule $f$, denoted $\mathcal{L}(f)$, is defined by

$$L \in \mathcal{L}(f) \Leftrightarrow [\forall x, y \in X, \ \forall \rho \in \mathcal{R}^n, \ xP_iy \ \forall i \in L \Rightarrow xPy]$$

and that the family $\mathcal{L}(f)$ is proper and monotonic (Lemma 2.2). Next, for any family of coalitions $\mathcal{L} \subseteq 2^N$ we can define an aggregation rule induced by $\mathcal{L}$, denoted $f_{\mathcal{L}}$, as

$$\forall x, y \in X, \ xP_{\mathcal{L}}y \Leftrightarrow [\exists L \in \mathcal{L} : \forall i \in L, \ xP_iy].$$

Note that the the induced aggregation rule $f_{\mathcal{L}}$ is only well-defined if $\mathcal{L}$ is proper.

Now consider the relationship between $f_{\mathcal{L}(f)}$, i.e. the aggregation rule generated by the decisive sets of some original aggregation rule $f$, and the original rule $f$ itself. Clearly, if $x$ is socially preferred to $y$ under the rule $f_{\mathcal{L}(f)}$ it will be under $f$ as well; however the converse need not hold.

**Definition 3.1** *An aggregation rule $f$ is a simple rule if $f = f_{\mathcal{L}(f)}$.*

Hence for simple rules knowledge of the decisive sets associated with the rule is equivalent to knowledge of the rule itself, and so focusing attention solely on the decisive sets is legitimate. Thus our first goal is to characterize simple rules. Example 3.1 both illustrates the preceding concepts and shows that not all rules are simple rules; i.e. knowledge of the decisive sets for some rules does not provide a complete description of those rules.

**Example 3.1** Let $f_p$ be *plurality rule*; i.e. $\forall x, y \in X, \ \forall \rho \in \mathcal{R}^n$,

$$xP_{f_p}y \Leftrightarrow |P(x, y; \rho)| > |P(y, x; \rho)|$$

Therefore, for plurality rule a coalition is decisive only if it contains more than half the members of $N$: $\mathcal{L}(f_p) = \{L \subseteq N : |L| > n/2\}$. Consider the rule $f_{\mathcal{L}(f_p)}$ induced by the family of decisive coalitions $\mathcal{L}(f_p)$. By definition

$$\forall x, y \in X, \ \forall \rho \in \mathcal{R}^n, \ xP_{\mathcal{L}(f_p)}y \Leftrightarrow |P(x, y; \rho)| > n/2.$$

And this rule is exactly *majority rule*, $f_m$. Now let $N = \{1, 2, 3\}$ and $\rho$ be such that for $x, y \in X : xP_1y$ and $xI_iy$, $i = 2, 3$. Then $xP_{f_p}y$ but $xI_{f_m}y$. Hence $f_p \neq f_{\mathcal{L}(f_p)}$ and plurality rule is *not* a simple rule; in particular, although individual 1's strict preference for $x$ over $y$ is the social preference at $\rho$, $\{1\} \notin \mathcal{L}(f_p)$ because, for $\rho'$ such that $xP_1'y$, $yP_2'x$, and $yP_3'x$, we have $yP_{f_p}'x$. On the other hand, suppose we begin with majority rule, $f_m$. Then $\mathcal{L}(f_m) \equiv \mathcal{L}(f_p)$ and we have $f_m = f_{\mathcal{L}(f_m)}$. So majority rule is simple.$\square$

Consider the following list of properties an aggregation rule might satisfy:

**Definition 3.2** *Given any profiles $\rho, \rho' \in \mathcal{R}^n$ and $x, y \in X$, an aggregation rule $f$ is:*

*(1) decisive if and only if*

$$[P(x, y; \rho) = P(x, y; \rho') \text{ and } xPy] \text{ imply } xP'y.$$

*(2) monotonic if and only if*

$$[P(x, y; \rho) \subseteq P(x, y; \rho'), R(x, y; \rho) \subseteq R(x, y; \rho') \text{ and } xPy] \text{ imply } xP'y.$$

Thus, if $f$ is decisive then as long as the set of individuals strictly preferring $x$ to $y$ remains the same, the social preference remains the same. In particular, the social preference of $x$ over $y$ is invariant to changes in which individuals who were originally indifferent between the two now favor $y$ over $x$. And $f$ monotonic implies that if $x$ is socially preferred to $y$, then increasing the support for $x$ over $y$, or decreasing the opposition, does not eliminate this social preference.

Although superficially similar, decisiveness and monotonicity are logically independent conditions. Moreover, each is likewise independent of the neutrality property introduced in Chapter 2, a property that appears to subsume both decisiveness and monotonicity. This is demonstrated in the following set of examples:

**Example 3.2** (1) Define the aggregation $f$ by: $xPy \Leftrightarrow |P(x, y; \rho)| > n/2$ and $|P(x, y; \rho)|$ is odd. $f$ is decisive and neutral, but is not monotonic: if $xPy$ & $|P(x, y; \rho)|$ is odd, then changing one individual's preference from $yR_i x$ to $xP_i y$ implies it is now no longer the case that $xPy$.

(2) Define the aggregation rule $f$ by: $\forall y \neq z$, $xPy \Leftrightarrow |P(x, y; \rho)| > n/2$ and $xPz \Leftrightarrow |P(x, z; \rho)| > 2n/3$. $f$ is decisive and monotonic, but not neutral: (strict) social preference for any alternative against alternative $z$ requires two-thirds of the population, while (strict) social preference against any other alternative merely requires a simple majority.

(3) Define the aggregation rule $f$ by: $xPy \Leftrightarrow$ either $xP_i y$ $\forall i \in N$, or $xP_1 y$ and $xR_i y$ $\forall i \neq 1$. $f$ is neutral and monotonic, but is not decisive: if the profile $\rho$ is such that $xP_1 y$ and $xI_i y$ for all $i \neq 1$, then $xPy$; yet under a profile $\rho'$ such that $xP_1' y$ and $yP_i' x$ for all $i \neq 1$ we have that $\sim [xP'y]$. $\square$

Which preference aggregation rules are simple and what set of properties must any such rule satisfy? The following characterization theorem provides answers to both questions.

**Theorem 3.1** *An aggregation rule is a simple rule if and only if it is decisive, neutral, and monotonic.*

**Proof.** (Sufficiency) First note that $\forall x, y \in X$, $xP_{\mathcal{L}(f)}y \Rightarrow xPy$. To prove the result, then, it suffices to show the converse statement must hold when $f$ satisfies the maintained properties. So suppose $f$ is decisive, neutral, and monotonic. Consider a profile $\rho$ and assume $xPy$. Let $L^* \equiv P(x, y; \rho)$. We wish to show that $L^* \in \mathcal{L}(f)$; to do this, we construct a sequence of profiles, $(\rho, \rho^1, \rho^2, \rho^*)$, such that $\rho^*$ is *any* profile with $aP_i^*b$ $\forall i \in L^*$, arbitrary $a, b \in X$, and $aP^*b$. So let $\rho^*$ be any profile such that, $\forall i \in L^*$, $aP_i^*b$ and let $L^+ = P(a, b; \rho^*) \backslash L^*$; note that $L^+$ might be empty. Consider any profile $\rho^1 \in \mathcal{R}^n$ such that $P(a, b; \rho^1) \equiv P(x, y; \rho) = L^*$ and $P(b, a; \rho^1) \equiv P(y, x; \rho)$. Then by neutrality, $aP^1b$. Now let $\rho^2 \in \mathcal{R}^n$ be the profile defined by $R_i^2|_{\{a,b\}} = R_i^*|_{\{a,b\}}$ iff $i \in L^* \cup L^+$ and $R_j^2|_{\{a,b\}} = R_j^1|_{\{a,b\}}$ otherwise. Thus the only individuals whose preferences over $\{a, b\}$ can change in moving from $\rho^1$ to $\rho^2$ are individuals $i \in L^+$, and the only possible change is one that moves $a$ up relative to $b$ in such individuals' rankings. By monotonicity, therefore, $aP^2b$. Because this inference depends on all individuals $i$ *not* in $L^* \cup L^+$ having $bR_i^2a$, it is premature to conclude $L^*$ is a decisive coalition. However, by construction, $P(a, b; \rho^*) \equiv P(a, b; \rho^2)$. Therefore, by $f$ decisive, $aP^*b$. Hence, since $\rho^*$ and $a, b$ are arbitrary save for $aP_i^*b$ if $i \in L^*$ and $aP^*b$, it must be that $L^* \in \mathcal{L}(f)$ as required.

(Necessity) To show necessity, it suffices to show that the induced rule $f_{\mathcal{L}(f)}$ is neutral, monotonic, and decisive since $f = f_{\mathcal{L}(f)}$. Neutrality follows since $\mathcal{L}(f)$ is defined without regard to alternatives; monotonicity follows from Lemma 2.2 and definition of $f_{\mathcal{L}(f)}$; and decisiveness follows directly from the definitions of $\mathcal{L}(f)$ and $f_{\mathcal{L}(f)}$.$\square$

Thus decisive, neutral, and monotonic aggregation rules are completely described by their associated decisive sets and are indeed the *only* aggregation rules having this property. In addition, by monotonicity we can without loss of generality characterize such rules by their minimal decisive sets:

**Definition 3.3** *Let $f$ be a preference aggregation rule with decisive coalitions $\mathcal{L}(f)$. A coalition $L \in \mathcal{L}(f)$ is a minimal decisive coalition if, for all $L' \subset L$, $L' \notin \mathcal{L}(f)$. Let $\mathcal{L}_{\min}(f) \subseteq \mathcal{L}(f)$ denote the set of minimal decisive coalitions for $f$.*

Finally, any individual $j$ in the collegium of a simple rule, i.e. $j \in L$ for all $L \in \mathcal{L}(f)$, has a veto with respect to the simple rule $f$. To see this, note that by definition $xP_{\mathcal{L}(f)}y$ implies $xP_iy$ for all $i \in L$, where $L$ is some decisive coalition, and hence $xP_{\mathcal{L}(f)}y$ implies $xP_jy$, since the presumption is that $j$ is in *all* decisive coalitions. Therefore, $xP_jy$ implies it cannot be the case that $yPx$, or, rather, $xP_jy$ implies $xR_{\mathcal{L}(f)}y$, thus establishing $j$'s veto.

Examples of simple rules include $q$-rules:

**Definition 3.4** *A simple rule $f$ is a $q$-rule if $q > n/2$ and $\mathcal{L}(f) = \{L \subseteq N : |L| \geq q\}$.*

Thus under a $q$-rule a coalition is decisive if and only if the number of members is at least $q$. We have already seen two examples of $q$-rules in the preceding chapter: when $q = n$ then we have the *weak Pareto rule*, requiring all individuals to strictly prefer $x$ to $y$ for society to strictly prefer $x$ to $y$. At the other extreme we have *majority rule*, defined as follows: for any $t \in \Re$ let $\lceil t \rceil$ be the smallest integer greater than or equal to $t$, and let $q_m = \lceil (n + 1)/2 \rceil$ (i.e. $q_m = (n + 1)/2$ when $n$ is odd and $(n/2) + 1$ when $n$ is even). Then majority rule is a $q$-rule with $q = q_m$. And in between unanimity and majority rule lie a sequence of supermajority rules. Empirical examples of $q$-rules are easy to come by. For instance, some criminal trials require unanimous juries to convict; committee decisions and elections are frequently via majority rule; and amending constitutions typically requires a supermajority but not unanimous consent (in the USA, for example, the required majority is 2/3's of the elected legislators in both chambers considered separately).

A more general class of simple rules than $q$-rules are *weighted $q$-rules*, characterized as follows: associate with each $i \in N$, a weight $w_i \geq 0$. Then $f$ is a weighted $q$-rule if $q > \sum_{i \in N} w_i/2$ and $\mathcal{L}(f) = \{L \subseteq N : \sum_{i \in L} w_i \geq q\}$, i.e. the set of decisive coalitions are those whose sum of weights equals or exceeds the critical level $q$. Hence $q$-rules can be thought of as weighted $q$-rules with the weight of each individual equal to one. Examples of asymmetric weighted rules can be found in the corporate world where individuals' votes are weighted by their stake in the company and international organizations, such as the World Bank, that allocates voting power in part according to the size of the contributions to the Bank's resources made by any member country.

It would be convenient if *all* simple rules could be characterized as weighted $q$-rules. However, this is not possible, as the following example makes clear.

**Example 3.3** Let $N = \{1, 2, 3, 4, 5\}$, $\mathcal{L}_{\min} = \{\{1, 2\}, \{1, 3, 4\}, \{2, 4, 5\}\}$, and define $f$ by:

$$\forall x, y \in X, \; xPy \Leftrightarrow [\exists L \in \mathcal{L}_{\min}(f) \text{ such that } L \subseteq P(x, y; \rho)].$$

By definition, $f$ is a simple rule. However, it is not a weighted $q$-rule. To see this, assume the contrary. Then there exists a set of nonnegative weights $\{w_1, w_2, ..., w_5\}$ and $q > \sum_{i \in N} w_i / 2$ such that

$$w_1 + w_3 + w_4 \geq q \text{ and } w_2 + w_4 + w_5 \geq q.$$

These inequalities imply,

$$(w_1 + w_4 + w_5) + (w_2 + w_3 + w_4) \geq 2q.$$

But by definition of $\mathcal{L}_{\min}$, $w_1 + w_4 + w_5 < q$ and $w_2 + w_3 + w_4 < q$ : contradiction.□

On the other hand, for $n \leq 4$ all simple rules can be characterized as weighted $q$-rules [Exercise].

## 3.2 Acyclic simple rules

In this section we focus on the acyclicity of simple rules, or equivalently, on properties of their associated decisive coalitions. Throughout we will assume that the simple rules are weakly Paretian, i.e. $N \in \mathcal{L}(f)$ (note that if $\mathcal{L}$ is monotonic, then $\mathcal{L} \neq \emptyset$ if and only if $N \in \mathcal{L}$).

Recall that $K(\mathcal{L}) \equiv \bigcap_{L_i \in \mathcal{L}} L_i$ is labeled the *collegium* of the family $\mathcal{L}$, and we say that a simple rule $f$ is *collegial* if $K(\mathcal{L}(f)) \neq \emptyset$, and is *noncollegial* otherwise.

**Definition 3.5** *The Nakamura number associated with a simple rule $f$, labeled $s(f)$, is equal to $\infty$ if $f$ is collegial; otherwise,*

$$s(f) = \min\{|\mathcal{L}| : \mathcal{L} \subseteq \mathcal{L}(f) \; \& \; K(\mathcal{L}) = \emptyset\}.$$

In words, the Nakamura number associated with a noncollegial simple rule $f$ is the number of coalitions in the smallest noncollegial subfamily, $\mathcal{L}$, of $\mathcal{L}(f)$ (and note that the Nakamura number can be defined for any preference aggregation rule, not just for simple rules). This is hardly an intuitive concept. Rather than discuss what it means here, however, it is convenient to defer any informal elucidation until after Theorem 3.2, below, which connects the Nakamura number to the acyclicity of simple rules.

In computing the Nakamura number for any noncollegial simple rule, it suffices to look only at the subfamily of minimal decisive coalitions for $f$. So, for example, if $n = 4$ and a simple rule $f$ is such that the minimal decisive coalitions are $\{1,4\}, \{2,4\}, \{3,4\}$, and $\{1,2,3\}$, then $s(f) = 3$. Note that if $f$ is noncollegial there must exist at least three distinct minimally decisive coalitions [Exercise].

**Lemma 3.1** *For any simple rule $f$, $s(f) \geq 3$; and $f$ noncollegial implies $s(f) \leq n$.*

**Proof.** We first show that $s(f) \geq 3$ for any simple rule $f$. If $|\mathcal{L}(f)| = 1$, then $f$ is collegial and $s(f) = \infty$. Suppose $|\mathcal{L}(f)| \geq 2$ and let $L_1, L_2 \in \mathcal{L}(f)$. Then since $\mathcal{L}(f)$ is proper (by Lemma 2.2), $L_1 \cap L_2 \neq \emptyset$. Since this is true for any $L_1, L_2 \in \mathcal{L}(f)$, it must be that $K(\mathcal{L}) \neq \emptyset$ when $|\mathcal{L}| = 2$ and $\mathcal{L} \subseteq \mathcal{L}(f)$; hence $s(f) \geq 3$.

Now assume $f$ is simple and noncollegial. By $f$ noncollegial, for every $i \in N$ there exists some $L \in \mathcal{L}(f)$ such that $i \notin L$. By monotonicity of $\mathcal{L}(f)$, therefore, $\forall i \in N$, $L_i \equiv N \backslash \{i\} \in \mathcal{L}(f)$. Let $\mathcal{L} = \{L_i : i \in N\}$. Then $\mathcal{L} \subseteq \mathcal{L}(f)$, $K(\mathcal{L}) = \emptyset$ and $|K(\mathcal{L})| = n$. Hence, $s(f) \leq n$.$\square$

Hence the function $s(\cdot)$ assigns an integer between 3 and $n$ to every noncollegial simple rule. For more specific examples of the Nakamura number, we compute below this number for $q$-rules (note that a $q$-rule is collegial, and hence has an infinite Nakamura number, if and only if $q = n$) and the special case of majority rule. To these we add the following class of simple rules:

**Definition 3.6** *A simple rule $f$ is strong if $L \notin \mathcal{L}(f)$ implies $N \backslash L \in \mathcal{L}(f)$.*

Notice that if $f$ is collegial and strong, then $f$ must be dictatorial. To see this, let $i \in K(\mathcal{L}(f))$; then $N \backslash \{i\} \notin \mathcal{L}(f)$, since $i$ is in all decisive coalitions. But then if $f$ is strong, $\{i\} \in \mathcal{L}(f)$, implying $i$ is a dictator. Also note that majority rule is strong if and only if $n$ is odd.

**Lemma 3.2** *(1) If $f$ is simple, noncollegial and strong, $s(f) = 3$.*

*(2) If $f$ is a $q$-rule with $q < n$, $s(f) = \lceil n/(n - q) \rceil$.*

*(3) If $f$ is majority rule, $s(f) = 3$ except when $n = 4$, in which case $s(f) = 4$.*

**Proof.** (1) Let $L_1$ and $L_2$ be distinct minimally decisive coalitions in $\mathcal{L}(f)$; since $\mathcal{L}(f)$ is proper, $A \equiv L_1 \cap L_2$ is nonempty; and since $L_1, L_2$ are distinct and minimally decisive, $A \notin \mathcal{L}(f)$. Now $f$ strong implies $N\backslash A \in \mathcal{L}(f)$ as well, and since the collegium of $\{L_1, L_2, N\backslash A\}$ is empty, it must be that $s(f) = 3$.

(2) Let $f$ be a $q$-rule and write $s(f) \equiv s(q)$. We first show that $s(q) \geq \lceil n/(n-q) \rceil$. To do this let $\{L_h\}_{h=1}^s$ be any family of coalitions such that $\cap_{h=1}^s L_h = \emptyset$ and, for all $h = 1, \ldots s$, $|L_h| = q$ (by definition of $s(\cdot)$, we can focus on minimal winning coalitions without loss of generality). For any set $Z \subseteq N$, let $Z^c \equiv N\backslash Z$ denote the complement of $Z$ in $N$. Then for all $h = 1, \ldots s$, $|L_h^c| = n - q$, and, since $\cap_{h=1}^s L_h \equiv [\cup_{h=1}^s L_h^c]^c$,

$$\bigcap_{h=1}^s L_h = \emptyset \Leftrightarrow \bigcup_{h=1}^s L_h^c = N.$$

Now

$$\bigcup_{h=1}^s L_h^c = N \Rightarrow n = \left| \bigcup_{h=1}^s L_h^c \right|$$

and

$$\left| \bigcup_{h=1}^s L_h^c \right| \leq \sum_{h=1}^s |L_h^c| = s(n - q).$$

Therefore, $\cap_{h=1}^s L_h = \emptyset$ implies $s \geq n/(n-q)$ and, since $\{L_h\}$ was arbitrary (save for being a family of minimal winning coalitions with empty intersection), it must be that $s(q) \geq n/(n-q)$; in particular, since $s(q)$ must be integer-valued, $s(q) \geq \lceil n/(n-q) \rceil$. Next, we show that $s(q) \leq \lceil n/(n-q) \rceil$ as well. To see this, let $t = \lceil n/(n-q) \rceil$; we construct a family of $t$ decisive coalitions $\{L_h\}$ with empty intersection. For integers $h < n/(n-q)$ define

$$L_1^c = \{1, \ldots, n - q\}$$
$$L_2^c = \{n - q + 1, \ldots, 2(n - q)\}$$
$$\cdots$$
$$L_h^c = \{(h - 1)(n - q) + 1, \ldots, h(n - q)\}.$$

Note that $h(n-q) < n$, so these sets have not exhausted the population. Now if $n/(n-q)$ is integer-valued, then $(t-1)(n-q) = q$ and we can choose $L_t^c = \{q+1, \ldots, n\}$; otherwise, let $L_t^c = \{(t-1)(n-q)+1, \ldots, n, 1, \ldots, t(n-q)-n\}$. Then (a) each set $L_h^c$ has $(n-q)$ members, and (b) each $i \in N$ is in (at least) one $L_h^c$; thus $\cup_{h=1}^t L_h^c = N$. Now set $L_h = N\backslash L_h^c$; then by construction, $\forall h$, $|L_h| = q$, and $\cap_{h=1}^t L_h = \emptyset$. Since $s(q)$ is the *minimal* size of such a family, then, $s(q) \leq t \equiv \lceil n/(n-q) \rceil$. Thus we have shown $s(q) \geq \lceil n/(n-q) \rceil$ and $s(q) \leq \lceil n/(n-q) \rceil$, implying $s(q) = \lceil n/(n-q) \rceil$.

(3) Follows from (2) [Exercise].□

It follows that the bounds on the Nakamura number described in Lemma 3.1 are "tight": any noncollegial and strong simple rule has a Nakamura number equal to 3, whereas a $q$-rule with $q = n - 1$ generates a Nakamura number equal to $n$ (since $\lceil n/(n - (n - 1)) \rceil = n$). Note also that we can rewrite $\lceil n/(n - q) \rceil$ as $\lceil 1/(1 - (q/n)) \rceil$. Hence the Nakamura number for a $q$-rule depends only on the ratio $q/n$; for example, the Nakamura number for a $q$-rule of 3 out of a population of size 4 is the same as the Nakamura number for a $q$-rule of 120 out of a population of 160.

The importance of the Nakamura number is seen in the following result (recall that a rule $f$ is acyclic if and only if $f(\rho)$ is acyclic for all $\rho \in \mathcal{R}^n$).

**Theorem 3.2** *A simple rule $f$ is acyclic if and only if $|X| < s(f)$.*

**Proof.** (Sufficiency) Suppose $|X| \equiv r < s(f)$, but for some profile $\rho$ we have that $x_1 P x_2$, $x_2 P x_3, \ldots$, $x_{t-1} P x_t$, & $x_t P x_1$. Since $f$ is a simple rule, $P(x_j, x_{j+1}; \rho) \in \mathcal{L}(f)$, $j = 1, \ldots, t - 1$, and $P(x_t, x_1; \rho) \in \mathcal{L}(f)$. Therefore, given the definition of $s(\cdot)$, $r < s(f)$ implies the existence of an individual $i \in N$ such that

$$i \in [\cap_j P(x_j, x_{j+1}; \rho)] \cap P(x_t, x_1; \rho).$$

But then $i$'s preferences over $\{x_1, ..., x_t\}$ are:

$$x_1 P_i x_2 P_i x_3 P_i \ldots P_i x_t P_i x_1.$$

Hence, $R_i \notin \mathcal{R}$ : contradiction.

(Necessity) Suppose $s(f) \leq r$: we construct a profile $\rho$ such that $f$ generates a cycle. To do this, let $\mathcal{L} = \{L_1, \ldots, L_r\}$ be a family of decisive coalitions with an empty intersection: $\mathcal{L} \subseteq \mathcal{L}(f)$ and $K(\mathcal{L}) = \emptyset$ (that such a family can be found follows from $s(f) \leq r$ and the definition of $s(\cdot)$). Let $L_k^c = N \backslash L_k$. Since $K(\mathcal{L}) = \emptyset$, $\cup_{k=1}^r L_k^c = N$. Therefore, there exists a family of (possibly empty) pairwise disjoint coalitions $\{D_1, ..., D_r\}$ such that, $\forall k = 1, \ldots, r$, $D_k \subseteq L_k^c$ and $\cup_{k=1}^r D_k = N$. Moreover, by monotonicity of decisive sets, $D_k^c = N \backslash D_k \supset L_k$ implies $D_k^c \in \mathcal{L}(f)$. By construction, $k \neq l$ implies $D_k \cap D_l = \emptyset$. Hence, there exists a profile $\rho$ such that $\rho|_{\{x_1,...,x_r\}}$ is given by:

$$\forall i \in D_1, \ x_r P_i x_{r-1} P_i \ldots P_i x_1$$
$$\forall i \in D_2, \ x_1 P_i x_r P_i \ldots P_i x_2$$
$$\ldots$$
$$\forall i \in D_j, \ x_{j-1} P_i x_{j-2} P_i \ldots P_i x_{j+1} P_i x_j$$
$$\ldots$$

$\forall i \in D_r,\ x_{r-1} P_i x_{r-2} P_i \ldots P_i x_1 P_i x_r.$

Then $P(x_1, x_r; \rho) = D_1^c \in \mathcal{L}(f)$ and, $\forall j = 1, \ldots, r-1,$ $P(x_{j+1}, x_j; \rho) = D_{j+1}^c \in \mathcal{L}(f)$. Hence $x_1 P x_r$ and $x_{j+1} P x_j$, all $j = 1, \ldots, r-1$. But this contradicts $f(\rho)$ acyclic.$\Box$

Theorem 3.2 shows that acylicity of any simple rule is assured if and only if the number of alternatives under consideration is strictly less than the Nakamura number for the rule being used. Thus the higher is the Nakamura number for a given rule, the larger the set of alternatives from which the rule can be used to generate a nonempty set of maximal elements. To see the intuition behind Theorem 3.2, let $\mathcal{L}$ be any family of $\ell$ decisive coalitions under some rule (simple or otherwise) and consider whether we can construct a profile such that there is a cycle on a set of alternatives $S$ generated by precisely the $\ell$ decisive coalitions in $\mathcal{L}$. The answer is evidently "no" if there is some individual $i$ who is a member of every set in $\mathcal{L}$ (i.e. if the collegium $K(\mathcal{L})$ is nonempty), for to do so would require $i$ to have cyclic preferences on the set. So assume there is no such individual. Then again the answer is "no" unless the set $S$ contains at least $\ell$ alternatives; for if there are fewer alternatives than the number of coalitions in $\mathcal{L}$ and we could construct a cycle on $S$, then at least one coalition in $\mathcal{L}$ would be irrelevant to the construction. On the other hand, if the collegium $K(\mathcal{L})$ is empty and $S$ contains at least $\ell$ alternatives then we can indeed construct a cycle on any subset of $S$ containing $\ell$ elements (see the construction in Example 3.4, below). Consequently, if we are to be able to construct a profile $\rho$ inducing a cycle under $f(\rho)$ on some set $S$ that involves exactly the $\ell$ coalitions in $\mathcal{L}$, then it must be that no individual is in all $\ell$ coalitions and that $S$ contains at least $\ell$ alternatives.

Now suppose $f$ is a simple rule and therefore completely characterized by its family of decisive coalitions, $\mathcal{L}(f)$. It follows from the preceding discussion that if $f$ is acyclic on $X$, there cannot exist a family of decisive coalitions $\mathcal{L}$ in $\mathcal{L}(f)$ that *(i)* has an empty collegium, and *(ii)* contains no more coalitions than there are alternatives in $X$. And this is precisely what Theorem 3.2 asserts. The Nakamura number, $s(f)$, of a simple rule $f$ is the cardinality of the smallest family of decisive coalitions with an empty collegium. To insure acylity of $f$, therefore, the number of available alternatives must be strictly smaller than $s(f)$; if it is not, then *(i)* and *(ii)* obtain and there can exist a cycle precipitated by precisely the $s(f)$ decisive coalitions with empty collegium. These observations are illustrated in Example 3.4.

**Example 3.4** Consider a society $N = \{1, \ldots, 100\}$ that determines its collective preferences over a set of alternatives $X$ using a $q$-rule. Then given $q = 51$, how many alternatives are required for us to construct a profile for the society that generates a preference cycle on $X$? Clearly, we need at least three alternatives, $x, y, z$. So let individuals $1, \ldots, 51$ strictly prefer $x$ to $y$, and let individuals $49, \ldots, 100$ strictly prefer $y$ to $z$. Then by transitivity of individual preferences, individuals $49, 50$, and $51$ strictly prefer $x$ to $z$, but all remaining 97 individuals are unconstrained. Hence we can assign them strict preferences for $z$ over $x$ thereby generating a social preference cycle: $xPyPzPx$. Indeed, this construction works for any value of $q$ up to and including $q = 66$. For example, at the boundary case $q = 66$, assign individuals $1, \ldots, 66$ strict preference for $x$ over $y$ and individuals $35, \ldots, 100$ strict preference for $y$ over $z$. Together with transitivity, these restrictions imply that individuals 35 through 66 strictly prefer $x$ to $z$, leaving the remaining 68 individuals unconstrained. So given $q = 66$, we have just enough freedom to construct the cycle $xPyPzPx$ by giving individuals $1, \ldots, 34$ and $67, \ldots, 100$ strict preferences for $z$ over $x$. And this is exactly what Theorem 3.2 implies: by Lemma 3.3(2), the Nakamura number for all $q$-rules with $q$ between 51 and 66 inclusive and $|N| = n = 100$ is equal to 3.

When $q = 67$, however, the preceding argument fails. Allocating preferences for $x$ over $y$ to individuals 1 through 67 and preferences for $y$ over $z$ to individuals 34 through 100, leaves only 66 individuals with unconstrained preferences over $x$ and $z$. Given $n = 100$ and $q = 67$, therefore, to create a preference cycle on $X$ it is necessary to have a fourth alternative available: the Nakamura number for this $q$-rule is 4. Assume there is such an alternative, say $w$, and assign a preference for $x$ over $y$ to $1, \ldots, 67$, and for $y$ over $z$ to $34, \ldots, 100$; then individuals $34, \ldots, 67$ strictly prefer $x$ to $y$, $y$ to $z$ and (by transitivity) $x$ to $z$. If we assign individuals 34 through 67 a preference for $z$ over $w$, therefore, there can be at most 66 people with a strict preference for $w$ over $x$, thus blocking the possibility of the resulting profile leading to a cyclic collective preference. However, suppose $1, \ldots, 33$ and $50, \ldots, 100$ strictly prefer $z$ to $w$; then only 18 individuals, $50, \ldots, 67$, are constrained to prefer $x$ to $w$ and we can assign individuals $1, \ldots, 49$ and $72, \ldots, 100$ a strict preference for $w$ over $x$. Doing this leads to the profile,

$$
\begin{aligned}
i &= 1, \ldots, 33 : & zP_iwP_ixP_iy \\
i &= 34, \ldots, 49 : & wP_ixP_iyP_iz \\
i &= 50, \ldots 67 : & xP_iyP_izP_iw \\
i &= 68, \ldots, 71 : & yP_ixP_izP_iw \\
i &= 72, \ldots, 100 : & yP_izP_iwP_ix
\end{aligned}
$$

and we generate a cycle, $xPyPzPwPx$. Moreover, since we have 84 individuals who strictly prefer $z$ to $w$ and 78 who strictly prefer $w$ to $x$, there is room to construct a cycle over four alternatives for higher values of $q$. In particular, for any $q$ less than or equal to 75 there exists a way of allocating preferences to yield a cycle over sets of four alternatives, but with $q = 76$ a fifth alternative is necessary for such an allocation. Similarly, when $q = 81$ (and there are a hundred individuals) a sixth alternative is required to construct a cycle; and so on. $\square$

Theorem 3.2 gives a complete characterization of the acyclicity of any simple rule in terms of its Nakamura number. Lemma 3.2 identifies this number for an important set of such rules. Together, therefore, the two results yield the following result.

**Corollary 3.1** *(1) A noncollegial strong simple rule is acyclic if and only if $|X| < 3$.*

*(2) A noncollegial q-rule is acyclic if and only if $|X| < \lceil n/(n-q) \rceil$.*

*(3) Majority rule (with $n \neq 4$) is acyclic if and only if $|X| < 3$.*

Notice that acyclicity is vacuously satisfied whenever there are less than three alternatives. Finally since, as remarked above, strong collegial simple rules are necessarily dictatorial, Corollary 3.1(1) is equivalent to claiming that any strong simple rule is acyclic on sets with at least three alternatives if and only if it is dictatorial.

From Corollary 3.1 we see that majority rule is not generally acyclic when the number of alternatives is at least 3. This fact has been known for some time, and is perhaps best illustrated by *Condorcet's Paradox*: let $X = \{x, y, z\}$, $N = \{1, 2, 3\}$ and consider the profile,

$$xP_1yP_1z$$
$$zP_2xP_2y$$
$$yP_3zP_3x.$$

Then majority rule yields the cycle $xP_myP_mzP_mx$. Theorem 3.2 demonstrates how this paradox is a consequence of a more general theory concerning aggregation rules; namely, for *any* noncollegial simple rule, we can identify a critical number of alternatives such that the rule is acyclic if and only if the number of alternatives is less than this critical number. Theorem 3.2 also fills in the gap left by Theorem 2.4 with respect to noncollegial simple rules, in the following sense: from Theorem 2.4, we know that *any* such rule will fail to be acyclic if the number of alternatives is at least as large as the number of individuals, whereas Theorem 3.2 and the subsequent corollary say that the critical number of alternatives generating this acyclicity (1) will depend on the specifics of the rule, and (2) is directly computable, and at times easily computable, from the nature of the rule.

## 3.3  Application: A comparison of simple rules

Given any logically possible preference profile of weak orderings is admissible, Theorem 3.2 provides a complete characterization of when any given simple rule will assuredly yield a nonempty choice set, a characterization in terms of the Nakamura number for the rule and the number of alternatives in question. We can think of the Nakamura number as providing a relative measure of the "collective rationality" different rules exhibit. For example, if we have two $q$-rules $f$ and $f'$, where $q > q'$ and hence $s(f) \geq s(f')$, then we can think of $f$ as being more "rational" in the sense of generating an acyclic relation (and, hence by Theorem 1.1, a nonempty maximal set) over larger sets of alternatives. In this sense then the class of $q$-rules are ordered in terms of their acyclicity by the value of $q$, with the extremes being given by the Pareto extension rule (with a value of $s(f) = \infty$) and majority rule (with a value of $s(f) = 3$ or $4$).

On the other hand, upon inspecting $q$-rules it is apparent that another difference between rules is also present; namely, that the increase in acyclicity for higher values of $q$ is accompanied by a *decrease* in the degree to which the rule is "resolute" in determining strict social preference. For example, compare a $q$-rule with $q = 2/3$ versus one with $q = 5/6$. While the 5/6-rule is necessarily more acyclic than the 2/3-rule, the 2/3-rule is a finer relation than the 5/6-rule: whenever $x$ is socially preferred to $y$ under the 5/6-rule, $x$ is likewise socially preferred to $y$ under the 2/3-rule, but the converse fails. In this sense then the $q = 2/3$ rule is *more resolute* than the $q = 5/6$ rule. More generally, we can define a binary relation, "more resolute than", on the set of all preference aggregation rules as follows.

**Definition 3.7** *Let $f$ and $f'$ be two distinct preference aggregation rules. Say that $f$ is more resolute than $f'$ if and only if for all $\rho \in \mathcal{R}^n$ and all $x, y \in X$, $x P_{f'} y$ implies $x P_f y$.*

Thus, as the Nakamura number provides an ordering among simple rules in terms of their acyclicity, this notion of resoluteness provides at least a partial ordering among rules. With regard to simple rules, the concept of resoluteness has an immediate application: a simple rule $f$ is more resolute than another simple rule $f'$ if and only if $\mathcal{L}(f') \subset \mathcal{L}(f)$. Hence the tension between any two $q$-rules is one between collective rationality on the one hand, and resoluteness on the other.

However, when we move beyond $q$-rules a further potential difference between simple rules exists, namely, the degree of "equality" among the individuals in terms of affecting social preference. For instance, we can think of $q$-rules as being the most equal, whereas dictatorship would be the most unequal. While several possible measures of inequality are plausible, we will not concern ourselves here with selecting such a measure. Yet even without a precise measure of equality, we can deduce the following: from Theorem 3.2 we know that the simple rules that are most acyclic are those that are collegial and, within this class, the rules that are most resolute turn out to be dictatorships. To see this, let $f$ be a nondictatorial but collegial simple rule, and let $i \in K(\mathcal{L}(f))$; then $i$'s assent is required for a strict social preference to be generated, i.e. $xPy$ implies $xP_iy$. Now if $f'$ is the dictatorial simple rule with $i$ as its dictator, then by definition $xP'y$ if and only if $xP_iy$. But then $f'$ is more resolute than $f$, since $xPy$ implies $xP_iy$, which in turn implies $xP'y$. In general, then, any collegial and nondictatorial simple rule is less resolute than some dictatorial rule, or alternatively, the most resolute acyclic rules are dictatorships.

Hence the quandry: (1) the simple rule that is the most acyclic as well as the most equal, the Pareto extension rule, is also the absolute weakest in terms of resoluteness (since *any* Paretian simple rule $f$ has by definition $N \in \mathcal{L}(f)$); (2) the simple rule that is most resolute among those that are most equal, majority rule, is also the absolute weakest in terms of acyclicity; and (3) the simple rule that is most resolute among those that are most acyclic, dictatorship, is also the most unequal. In this sense then a fundamental tension exists between the three criteria of equality, resoluteness, and collective rationality: any rule which is "best" with respect to two of the criteria must necessarily be "worst" with respect to the remaining criterion. Further, one can in principle view *all* simple rules as satisfying to a greater-or-lesser extent these three criteria.

## 3.4  Voting rules

The characterization of simple rules developed above excludes some aggregation procedures that are colloquially considered to be "simple". In particular, as shown in Example 3.1, plurality rule, (whereby $xPy$ if and only if

$|P(x,y;\rho)| > |P(y,x;\rho)|$) is *not* a simple rule because, unlike majority rule, plurality rule ignores indifferent individuals when ranking any pair of alternatives. Thus while plurality rule is monotonic and neutral, it is not decisive and hence Theorem 3.2 above does not say anything about the acyclicity properties of plurality rule. In this section, therefore, we drop the condition of decisiveness, and examine the acyclicity of neutral and monotonic aggregation rules. Our first goal is to characterize such rules in a convenient format.

For any aggregation rule $f$, define the *decisive structure* of $f$, $\mathcal{D}(f)$, to be a family of ordered pairs of coalitions $(S, W) \subseteq N \times N$ such that,

$$(S, W) \in \mathcal{D}(f) \Leftrightarrow S \subseteq W \text{ and } \forall x, y \in X, \forall \rho \in \mathcal{R}^n,$$

$$[xP_iy, \forall i \in S \text{ and } xR_jy, \forall j \in W] \Rightarrow xPy.$$

Think of the individuals in $S$ as those who strictly prefer one alternative to another, whereas those in $W$ weakly prefer one alternative to another. Thus the decisive structure of $f$ is a set of pairs of coalitions, with one coalition a subset of the other, such that when all individuals in the smaller coalition strictly prefer alternative $x$ to alternative $y$ and all individuals in the larger coalition weakly prefer $x$ to $y$, then society strictly prefers $x$ to $y$. To see the difference between $\mathcal{D}(f)$ and $\mathcal{L}(f)$, i.e. the set of decisive coalitions associated with the aggregation rule $f$, note that $\mathcal{L}(f)$ is the family of coalitions $L \subseteq N$ such that $(L, L) \in \mathcal{D}(f)$: as long as the members in $L$ strictly prefer (say) $x$ to $y$, then society strictly prefers $x$ to $y$ irrespective of the preferences of the remaining individuals.

**Example 3.5** Let $f_p$ be plurality rule. Then:

$$\mathcal{L}(f_p) = \{L \subseteq N : |L| > n/2\}$$

and

$$\mathcal{D}(f_p) = \{(S, W) \subseteq N \times N : S \subseteq W \ \& \ |S| > |N \backslash W|\}.$$

Clearly, $|L| > n/2$ if and only if $|L| > |N \backslash L|$. Hence $L \in \mathcal{L}(f_p)$ if and only if $(L, L) \in \mathcal{D}(f_p)$; but $(S, W) \in \mathcal{D}(f_p)$ does not imply $S \in \mathcal{L}(f_p)$. On the other hand, if $f_m$ is majority rule, we have $\mathcal{L}(f_m) \equiv \mathcal{L}(f_p)$ and,

$$\mathcal{D}(f_m) = \{(L, L') \subseteq N \times N : L \in \mathcal{L}(f_m), \ L \subseteq L'\}.\square$$

Now for any set $\mathcal{D} \subseteq 2^N \times 2^N$ such that $(S, W) \in \mathcal{D}$ implies $S \subseteq W$, define the aggregation rule $f_{\mathcal{D}}$ induced by $\mathcal{D}$ as

$$\forall x, y \in X, xPy \Leftrightarrow [\exists (S, W) \in \mathcal{D} : \forall i \in S, \ xP_iy \text{ and } \forall i \in W, \ xR_iy].$$

**Definition 3.8** *An aggregation rule $f$ is a voting rule if $f = f_{\mathcal{D}(f)}$.*

Thus, voting rules are completely characterized by their decisive structures, in the same way that simple rules are completely characterized by their decisive sets.

**Definition 3.9** *A set $\mathcal{D} \subset 2^N \times 2^N$ is*

*(1) monotonic if $(S, W) \in \mathcal{D}$, $S \subseteq S' \subseteq W'$ and $S \subseteq W \subseteq W'$ imply $(S', W') \in \mathcal{D}$.*

*(2) proper if $(S, W) \in \mathcal{D}$, $S' \subseteq N \backslash W$ and $W' \subseteq N \backslash S$ imply $(S', W') \notin \mathcal{D}$.*

These conditions are analogues to those for decisive sets, introduced in Chapter 2. Although this is immediate for the monotonicity part of the definition, it may not be quite so transparent for the properness part. To check that it is indeed the appropriate analogue, simply set $S = W = L$ and $S' = W' = L'$ in (2). And note that, as before, $f_{\mathcal{D}}$ is a well-defined binary relation only if $\mathcal{D}$ is proper. Figure 3.2 illustrates the definition of properness for decisive structures.

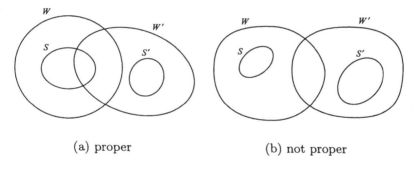

(a) proper           (b) not proper

Figure 3.2: Properness of decisive structures

We can now state the analogue to Theorem 3.1.

**Theorem 3.3** *An aggregation rule is a voting rule if and only if it is neutral and monotonic.*

**Proof.** (Necessity) Let $f$ be a voting rule. Then $\mathcal{D}(f)$ is necessarily proper since $f$ maps into binary relations. And since $f = f_{\mathcal{D}(f)}$ by definition, to check $f$ monotonic it suffices to show $\mathcal{D}(f)$ monotonic. To do this, let $S \subseteq S'$ and $W \subseteq W'$. Then: $[\forall i \in S', \ x P_i y] \Rightarrow [\forall i \in S, \ x P_i y]$, and

$[\forall i \in W', \ xR_iy] \Rightarrow [\forall i \in W, \ xR_iy]$. Hence, if $(S, W) \in \mathcal{D}$ then $xPy$, implying $(S', W') \in \mathcal{D}$ as well. And neutrality of $f$ is immediate since $\mathcal{D}(f)$ is not defined in terms of alternatives.

(Sufficiency) Note first that for *any* aggregation rule $f$, $f$ is more resolute than $f_{\mathcal{D}(f)}$, and hence $xP_{\mathcal{D}(f)}y$ implies $xPy$. Now suppose $\rho$ is such that $xPy$ under $f$. Let $S = P(x, y; \rho)$ and $W = R(x, y; \rho)$. We wish to show $(S, W) \in \mathcal{D}(f)$ and hence $xP_{\mathcal{D}(f)}y$ as well. Choose $a, b \in X$ arbitrarily, and let $\rho'$ be such that $aP_i'b \Leftrightarrow i \in S$, and $aR_i'b \Leftrightarrow i \in W$, i.e. $P(a, b; \rho') = S$ and $R(a, b; \rho') = W$. Since $f$ is neutral, then, $aP'b$. Now let $\rho''$ be any profile such that $P(a, b; \rho') \subseteq P(a, b; \rho'')$ & $R(a, b; \rho') \subseteq R(a, b; \rho'')$. Since $f$ is monotonic, $aP''b$. But then we have shown that $[aP_ib \ \forall i \in S \ \& \ aR_ib \ \forall i \in W]$ implies $aPb$; and since $a, b$ were chosen arbitrarily, we have that $(S, W) \in \mathcal{D}(f)$ and hence $xP_{\mathcal{D}(f)}y$, as required.□

Therefore neutral and monotonic aggregation rules are voting rules, and hence are completely described by their decisive structures. Comparing Theorems 3.1 and 3.3 directly yields that the class of voting rules contains all simple rules.

Next we turn to the acyclicity of voting rules and look for a generalization of Theorem 3.2. For any subset $\mathcal{D} = \{(S^1, W^1), ..., (S^m, W^m)\} \subseteq \mathcal{D}(f)$, the *collegium* of $\mathcal{D}$ is given by,

$$K(\mathcal{D}) = \{i \in N : \forall j, \ i \in W^j \text{ and, for some } k, \ i \in S^k\}.$$

So the collegium of the collection $\mathcal{D}$ consists of those individuals in all "weak" coalitions and in at least one "strict" coalition.

**Definition 3.10** *For any voting rule $f$, define the Nakamura number for $f$, $v(f)$, to be $\infty$ if, for all subsets $\mathcal{D} \subseteq \mathcal{D}(f)$, $K(\mathcal{D}) \neq \emptyset$; otherwise,*

$$v(f) = \min\{|\mathcal{D}| : \mathcal{D} \subseteq \mathcal{D}(f) \ \& \ K(\mathcal{D}) = \emptyset\}.$$

Say that a voting rule is *collegial* if $v(f) = \infty$ and is *noncollegial* otherwise. Because a simple rule is a particular sort of voting rule, we expect $v(f)$ to coincide with the Nakamura number $s(f)$ when $f$ is simple and it does [Exercise]. In view of this coincidence, therefore, Theorem 3.2 is in fact a special case of the following result.

**Theorem 3.4** *A voting rule $f$ is acyclic if and only if $|X| < v(f)$.*

**Proof.** (Sufficiency) Suppose $|X| \equiv r < v(f)$, but for some profile $\rho$ we have

$$x_1 P x_2, x_2 P x_3, ..., x_{s-1} P x_s, \text{ and } x_s P x_1$$

where without loss of generality we can take $s \leq r$. Since $f$ is a voting rule, $(P(x_j, x_{j+1}; \rho), R(x_j, x_{j+1}; \rho)) \in \mathcal{D}(f)$ for $j = 1, ..., s - 1$, and $(P(x_s, x_1; \rho), R(x_s, x_1; \rho)) \in \mathcal{D}(f)$ as well. By the definition of $v(f)$, and the fact that $s \leq r < v(f)$, there must exist $i \in N$ such that $i \in R(x_j, x_{j+1})$, $j = 1, ..., s-1$, $i \in R(x_s, x_1; \rho)$, and if $i \notin P(x_s, x_1; \rho)$ then $i \in P(x_j, x_{j+1}; \rho)$ for some $j$. Without loss of generality assume the latter case holds for $j = 1$; then $x_1 P_i x_2$, and since $x_2 R_i x_3$ we have by transitivity $x_1 P_i x_3$. Repeating this argument, we get that $x_1 P_i x_s$, contradicting $i \in R(x_s, x_1; \rho)$, and thereby proving sufficiency.

(Necessity) Suppose $v(f) \leq r \equiv |X|$; we construct a profile $\rho$ which generates a cycle under $f(\rho)$. Let $\mathcal{D} = \{(S^1, W^1), ..., (S^k, W^k)\}$ be any subset of $\mathcal{D}(f)$ such that $k \leq r$ and where $K(\mathcal{D}) = \emptyset$ (which exists by the definition of $v(\cdot)$), and define $I = \cap W^k$; note that $I$ may be empty, but in any case $I \cap \{\cup S^j\} = \emptyset$ since $K(\mathcal{D}) = \emptyset$. For $j = 1, ..., k$ let $L_j = W^j \backslash I$; then

(1) $\forall j, S^j \subseteq L_j$ and, therefore
(2) $\forall j, (L_j, L_j \cup I) \in \mathcal{D}(f)$ (by the monotonicity of $f$); and
(3) $\cap L_j = \emptyset$.

Now let the profile $\rho$ be such that $\forall i \in I, \forall x, y \in X, x I_i y$ and let $N' = N \backslash I$. Next, define $L_j^c = N' \backslash L_j$; thus $\cup L_j^c = N'$ (since $\cap L_j = \emptyset$). Therefore we can identify a family of pairwise disjoint (possibly empty) coalitions $\{D_j\}$ such that, $\forall j, D_j \subseteq L_j^c$ and $\cup D_j = N'$. See Figure 3.3. Further, since $(L_j, L_j \cup I) \in \mathcal{D}(f)$ and $D_j^c \equiv N' \backslash D_j \supseteq L_j$, we have by monotonicity that $(D_j^c, D_j^c \cup I) \in \mathcal{D}(f)$ as well.

Now let the outcomes in $X$ be ordered as $\{x_1, ..., x_r\}$. We construct the remainder of the profile $\rho$ as follows (recall the $D_j$'s are pairwise disjoint):

$$\forall i \in D_1, x_r P_i x_{r-1} P_i ... P_i x_1$$
$$\forall i \in D_2, x_1 P_i x_r P_i x_{r-1} P_i ... P_i x_2$$
$$...$$
$$\forall i \in D_j, x_{j-1} P_i x_{j-2} P_i ... P_i x_1 P_i x_r P_i ... P_i x_{j+1} P_i x_j$$
$$...$$
$$\forall i \in D_r, x_{r-1} P_i x_{r-2} P_i ... P_i x_1 P_i x_r.$$

Then,

$$P(x_2, x_1; \rho) = D_2^c, \text{ implying (since } (D_2^c, D_2^c \cup I) \in \mathcal{D}(f)) \ x_2 P x_1,$$
$$...$$

$$P(x_{j+1}, x_j; \rho) = D^c_{j+1}, \text{ implying } x_{j+1} P x_j,$$

...

$$P(x_1, x_r; \rho) = D^c_1, \text{ implying } x_1 P x_r.$$

Therefore we have a cycle $x_1 P x_r P x_{r-1} P...P x_2 P x_1$. $\square$

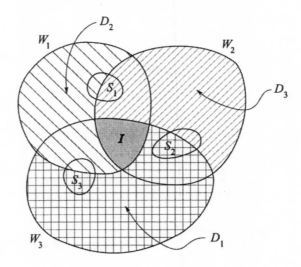

Figure 3.3: Construction of $\{D_j\}$ in the argument for Theorem 3.4

For a concrete illustration of this result, recall first the discussion of the pre-1965 UN Security Council aggregation rule, say $f_u$, in the previous chapter. Under that rule $N = \{1, \ldots, 11\}$ with individuals $1, \ldots, 5$ comprising the permanent members. The decisive structure for this rule is given by

$$\mathcal{D}(f_u) = \{(S, W) : S \subseteq W, |S| \geq 7 \ \& \ i \in W, \ all \ i = 1, \ldots, 5\}.$$

The collegium for this rule is nonempty, since $|S| \geq 7$ and $|N| = n = 11$ requires at least one permanent member to be in each set $S$. Therefore the Nakamura number is infinite and so, by Theorem 3.4, $f_u(\rho)$ is acyclic for every profile $\rho$ and any number of alternatives.

After 1965, the Security Council membership was expanded to include the same five permanent members ($i = 1, ..., 5$) and ten others ($i = 6, ..., 15$); so now $N = \{1, \ldots, 15\}$. Since this change, the aggregation rule, $f'_u$, has been:

$$\forall x, y \in X, \ xPy \Leftrightarrow |P(x, y; \rho)| \geq 9 \ and \ x R_i y \ i = 1, ..., 5.$$

The decisive structure for the post-1965 rule, therefore, is

$$\mathcal{D}(f'_u) = \{(S, W) : S \subseteq W, |S| \geq 9 \ \& \ i \in W, \ all \ i = 1, \ldots, 5\}.$$

But in contrast with the pre-1965 rule, it is now logically possible for there to be a cycle; i.e. the Nakamura number of $f'_u$ is finite. To see this, consider the following family of ten decisive pairs: for all $j = 6, \ldots, 15$, let $W^j = N\backslash\{j\}$ and $S^j = W^j\backslash\{1, \ldots, 5\}$; then $\mathcal{D} \equiv \{(S^j, W^j)\} \subset \mathcal{D}(f'_u)$. By construction, only the five permanent members are in all coalitions $W^j$, and none of the permanent members are in any coalition $S^j$. Consequently $K(\mathcal{D}) = \emptyset$ and, therefore, $v(f'_u)$ is less than or equal to ten (the precise value is left as an exercise). Hence, Theorem 3.4 says that there exists a ten-alternative example on which $f'_u(\rho)$ is cyclic for some profile $\rho$. For instance, let $|X| = 10$ and consider the following profile $\rho$ on $\{x_1, x_2, \ldots, x_{10}\} = X$:

$$\forall i \in \{1, \ldots, 5\}, \ \forall s, t \in \{1, \ldots, 10\}, \ x_s I_i x_t,$$

and

$$x_1 P_6 x_2 P_6 \ldots x_9 P_6 x_{10}$$
$$x_{10} P_7 x_1 P_7 x_2 P_7 \ldots x_8 P_7 x_9$$
$$x_9 P_8 x_{10} P_8 x_1 P_8 \ldots x_7 P_8 x_8$$
$$\ldots$$
$$x_2 P_{15} x_3 P_{15} \ldots x_{10} P_{15} x_1.$$

Because all the permanent members are indifferent over these ten alternatives and, among the ten non-permanent members, there are always nine who strictly prefer $x_1$ to $x_2$, and nine who strictly prefer $x_2$ to $x_3$, ..., there is a cycle under the post-1965 rule on $\{x_1, x_2, \ldots, x_{10}\}$.

The post-1965 UN Security Council rule $f'_u$ also shows that the converse of Theorem 2.4 is not true: there exist cyclic aggregation rules for which the intersection of all decisive coalitions is not empty. To see this, note that $\mathcal{L}(f'_u)$ consists of all coalitions of size at least nine that include all permanent members of the Council.

## 3.5 Counting rules

While Theorem 3.4 provides a general result concerning the acyclicity of neutral and monotonic aggregation rules, its application is admittedly somewhat awkward for non-simple rules. However for voting rules that treat individuals symmetrically (e.g. plurality rule), an easier characterization is available.

Let $\sigma : N \to N$ be a permutation of the set of individuals. A profile $\rho' \in \mathcal{R}^n$ is a $\sigma$-*permutation* of another profile $\rho \in \mathcal{R}^n$ if and only if, for all individuals $i \in N$, $R_i' \equiv R_{\sigma(i)}$. In other words, the lists of preferences under $\rho$ and $\rho'$ are identical up to the identity of the particular individuals holding particular preferences. To save on notation, we also refer to such a pair $(\rho, \rho')$ as a $\sigma$-permutation.

**Definition 3.11** *An aggregation rule $f$ is anonymous if and only if for all $\sigma$-permutations $(\rho, \rho')$, $f(\rho) \equiv f(\rho')$.*

So if $f$ is anonymous, the names of individuals holding particular preferences are immaterial in deriving social preference. To all intents and purposes, therefore, anonymity is a neutrality-like property on the set of individuals: whereas neutral aggregation rules ignore the names of alternatives, anonymous rules ignore the names of individuals.

From section 3.4 above we know that any neutral and monotonic aggregation rule is characterized by its decisive structure $\mathcal{D}(f)$ identifying pairs of coalitions which strictly and weakly prefer one alternative to another. If in addition the rule is anonymous, then the only relevant criterion for such coalitions is their *size*; that is, how many individuals strictly prefer, and weakly prefer, one alternative to another. This we state formally (and without proof) as follows:

**Theorem 3.5** *If a voting rule $f$ is anonymous, then $(S, W) \in \mathcal{D}(f)$, $|S| = |S'|$ and $|W| = |W'|$ imply $(S', W') \in \mathcal{D}(f)$.*

Let $\mathbf{Z}_+ = \{0, 1, 2, ...\}$ and define the set

$$E = \{(p, a) \in \mathbf{Z}_+ \times \mathbf{Z}_+ : p + a \leq n\}.$$

Throughout we will think of $p$ as denoting the number of individuals who strictly prefer one alternative to another ($p =$ "*pro*"), whereas $a$ will denote the number of individuals with the opposing *strict* preference over the pair ($a =$ "*anti*"). Any aggregation rule $f$ determines a (possibly empty) subset of *decisive numbers* in $E$, denoted $\mathcal{N}(f)$, in the following manner:

$$(p, a) \in \mathcal{N}(f) \Leftrightarrow \forall x, y \in X, \ \forall \rho \in \mathcal{R}^n,$$

$$[|P(x, y; \rho)| \geq p \ \& \ |P(y, x; \rho)| \leq a] \Rightarrow xPy.$$

Similarly, for any subset $\mathcal{N}$ of $E$ we can describe the aggregation rule induced by $\mathcal{N}$, denoted $f_{\mathcal{N}}$, by

$$\forall x, y \in X, \ xPy \Leftrightarrow [\exists (p, a) \in \mathcal{N} : |P(x, y; \rho)| \geq p \ \& \ |P(y, x; \rho)| \leq a].$$

**Definition 3.12** *A subset $\mathcal{N}$ of $E$ is*

*(1) monotonic if $(p,a) \in \mathcal{N}$, $p' \geq p$, $a' \leq a$ and $(p',a') \in E$ imply $(p',a') \in \mathcal{N}$*

*(2) proper if $a \geq p$ implies $(p,a) \notin \mathcal{N}$.*

Note that $f_{\mathcal{N}}$ is well-defined if and only if $\mathcal{N}$ is proper.

Figure 3.4 illustrates these definitions. Monotonicity means that if $(p,a) \in \mathcal{N}$ then all points in $E$ below and to the right of $(p,a)$ are in $\mathcal{N}$: see Figure 3.4(a). Properness means that $\mathcal{N}$ lies everywhere below the 45° line: see Figure 3.4(b).

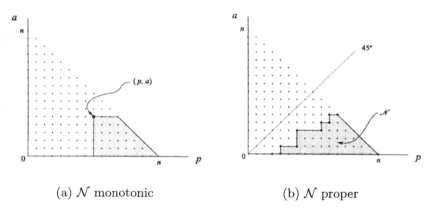

(a) $\mathcal{N}$ monotonic          (b) $\mathcal{N}$ proper

Figure 3.4: Monotonicity and properness of $\mathcal{N}$

**Definition 3.13** *A counting rule is an aggregation rule $f$ such that $f = f_{\mathcal{N}(f)}$.*

Thus counting rules are those aggregation rules completely characterized by their decisive numbers, $\mathcal{N}(\cdot)$.

**Theorem 3.6** *An aggregation rule is a counting rule if and only if it is anonymous, neutral, and monotonic.*

**Proof.** (Necessity) By definition, $f = f_{\mathcal{N}(f)}$. Assume for the moment that $\mathcal{N}(f)$ is proper and monotonic. Then we show that $f_{\mathcal{N}(f)}$, and hence $f$, is anonymous, neutral and monotonic. The aggregation rule $f_{\mathcal{N}(f)}$ is clearly anonymous and neutral because $f_{\mathcal{N}(f)}$ depends only on the *number*, not the *identity*, of individuals favoring one alternative over another and any pair of alternatives is treated the same as any other pair. To see that $f_{\mathcal{N}(f)}$ satisfies monotonicity, let $\rho$ be such that $xP_{\mathcal{N}(f(\rho))}y$; then by definition $|P(x,y;\rho)| \geq p$ and $|P(y,x;\rho)| \leq a$ for some $(p,a) \in \mathcal{N}(f)$. If then $\rho'$ is such that $P(x,y;\rho) \subseteq P(x,y;\rho')$ and $P(y,x;\rho') \subseteq P(y,x;\rho)$, then it must be that $|P(x,y;\rho')| \geq p$ and $|P(y,x;\rho')| \leq a$. And since $\mathcal{N}(f)$ is monotonic by assumption, this implies $xP'_{\mathcal{N}(f(\rho'))}y$ thereby establishing the monotonicity of $f_{\mathcal{N}(f)}$.

It remains to check that $\mathcal{N}(f)$ is indeed proper and monotonic, as presumed. To show $\mathcal{N}(f)$ proper, let $(p,a) \in \mathcal{N}(f)$ and suppose to the contrary that $a \geq p$. Let $\rho$ be such that $|P(x,y;\rho)| = |P(y,x;\rho)| = p$ (which is possible since $p+a \leq n$ and hence $a \geq p$ implies $2p \leq n$). But then $|P(x,y;\rho)| \geq p$ and $|P(y,x;\rho)| \leq a$, implying (since $(p,a) \in \mathcal{N}(f)$) $xPy$, while at the same time $|P(y,x;\rho)| \geq p$ and $|P(x,y;\rho)| \leq a$, implying $yPx$, thereby contradicting $f(\rho)$ being a binary relation; thus $\mathcal{N}(f)$ must be proper. To see that $\mathcal{N}(f)$ is monotonic, let $(p,a) \in \mathcal{N}(f)$, and $p' \geq p$, $a' \leq a$, and $(p'a') \in E$. Then for all $x,y \in X$, $\rho \in \mathcal{R}^n$, $|P(x,y;\rho)| \geq p'$ and $|P(y,x;\rho)| \leq a'$ imply $|P(x,y;\rho)| \geq p$ and $|P(y,x;\rho)| \leq a$. And since $(p,a) \in \mathcal{N}(f)$, by definition we have therefore have $xPy$. Hence $(p',a') \in \mathcal{N}(f)$ as well.

(Sufficiency) Suppose $f$ is anonymous, neutral, and monotonic; we wish to show that $f = f_{\mathcal{N}(f)}$. (1) If $\rho$ is such that $xP_{\mathcal{N}(f)}y$, then $xPy$ as well. (2) Suppose $\rho$ is such that $xPy$, and let $p^* = |P(x,y;\rho)|$, $a^* = |P(y,x;\rho)|$. We wish to show $(p^*,a^*) \in \mathcal{N}(f)$, and hence $xP_{\mathcal{N}(f)}y$ as well. So let $z,w \in X$, and $\rho' \in \mathcal{R}^n$ be such that $|P(z,w;\rho')| \geq p^*$ and $|P(w,z;\rho')| \leq a^*$. Define $\rho^+$ to be a profile which differs from $\rho'$ in that $|P(z,w;\rho^+)| = p^*$ and $|P(w,z;\rho^+)| = a^*$. Since $f$ is anonymous and neutral, $xPy$ implies $zP^+w$; and since $f$ is monotonic, $zP^+w$ implies $zP'w$. Therefore, $|P(z,w;\rho')| \geq p^*$ and $|P(w,z;\rho')| \leq a^*$ imply $zPw$, and since $w,z,\rho'$ are arbitrary, we have that $(p^*,a^*) \in \mathcal{N}(f)$.$\square$

Thus for anonymous, neutral, and monotonic rules we can without loss of generality focus on the set of decisive numbers, $\mathcal{N}(f)$, associated with the rule.

One previous example of a counting rule is majority rule, characterized as a counting rule by the set $\mathcal{N} = \{(p,a) \in E : p \geq \lceil (n+1)/2 \rceil\}$. In general, any $q$-rule is a counting rule defined by $\mathcal{N} = \{(p,a) \in E : p \geq q\}$. In fact, because $q$-rules constitute the intersection of simple rules and counting rules, we have the following immediate characterization of $q$-rules.

**Theorem 3.7** *A preference aggregation rule is decisive, neutral, monotonic, and anonymous if and only if it is a $q$-rule.*

Some important examples of counting rules other than $q$-rules are given in the following definition.

**Definition 3.14** *A counting rule $f$ is*

*(1) plurality rule if $\mathcal{N}(f) = \{(p,a) \in E : p > a\}$;*

*(2) an extended $q$-rule if $\mathcal{N}(f) = \{(p,a) \in E : p \geq q(p+a)/n\}$ (where $q$ is a real number such that $n/2 < q \leq n$).*

Figure 3.5 illustrates the sets of decisive numbers, $\mathcal{N}(f)$, for $f$ being a $q$-rule (Figure 3.5(a)) and an extended $q$-rule with the same value of $q$ (Figure 3.5(b)). In each case, $\mathcal{N}(f)$ is the set of points defined by the solid triangle.

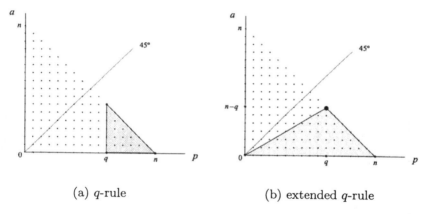

(a) $q$-rule          (b) extended $q$-rule

Figure 3.5: $\mathcal{N}(f)$ for a $q$-rule and an extended $q$-rule

Note that if $f$ is an extended $q$-rule with $q = n$, then $(p,a) \in \mathcal{N}(f)$ implies $a = 0$, and hence $f$ is the *Pareto extension rule*: $xPy$ if and only if $xR_iy$ for all $i \in N$ and $xP_jy$ for some $j \in N$. Similarly, plurality rule is essentially an extended $q$-rule with $q \approx n/2$. Figure 3.6 shows the sets of decisive numbers for plurality rule and the Pareto extension rule: for plurality rule the set $\mathcal{N}(f)$ consists of all integer-pairs $(p,a)$ below the $45°$ line with $0 < p + a \leq n$ and $a \geq 0$ (Figure 3.6(a)); for the Pareto extension rule, the set $\mathcal{N}(f)$ consists of all integer-pairs $(p,0)$ with $n \geq p > 0$ (Figure 3.6(b)).

There are some counting rules that are not extended $q$-rules; for example,

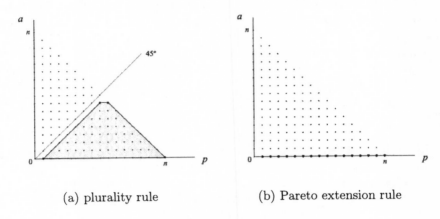

(a) plurality rule                    (b) Pareto extension rule

Figure 3.6: $\mathcal{N}(f)$ for two counting rules

let $f$ be a counting rule defined by the following set of decisive numbers:

$$\mathcal{N}(f) = \{(p,a) \in E : p \geq 2, a \leq 1\}.$$

Note that the set of decisive coalitions from this rule is $\mathcal{L}(f) = \{L \subseteq N : |L| \geq n - 1\}$; the only coalitions that can dictate the social preference regardless of others' preferences are coalitions of at least $n - 1$ members. But $f$ is not decisive and so it is not characterized by the set $\mathcal{L}(f)$. Also note that this set of decisive coalitions is the same as that generated by an extended $q$-rule with $q = n - 1$; hence two different counting rules can generate the same set of decisive coalitions.

Next, we consider the acylicity of counting rules.

**Definition 3.15** *For any counting rule $f$, define the Nakamura number for $f$, $c(f)$ as equal to $\infty$ if $(p,a) \in \mathcal{N}(f)$ implies $a = 0$; otherwise,*

$$c(f) = \min\{\lceil (p+a)/a \rceil : (p,a) \in \mathcal{N}(f), a \geq 1\}.$$

That is, for each $(p,a) \in \mathcal{N}(f)$, compute the Nakamura number as if the rule was a $q$-rule with $q = p$ and the population was of size $p+a$, and then choose the lowest such number. As with the Nakamura number for simple rules, where without loss of generality we need only consider minimally decisive coalitions, here we need only consider *boundary points* in $\mathcal{N}(f)$, i.e. $(p,a)$ such that $(p, a + 1) \notin \mathcal{N}(f)$.

The Nakamura number for a counting rule can be illustrated graphically. For each $(p, a) \in \mathcal{N}(f)$ with $a \geq 1$ we can locate the point $(a, p+a)$ and find the slope of the line connecting 0 and $(a, p+a)$. The minimum slope of such a line is associated with some $(\hat{p}, \hat{a}) \in \mathcal{N}(f)$, and then $c(f) = \lceil (\hat{p} + \hat{a})/\hat{a} \rceil$. To find this particular pair $(\hat{p}, \hat{a})$ we can use the fact that for any two pairs $(p, a)$ and $(p', a')$, $(p + a)/a \leq (p' + a')/a'$ if and only if $p/a \leq p'/a'$, which is true if and only if $a/p \geq a'/p'$. Thus, given a counting rule $f$ the relevant $(\hat{p}, \hat{a}) \in \mathcal{N}(f)$ are the ones with maximal $a/p$ ratio: see Figure 3.7 in which $\mathcal{N}(f)$ is the region enclosed by solid lines.

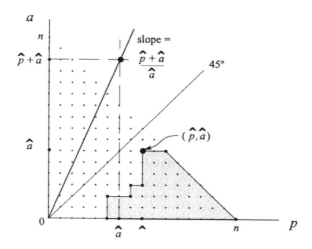

Figure 3.7: Geometric representation of $c(f)$

That the definition of the Nakamura number for counting rules, $c(f)$, is the "correct" specification of $v(f)$ for anonymous voting rules, is demonstrated in the next result.

**Lemma 3.3** *If $f$ is a counting rule, then $c(f) = v(f)$.*

**Proof.** If $c(f) = \infty$ then $(p, a) \in \mathcal{N}(f)$ implies $a = 0$. Hence, for all $(S, W) \in \mathcal{D}(f)$, $W = N$. Therefore, $\forall \mathcal{D} \subseteq \mathcal{D}(f)$, $K(\mathcal{D}) \neq \emptyset$ implying $v(f) = \infty$. Conversely, if $v(f) = \infty$ and $f$ is anonymous, then $(p, a) \in \mathcal{N}(f)$ implies $a = 0$, and hence $c(f) = \infty$.

Now suppose $c(f) < \infty$ and $v(f) < \infty$; then we claim $v(f) \geq c(f)$. Choose any family of $k$ ordered pairs $\mathcal{D} = \{(S^1, W^1), ..., (S^k, W^k)\} \subseteq \mathcal{D}(f)$

such that $k < c(f)$; if $K(\mathcal{D}) \neq \emptyset$ the claim follows from definition of $v(f)$. We now show $K(\mathcal{D}) \neq \emptyset$. To do this, define

$$\bar{a} = \max\{n - |W^j| : j = 1, ..., k\}$$
$$\bar{p} = \min\{|S^j| : n - |W^j| = \bar{a}, j = 1, ..., k\}.$$

Then $\forall (S, W) \in \mathcal{D}$, $|W| \geq n - \bar{a}$. Now $k < c(f)$ by assumption, and $c(f) \leq \lceil (\bar{p} + \bar{a})/\bar{a} \rceil$ by definition. Further, $\bar{p} + \bar{a} \leq n$ implies $\lceil (\bar{p} + \bar{a})/\bar{a} \rceil \leq \lceil n/\bar{a} \rceil$. Hence $k < \lceil n/\bar{a} \rceil$. Now, for any family of $\{L_j\}$ in $N$, $\cap L_j = \emptyset$ iff $\cup L_j^c = N$ and $|L_j| \geq n - \bar{a}$ iff $|L_j^c| \leq \bar{a}$. So there exists a family of coalitions $\{L_j\}$ in $N$ with empty intersection and $|L_j| \geq n - \bar{a}$ each $j$, if and only if there exists a family of coalitions $\{M_j\}$ in $N$ with union equal to $N$ and $|M_j| \leq \bar{a}$ each $j$. Hence, the minimum number of coalitions of size (at least) $n - \bar{a}$ out of a population of $n$ with an empty intersection is identical to the minimum number of coalitions of size (at most) $\bar{a}$ out of a population of $n$ with union equal to $N$. Therefore, $\lceil n/\bar{a} \rceil$ gives the minimum number of coalitions of size (at least) $n - \bar{a}$ out of a population of $n$ with an empty intersection. So $k < \lceil n/\bar{a} \rceil$ implies $\cap W^j \neq \emptyset$. Next, define $I = \{i \in N : i \in \cap W^j \ \& \ i \notin \cup S^j\}$, where $I$ may be empty; and let $|I| = t$. Ignoring these individuals we have $k$ coalitions of size (at least) $n - \bar{a} - t$ out of $n - t$; and since (by the definition of the set $I$) $\lceil (\bar{p} + \bar{a})/\bar{a} \rceil \leq \lceil (n - t)/\bar{a} \rceil$ we have that $\cap (W^j \backslash I) \neq \emptyset$, and hence $K(\mathcal{D}) \neq \emptyset$. Further, because $\mathcal{D}$ was arbitrary save for the assumption that $|\mathcal{D}| < c(f)$, we have from the definition of $v(f)$ that $v(f) \geq c(f)$.

Finally, we show that $c(f) \geq v(f)$ as well. So let $(\underline{p}, \underline{a})$ be such that $k \equiv c(f) = \lceil (\underline{p} + \underline{a})/\underline{a} \rceil$. Define $t = n - (\underline{p} + \underline{a})$, and let $I = \{1, ..., t\}$ be the first $t$ individuals. Now $\lceil (\underline{p} + \underline{a})/\underline{a} \rceil$ gives the minimum number of coalitions of size $\underline{p}$ out of a population of size $(\underline{p} + \underline{a})$ with an empty intersection; hence among $N \backslash I$ we can construct $k$ coalitions, each of size $\underline{p}$, with an empty intersection; label these $\{S^1, ..., S^k\}$. For each $j = 1, ..., k$, let $W^j = S^j \cup I$, and define $\mathcal{D} = \{(S^j, W^j)^k_{j=1}\}$; then since $(\underline{p}, \underline{a}) \in \mathcal{N}(f)$, we have that $\mathcal{D} \subseteq \mathcal{D}(f)$. And by construction, $\cap W^j = I$, and for all $i \in I$, $i \notin \cup S^j$. Therefore $K(\mathcal{D}) = \emptyset$ and, since $v(f)$ is the *minimum* of all such collegial subfamilies, we have that $v(f) \leq k = c(f)$.□

Some important special cases are given in

**Lemma 3.4** *(1) For any counting rule $f$, $c(f) \geq 3$.*
*(2) If $f$ is plurality rule, then $c(f) = 3$.*
*(3) If $f$ is an extended $q$-rule with $q < n$, then $c(f) = \lceil n/(n - q) \rceil$.*

**Proof.** (1) Follows from the requirement that $\mathcal{N}(f)$ be proper.

(2) Under plurality rule the boundary points of $\mathcal{N}(f)$ are given by $p = a + 1$, and hence for all such $(p, a)$ (with $a \geq 1$) we have that $\lceil (p+a)/a \rceil = \lceil (2a+1)/a \rceil = \lceil 2 + 1/a \rceil = 3$.

(3) Suppose $(p, a)$ is such that $a \geq 1$ and $p \geq q(p+a)/n$; then

$$
\begin{array}{rcl}
p & \geq & q(p+a)/n \\
\Leftrightarrow \quad p(n-q) - qa & \geq & 0 \\
\Leftrightarrow \quad p(n-q) - qa + na & \geq & na \\
\Leftrightarrow \quad (p+a)(n-q) & \geq & na \\
\Leftrightarrow \quad (p+a)/a & \geq & n/(n-q);
\end{array}
$$

and hence $\lceil (p+a)/a \rceil \geq \lceil n/(n-q) \rceil$ Finally, there exists $(p,a)$ such that this holds with equality, namely, when $p = q$ and $a = n - q$.$\square$

Hence $c(f)$ for plurality rule is 3, while for an extended $q$-rule the number is equal to the Nakamura number of its associated simple rule.

In view of Theorem 3.4 and Lemma 3.3, we have the following result.

**Theorem 3.8** *A counting rule is acyclic if and only if $|X| < c(f)$.*

Combining this theorem with Lemma 3.4 then gives

**Corollary 3.2** *(1) Plurality rule is acyclic if and only if $|X| < 3$;*
*(2) An extended $q$-rule is acyclic if and only if $|X| < \lceil n/(n-q) \rceil$.*

In section 3.3 we saw how simple rules potentially differed along three dimensions: collective rationality, resoluteness, and equality. With regard to counting rules, it is clear that only the first two dimensions are germane, since by Theorem 3.3 all counting rules are anonymous and hence possess a common level of equality. On the other hand, there exist some counting rules which are more resolute than others, without entailing an associated lower degree of collective rationality. To see this, note first that the definition of resoluteness has the following simple application for counting rules: a counting rule $f$ is more resolute than another counting rule $f'$ if and only if $\mathcal{N}(f') \subset \mathcal{N}(f)$. Thus, for example, plurality rule is easily seen to be the *most* resolute counting rule, whereas the Pareto extension rule is the most resolute among those requiring $a = 0$ (because $(1, 0)$ is a decisive number for the Pareto extension rule and properness requires $p > a$ for all $(p, a) \in \mathcal{N}(f)$ and all aggregation rules $f$.) Also, for a given value of $q$, an extended $q$-rule is more resolute than a $q$-rule: if $p \geq q$ then necessarily $p \geq q(p+a)/n$, because $p + a \leq n$.

**Definition 3.16** *A counting rule $f$ dominates another counting rule $f'$ if $c(f) \geq c(f')$ and $\mathcal{N}(f) \supset \mathcal{N}(f')$. A counting rule is efficient if it is undominated.*

Clearly, then, plurality rule is an efficient counting rule, for any gains in acyclicity are at the expense of resoluteness. Also, $q$-rules are *not* efficient, since an extended $q$-rule gives the same level of acyclicity but is more resolute. Indeed, a necessary condition for any counting rule to be efficient is that it is an extended $q$-rule.

**Theorem 3.9** *A counting rule $f$ is efficient only if it is an extended $q$-rule.*

**Proof.** Suppose that $f$ is a counting rule but not an extended $q$-rule; i.e. for every $q \in (n/2, n]$, there exist $(p', a')$ with $p' > a'$, $p' \geq q(p' + a')/n$ and $(p', a') \notin \mathcal{N}(f)$. We show there exists an extended $q$-rule $f'$ such that $c(f') \geq c(f)$ and $\mathcal{N}(f) \subset \mathcal{N}(f')$. So let $f$ be such a rule. If $c(f) = \infty$ then, as noted above, the Pareto extension rule is more resolute than $f$. Suppose $c(f) < \infty$ and let $(\underline{p}, \underline{a})$, $\underline{p} > \underline{a}$, be such that $\lceil (\underline{p} + \underline{a})/\underline{a} \rceil = c(f)$. Define $f'$ to be the extended $q$-rule with $q = n\underline{p}/(\underline{p} + \underline{a})$; since $\underline{p} > \underline{a}$, necessarily $n/2 < q \leq n$ and $f'$ is well defined. If $(p, a) \in \mathcal{N}(f)$ is such that $a = 0$, it follows that $p \geq q(p+a)/n$ and hence, by $q \leq n$, $(p, a) \in \mathcal{N}(f')$. And for all $(p, a) \in \mathcal{N}(f)$ where $a \geq 1$,

$$
\begin{aligned}
&& (p + a)/a &\geq (\underline{p} + \underline{a})/\underline{a} \\
&\Leftrightarrow& \underline{a}/(\underline{p} + \underline{a}) &\geq a/(p + a) \\
&\Leftrightarrow& 1 - a/(p + a) &\geq 1 - \underline{a}/(\underline{p} + \underline{a}) \\
&\Leftrightarrow& p/(p + a) &\geq \underline{p}/(\underline{p} + \underline{a}).
\end{aligned}
$$

But by construction, $\underline{p}/(\underline{p}+\underline{a}) = q/n$ and hence $(p, a) \in \mathcal{N}(f')$ again. Finally, since by supposition $f$ is not an extended $q$-rule, there must exist some pair $(p', a') \in \mathcal{N}(f')$ such that $(p', a') \notin \mathcal{N}(f)$. Therefore $\mathcal{N}(f) \subset \mathcal{N}(f')$, implying $f'$ is more resolute than $f$. Furthermore, by Lemma 3.4(3),

$$
c(f') = \lceil \frac{n}{n - q} \rceil = \lceil n/(n - \lceil n\underline{p}/(\underline{p} + \underline{a}) \rceil) \rceil = \lceil (\underline{p} + \underline{a})/\underline{a} \rceil = c(f).
$$

Thus any counting rule that is not an extended $q$-rule is dominated by some extended $q$-rule and so only extended $q$-rules are efficient.□

Hence efficient counting rules must be extended $q$-rules; the converse, however, is not true [Exercise]. And within the class of extended $q$-rules, there is a tension between increased acyclicity from *higher* values of $q$ and increased resoluteness from *lower* values of $q$.

Finally, within the class of efficient counting rules (in fact, counting rules more generally) there exists exactly one which satisfies the following property:

**Definition 3.17** *An aggregation rule is positively responsive if and only if, for all profiles $\rho, \rho' \in \mathcal{R}^n$ and all $x, y \in X$, if $xRy$, $P(x, y; \rho) \subseteq P(x, y; \rho')$ and $P(y, x; \rho) \supseteq P(y, x; \rho')$ with at least one inclusion being strict, then $xP'y$.*

In other words, if $f$ is positively responsive then by changing (at least) one individual's preference from $xI_iy$ to $xP_i'y$ or from $yP_ix$ to $xR_i'y$, $x$ remains socially preferred to $y$ if it originally was, and becomes socially preferred to $y$ if originally indifferent. Hence with positively responsive aggregation rules individuals can break ties in social preference.

**Theorem 3.10** *A counting rule is positively responsive if and only if it is plurality rule.*

**Proof.** Sufficiency follows by the definition of plurality rule. To prove necessity, first note that since $f$ is a counting rule, $f$ is anonymous and neutral. Hence if $|P(x, y; \rho)| = |P(y, x; \rho)|$ it must be that $xIy$. Then by positive responsiveness, if $|P(x, y; \rho)| > |P(y, x; \rho)|$ it must be that $xPy$; and therefore (taking the contrapositive of this statement) $xRy$ implies $|P(x, y; \rho)| \geq |P(y, x; \rho)|$. Hence $xIy$ if and only if $|P(x, y; \rho)| = |P(y, x; \rho)|$, and $xPy$ if and only if $|P(x, y; \rho)| > |P(y, x; \rho)|$. And this is precisely the definition of plurality rule.$\square$

Theorem 3.10 along with Theorem 3.6 give *May's Theorem*: the only aggregation rule which is anonymous, neutral, and positively responsive is plurality rule. To illustrate May's Theorem, assume to the contrary that $f$ is anonymous, neutral, and positively responsive, but $f$ is *not* plurality rule. Then there must exist some profile $\rho$ for which a plurality strictly prefers $x$ to $y$, say, but $f(\rho)$ ranks $yRx$. Specifically, let $N = \{1, 2, 3\}$ and consider the following sequence of profiles:

$$\rho \;\; : \;\; xP_1y, \; xP_2y, \; yP_3x$$
$$\rho' \;\; : \;\; xP_1'y, \; yP_2'x, \; xP_3'y$$
$$\rho'' \;\; : \;\; yP_1''x, \; xP_2''y, \; yP_3''x.$$

By hypothesis, $yRx$ under profile $\rho$. Since $(\rho, \rho')$ is a $\sigma$-permutation with $\sigma(1) = 1$, $\sigma(2) = 3$, $\sigma(3) = 2$, anonymity implies $yR'x$. And neutrality then requires $xR''y$ (to see this, suppose not: then $yP''x$ by $f$ complete and, therefore, because $P(x, y; \rho') = P(y, x; \rho'')$ and $P(y, x; \rho') = P(x, y; \rho'')$, neutrality implies $xP'y$; contradiction). Now the only difference between $\rho''$ and $\rho$ is that individual 1 strictly prefers $y$ to $x$ under $\rho''$ and $x$ to $y$ under $\rho$. So by positive responsiveness, $xR''y$ implies $xPy$. But this contradicts the hypothesis and therefore $f$ must be plurality rule.

## 3.6  Discussion

Theorem 2.4 on aggregation to acyclic preference aggregation rules is, as remarked earlier, a qualitatively different result from those on transitive and quasi-transitive aggregation rules, in that the result requires the existence of more alternatives than individuals. And since acyclicity of a preference relation is the fundamental requirement for consistent choice from a finite set (Theorem 1.1), it is clearly important to understand the structure of acyclic rules more fully. To this end, the current chapter studies in considerable detail three wide (and related) classes of aggregation rules: simple rules, voting rules, and counting rules.

In Chapter 2, we saw how an aggregation rule induces a family of (proper and monotonic) decisive coalitions. Conversely, any (proper and monotonic) family of coalitions from the population induces a preference aggregation rule. In general, if we start with an aggregation rule, derive (for instance) the implicit set of decisive coalitions, and then define a second aggregation rule exclusively in terms of this set of coalitions, the two rules do not coincide (Example 3.1). Each of the three classes of rule studied here, however, has a self-referential property. With respect to simple rules (respectively, voting rules; counting rules), the self-referential property is the following: if we derive the induced decisive sets (respectively, decisive structures; decisive numbers) from the aggregation rule and then use this family to define a new aggregation rule, we recover exactly the aggregation rule with which we began. Such a self-referential property is not very intuitive beyond the observation that it means the rule is fully identified by its family of decisive sets (or structures or numbers). Thus, the first set of main results in the chapter are theorems that completely characterize each class of rule by a list of substantively interpretable axioms (Theorems 3.1, 3.3, and 3.6). Importantly, it turns out that the aggregation rules captured in these classes are empirically significant: among such rules are simple majority rule, all

$q$-rules (i.e. supermajority rules), extended and weighted $q$-rules, plurality rule, and rules in which there exist identified individuals with veto-power (as, for example, is the case with the UN Security Council decision rule).

Although the characterization theorems for (*inter alia*) the three classes of rule are useful and of independent interest, the main motivation for studying them derives from the observation in Chapter 2 that the structure of the family of decisive coalitions is closely related to the rationality properties of the associated collective preference relation (Section 2.4). When an aggregation rule is exhaustively characterized by its decisive sets (structure, numbers), therefore, the rationality properties of the rule can be analyzed directly in terms of these decisiveness properties. Hence, the second set of main results in the chapter are theorems that completely characterize the acyclicity of any rule in each class in terms of the relationship between a critical number for the rule – its Nakamura number – and the number of alternatives under consideration (Theorems 3.2, 3.4, and 3.8). Moreover, the Nakamura number of a rule is exclusively a property of the family of decisive sets (structures, numbers) of the rule in question. In sum, so long as the number of alternatives in $X$ is strictly less than the Nakamura number of a rule, then that rule is assuredly acyclic on $X$. Intuitively, the Nakamura number (which lies between 3 and the total number of individuals for every noncollegial rule) is an indicator of the extent to which a given aggregation rule can yield well-defined choices: the larger the number, the larger the sets of alternatives over which individual preferences aggregate to an acyclic social preference relation.

Finally, it is worth noting the difference between the characterization results of this chapter and the theorems of Chapter 2. There, the main results give a necessary, but not sufficient, condition for a particular type of rule to satisfy a given rationality property. So, for example, Theorem 2.1 states that if a preference aggregation rule satisfies weak Pareto and independence of irrelevant alternatives, then it is transitive only if it is dictatorial (i.e. only if there is a unique decisive coalition that contains exactly one individual); and Theorem 2.4 says that if a preference aggregation rule satisfies weak Pareto and there are at least as many alternatives as individuals, then it is acyclic only if it is collegial (i.e. only if there is a subset of individuals who are members of all decisive coalitions). By suitably restricting the classes of aggregation rule to those completely described by their decisiveness properties, we are able to provide a full characterization of when any rule in the class is acyclic and, therefore, when application of such rules is guaranteed to yield a nonempty set of maximal elements.

## 3.7   Exercises

**3.1.** Prove that if $n \leq 4$, all simple rules are weighted $q$-rules.

**3.2.** Lemma 3.2(1) showed all strong simple rules have Nakamura number equal to 3. Is the converse true (i.e. are all simple rules with Nakamura number equal to 3 strong)?

**3.3.** Prove that any noncollegial simple rule must have at least three distinct minimally decisive coalitions.

**3.4.** (a) Provide a direct proof (i.e. one that does not invoke Lemma 3.2(2)) for the fact that the Nakamura number for majority rule is 3 for $n \neq 4$ and is 4 for $n = 4$.
   (b) Let $n = 4$, and construct a simple rule $f$ such that $s(f) = 3$.

**3.5.** (a) Prove the following claim: "For any preference aggregation rule $f$, $\mathcal{L}(f)$ nonempty and $f$ acyclic imply $|X| < s(f)$".
   (b) Compare and contrast this claim with Theorem 3.2.

**3.6.** Let $f$ and $f'$ be $q$-rules. Prove or provide a counterexample to the claim that $s(f) > s(f')$ implies

$$\{\rho \in \mathcal{R}^n : f(\rho) \in \mathcal{A}\} \supset \{\rho \in \mathcal{R}^n : f'(\rho) \in \mathcal{A}\}.$$

Answer the same question assuming only that $f$ and $f'$ are simple rules.

**3.7.** Prove that if $f$ is a simple rule, then $s(f) = v(f)$.

**3.8.** Compute the Nakamura number for the post-1965 UN Security Council rule. Identify at least one other voting rule in use that is neither a simple rule nor a counting rule (justify your answer formally).

**3.9.** Provide a counter example to the converse of Theorem 3.9; i.e. if $f$ is an extended $q$-rule then $f$ is efficient.

**3.10.** Suppose a group $N = \{1, 2, 3, 4, 5\}$ makes collective decisions using a weighted $q$-rule with weights given by: $w_1 = w_2 = 0.35$ and $w_3 = w_4 = w_5 = 0.10$. For each value of $q \in (1/2, 1]$, identify as many of the formal properties of the aggregation rule and its underlying family of decisive coalitions as you can. Comment on any patterns you observe as $q$ increases parametrically from $1/2$ to $1$. [HINT: the material of Section 2.4 (filters) should prove useful here.]

## 3.8 Further reading

Nakamura [54] proved the general result relating the number of alternatives to the acyclicity of simple preference aggregation rules in general; see also Brown [15]. Ferejohn and Grether [29] proved Theorem 3.2 for $q$-rules. Extensions to voting rules and counting rules are due to Ferejohn and Fishburn [28] and to Banks [5]. May [46] first axiomatized plurality rule (which he referred to as the *method of majority decision*).

# Chapter 4

# Restricting Preferences

Theorem 3.10 provided an axiomatic foundation for plurality rule; yet Corollary 3.2 demonstrated that unless the feasible set consists of only two alternatives, plurality rule can be "badly behaved" in that it can fail to generate a well-defined choice in all circumstances. One popular avenue out of this predicament comes from weakening the requirement of acyclicity over *all* logically possible preference profiles to requiring acyclicity only over some well-motivated (and with luck, common) subset of profiles. The hope is that certain rules, in particular plurality and majority rule, will be acyclic on such a subset and hence their appealing equity and resoluteness properties are not invariably at the expense of a loss in collective rationality. This is the topic of the current chapter. We begin by introducing an important class of preference profiles for applied political theory, the class of *single-peaked* profiles. Intuitively, a single-peaked profile is one in which the set of alternatives can be ordered along a left-right scale in such a way that each individual has a unique most preferred alternative (or *ideal point*) and the individual's ranking of other alternatives falls as one moves away from her ideal point. Such profiles capture the common intuition that, for example, an individual has a most preferred ideological position on some liberal-conservative spectrum and the more distant is a candidate's ideological position from this most preferred point the more the individual dislikes the candidate. Furthermore, as this example suggests, the concept of single-peaked preferences extends naturally to infinite sets of alternatives representable by points along a line. We exploit this extension later in the chapter to provide an introduction to the spatial model, studied extensively in Chapters 5 and 6.

A second class of preference profiles is also analyzed which is characterized, not by an ordering of *alternatives*, but rather by an ordering of

*individuals.* Under *order-restricted* preferences, individuals are assigned a
position along a left-right scale with the condition being that, for any pair
of alternatives, the set of individuals preferring one of the alternatives all
lie to one side of those who prefer the other. While similar in spirit to
single-peaked preferences, examples are given to show that neither set of restricted profiles contains the other. Furthermore, an application shows how
order-restricted preferences can arise naturally in economic settings.

## 4.1   Single-peaked preferences

As in Chapter 3, our first goal is to identify restrictions under which various
classes of aggregation rules are acyclic, thereby guaranteeing from Theorem
1.1 the existence of a maximal outcome under the social preference relation.
Consider first the following:

**Definition 4.1** *Let $|X| = r \geq 2$; let $Q$ be a strict ordering of $X$ and label
$X$ so that $a_{t+1}Qa_t$ for all $t = 1, \ldots, r - 1$. $R_i \in \mathcal{R}$ is single-peaked on $X$
with respect to $Q$ if and only if there exists $t \in \{1, \ldots, r\}$ such that*

$$a_t P_i a_{t+1} P_i a_{t+2} P_i \ldots P_i a_r \ \& \ a_t P_i a_{t-1} P_i a_{t-2} \ldots P_i a_1.$$

As remarked in Chapter 1, an example of a strict ordering is the strict inequality ">" on the set of natural numbers 1,2,... . Therefore, single-peaked
preferences have the property that we can assign each of the $r$ outcomes
uniquely to one of the first $r$ natural numbers and then moves away from
the individual's most preferred outcome are associated with moves down the
individual's preference ordering.

   Now an assumption that each individual's preference ordering be single-
peaked is not much of a restriction, for it only disallows there being too
much indifference in any such ordering; that is, if $xI_iy$ and $R_i$ is single-
peaked, then necessarily $x$ and $y$ are on opposite sides of $i$'s most preferred
alternative. The next condition, however, requires there to be a certain
amount of homogeneity across the individuals' preferences.

**Definition 4.2** *A profile $\rho \in \mathcal{R}^n$ is single-peaked on $X$ if and only if there
is a strict ordering $Q$ of $X$ such that, for all $i \in N$, $R_i$ is single-peaked on
$X$ with respect to $Q$.*

Let $\mathcal{S} \subset \mathcal{R}^n$ denote the set of single-peaked preference profiles.

**Example 4.1** $N = \{1, 2, 3\}$, $X = \{x, y, z\}$, and $\rho \in \mathcal{R}^n$ is given by

$$xP_1yP_1z$$
$$yP_2xP_2z$$
$$zP_3yP_3x$$

Ordering the alternatives as $zQyQx$, we see that individuals' preferences are single-peaked with respect to $Q$: see Figure 4.1.$\square$

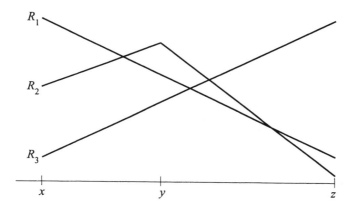

Figure 4.1: Preference profile for Example 4.1

The set of profiles in $\mathcal{S}$ thus contains two sorts of restrictions. The first is that each individual preference does not possess too much indifference, allowing $R_i$ to be single-peaked according to some ordering of the alternatives. The second is that there exists such an ordering common among all of the individuals: single-peakedness is a property of profiles and not of individual preference orderings considered one at a time. So it is quite possible for each individual to have single-peaked preferences on the set of alternatives, but for the profile not to be single-peaked. (This last restriction then implies that the set $\mathcal{S}$ is not "rectangular", i.e. $\mathcal{S}$ is not of the form $\mathcal{S} = \mathcal{S}_1 \times \mathcal{S}_2 \times \ldots \times \mathcal{S}_n$.) In particular, single-peaked preferences do not allow profiles of the form:

$$xP_iyP_iz$$
$$yP_jzP_jx$$
$$zP_kxP_ky$$

where these are precisely the kinds of profiles that generate cycles under majority rule.

In turns out that allowing for only single-peaked profiles implies that for *any* voting rule, the induced social preference relation is not only acyclic, but quasi-transitive as well.

**Theorem 4.1** *Let $f$ be a voting rule; then for all $\rho \in \mathcal{S}$, $f(\rho)$ is quasi-transitive.*

**Proof.** Let $x, y, z \in X$, $\rho \in \mathcal{S}$ and, without loss of generality, let $zQyQx$ in the single-peaked ordering. Then by single-peakedness we have the following inclusions:

$$(1)\ P(x, y; \rho) \subseteq P(x, z; \rho)\ \&\ P(z, x; \rho) \subseteq P(y, x; \rho)$$

$$(2)\ P(z, y; \rho) \subseteq P(z, x; \rho)\ \&\ P(x, z; \rho) \subseteq P(y, z; \rho).$$

There are six cases.

(i) If $xPy$ then $(P(x, y; \rho), R(x, y; \rho)) \in \mathcal{D}(f)$ by definition of a voting rule. Since $\mathcal{D}(f)$ is monotonic (by the proof to Theorem 3.3) and $f$ is neutral (Theorem 3.3), (1) implies $(P(x, z; \rho), R(x, z; \rho)) \in \mathcal{D}(f)$; therefore, $xPz$. Hence, $xPy$ and $yPz$ imply $xPz$.

(ii) If $xPz$ then $(P(x, z; \rho), R(x, z; \rho)) \in \mathcal{D}(f)$. Arguing exactly as for (i), we conclude that (2) implies $(P(y, z; \rho), R(y, z; \rho)) \in \mathcal{D}(f)$; therefore, $yPz$. Hence, $yPx$ and $xPz$ imply $yPz$.

(iii) If $zPx$ then $(P(z, x; \rho), R(z, x; \rho)) \in \mathcal{D}(f)$. Arguing exactly as for (i), we conclude that (1) implies $(P(y, x; \rho), R(y, x; \rho)) \in \mathcal{D}(f)$; therefore, $yPx$. Hence, $yPz$ and $zPx$ imply $yPx$.

(iv) If $zPy$ then $(P(z, y; \rho), R(z, y; \rho)) \in \mathcal{D}(f)$. Arguing exactly as for (i), we conclude that (2) implies $(P(z, x; \rho), R(z, x; \rho)) \in \mathcal{D}(f)$; therefore, $zPx$. Hence, $zPy$ and $yPx$ imply $zPx$.

(v) $xPz$ and $zPy$ cannot hold, since from (ii) $xPz$ implies $yPz$.

(vi) $zPx$ and $xPy$ cannot hold, since by (iii) $zPx$ implies $yPx$. Hence all six possible pairs of strict relations have been checked, and since $\{x, y, z\}$ are arbitrary, we have that $f(\rho)$ is quasi-transitive. $\square$

To see that this result cannot be strengthened to transitivity, consider the following:

**Example 4.2** Suppose $f$ is plurality rule; $N = \{1, 2, 3, 4\}$; $X = \{x, y, z\}$ and the preferences are

$$zP_1yP_1x$$
$$zP_2yP_2x$$
$$xP_3yP_3z$$
$$yP_4xP_4z.$$

Then the ordering $zQyQx$ is such that the above are single-peaked, yet $xIz$ and $zIy$, while $yPx$, i.e. indifference is not transitive.□

However, if $n$ is odd, then plurality rule *is* transitive for all $\rho \in S$ [Exercise].

For all $\rho \in \mathcal{R}^n$, all $V \in \mathcal{X}$, recall $M(f(\rho), V)$ consists of those alternatives in $V$ that are unbeaten under the preference aggregation rule $f$ at profile $\rho$. From Theorems 1.1 and 4.1, we have

**Corollary 4.1** *Let $f$ be a voting rule; then for all $\rho \in S$, all $V \in \mathcal{X}$, $M(f(\rho), V) \neq \emptyset$.*

Single-peaked preferences require individual preferences to be strictly decreasing as one moves away from an individual's unique ideal outcome. Can this be weakened? The following example says, in general, no:

**Example 4.3** Let $f$ be plurality rule; $N = \{1, 2, 3, 4, 5\}$; $X = \{x, y, z\}$ and the preferences are

$$i = 1, 2: \quad xP_iyI_iz$$
$$yP_3xP_3z$$
$$i = 4, 5: \quad zP_iyP_ix$$

The only possible single-peaked ordering is $zQyQx$ or the reverse, so assume the former ordering. (The preference profile is not single-peaked, since individuals' 1 and 2 have a "flat spot" to the right of their best policy $x$). Now plurality rule has $xPz$ by $\{1,2,3\}$ strictly preferring $x$ to $z$; $zPy$ by $\{4,5\}$ strictly preferring $z$ to $y$ with 1 and 2 indifferent; and $yPx$ by $\{3,4,5\}$ strictly preferring $y$ to $x$. Hence with a flat spot plurality rule is not even acyclic.□

On the other hand, if we consider majority rule in this example, we get that $yPx$ and $xPz$, but now $zIy$ (since there does not exist at least three individuals strictly favoring $z$ over $y$ or $y$ over $z$). Therefore, while plurality rule is cyclic in this example, majority rule is not. With this as motivation, consider the following weakened version of single-peakedness:

**Definition 4.3** *Let* $|X| = r \geq 2$; *let* $Q$ *be a strict ordering of* $X$ *and label* $X$ *so that* $a_{t+1}Qa_t$ *for all* $t = 1, \ldots, r - 1$. $R_i \in \mathcal{R}$ *is weakly single-peaked on* $X$ *with respect to* $Q$ *if and only if there exists* $t \in \{1, \ldots, r\}$ *such that,*

$$a_t R_i a_{t+1} R_i a_{t+2} R_i \ldots R_i a_r \ \& \ a_t R_i a_{t-1} R_i a_{t-2} \ldots R_i a_1.$$

Therefore, moves away from an individual's best outcome entail only weak moves down the preference order; that is, weakly single-peaked preferences allow for "flat spots" at the peak of the preference order, as well flat spots to either side. In general more indifference is admissible under weak than under strict single-peakedness.

**Definition 4.4** *A profile* $\rho \in \mathcal{R}^n$ *is weakly single-peaked on* $X$ *if and only if there is a strict ordering* $Q$ *of* $X$ *such that, for all* $i \in N$, $R_i$ *is weakly single-peaked on* $X$ *with respect to* $Q$.

Let $\mathcal{S}_w \subset \mathcal{R}^n$ denote the set of weakly single-peaked preference profiles.

**Theorem 4.2** *Let* $f$ *be a simple rule; then for all* $\rho \in \mathcal{S}_w$, $f(\rho)$ *is acyclic.*

**Proof.** The idea of the proof is to use Theorem 1.1 by first showing that under weak single-peakedness, $M(f(\rho), V)$ is nonempty for every $V \in \mathcal{X}$. Specifically, let $V \in \mathcal{X}$ and, without loss of generality, relabel $V$ so that $V = \{a_1, \ldots, a_s\}$ and $a_{t+1}Qa_t \ \forall t = 1, \ldots, s - 1$, where $Q$ is a strict ordering of $X$ with respect to which $\rho \in \mathcal{S}_w$. For any $x \in V$, let

$$G(x) = \{i \in N : \forall y \in V, \ xR_iy \text{ or } \exists z \in V \text{ such that } xQz \ \&, \ \forall y \in V, \ zR_iy\}.$$

Thus $G(a_1)$ constitutes the set of all individuals with $a_1$ as a most preferred alternative, $G(a_2)$ is the set of all individuals with $a_1$ or $a_2$ as a most preferred alternative, etc. Note that $G(a_t) \subseteq G(a_{t+1}) \ \forall t = 1, \ldots, s - 1$, and $G(a_s) = N$; further, if $i \in G(a_t)$ then $i$ weakly prefers $a_t$ to $a_\tau$ where $\tau > t$. The construction is illustrated in Figure 4.2. Let $x^* = \min\{x \in V : G(x) \in \mathcal{L}(f)\}$; this set is nonempty since in particular $G(a_s) = N \in \mathcal{L}(f)$. The claim then is that, $\forall y \in V$, $x^*R_{f(\rho)}y$; i.e. $x^* \in M(f(\rho), V)$. To see this let $y \neq x^*$ and assume $x^*Qy$. Then by the definition of $x^*$, $P(y, x^*; \rho) \notin \mathcal{L}(f)$, and since $f$ is a simple rule then it cannot be the case that $yP_{f(\rho)}x^*$; therefore $x^*R_{f(\rho)}y$. Next, let $yQx^*$; then $R(x^*, y; \rho) \in \mathcal{L}(f)$, and therefore by the properness of $f$, $P(y, x^*; \rho) \notin \mathcal{L}(f)$, implying again that $x^*R_{f(\rho)}y$. Since $V$ is arbitrary, therefore, $\forall V \in \mathcal{X}$, $M(f(\rho), V) \neq \emptyset$. The result now follows from Theorem 1.1.$\square$

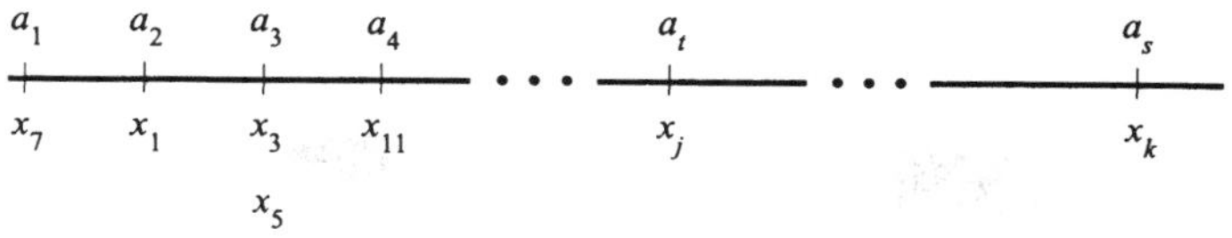

$$G(a_1) = \{7\}$$
$$G(a_2) = \{7,1\}$$
$$G(a_3) = \{7,1,3,5\}$$
$$\cdots$$
$$G(a_t) = \{7,1,3,5,11, \cdots ,j\}$$
$$\cdots$$
$$G(a_s) = N$$

Figure 4.2: Construction of $G(\cdot)$ in proof to Theorem 4.2

Thus, so long as individuals' preferences over $X$ constitute a weakly single-peaked profile, any simple rule will be acyclic on $X$. While insuring the existence of a nonempty maximal set is important, it is most useful for applied work to know something about what these maximal sets look like given existence. This issue is addressed in the next section.

## 4.2  Core characterization

In Chapter 3 the set of alternatives $X$ was not assumed to possess any structure vis-à-vis individuals' preferences and hence the sole identifying characteristic of maximal outcomes is given by their definition: $xR_{f(\rho)}y$ for all $y \in X$. With single-peaked preferences however this is no longer true; that is, we can locate the maximal outcomes with respect to the underlying ordering $Q$ rendering preferences single-peaked.

**Definition 4.5** *Let $f$ be a preference aggregation rule and $\rho \in \mathcal{R}^n$. The core of $f$ at $\rho$, $C_f(\rho)$ is defined by $C_f(\rho) \equiv M(f(\rho), X)$.*

So the core of a preference aggregation rule $f$ at any profile $\rho$ is simply the set of maximal elements in $X$ under the binary relation $f(\rho)$. In view of Theorem 1.1, therefore, earlier results on the existence of acyclic aggregation rules can be restated as results on the existence of aggregation rules with nonempty cores.

For any $\rho \in S$ let $x_i$ be individual $i$'s most preferred alternative from $X$, and for all $z \in X$ let $L^-(z) = \{i \in N : zQx_i\}$ and $L^+(z) = \{i \in N : x_iQz\}$, where $Q$ denotes the strict ordering of $X$ under which $\rho$ is single-peaked. Thus, $L^-(z)$ denotes those individuals who have ideal points to the left of $z$, and $L^+(z)$ denotes those with ideal points to the right of $z$. It is apparent that these sets depend on the particular choice of strict order $Q$; however, to save on notation, we leave this dependency implicit.

For any voting rule $f$, let $f' \equiv f_{\mathcal{L}(f)}$ be the simple rule associated with $f$ (for example, if $f$ is plurality rule then $f'$ is majority rule). Now in general $f$ is more resolute than $f'$, implying $C_f(\rho) \subseteq C_{f'}(\rho)$. On the other hand, when we restrict preferences to be single-peaked, we get equivalence.

**Theorem 4.3** *For any voting rule $f$, let $f' \equiv f_{\mathcal{L}(f)}$; then for all $\rho \in S$, $C_f(\rho) = C_{f'}(\rho)$.*

**Proof.** As noted above $C_f(\rho) \subseteq C_{f'}(\rho)$ holds generally, so we need only prove the converse. Let $a_t \in C_{f'}(\rho)$; then it must be the case that $L^-(a_t) \notin \mathcal{L}(f')$ and $L^+(a_t) \notin \mathcal{L}(f')$, since otherwise a decisive coalition would prefer either $a_{t-1}$ or $a_{t+1}$ to $a_t$. Further, by single-peakedness we know that for any $x, y \in X$, either $R(y, x; \rho) \subseteq L^-(x)$ or $R(y, x; \rho) \subseteq L^+(x)$, depending on whether $xQy$ or $yQx$, respectively. Thus $a_t R_{f'(\rho)} y$ for all $y \in X$ implies $R(y, a_t; \rho) \notin \mathcal{L}(f')$ for all $y \in X$; and since $\mathcal{L}(f')$ is defined to be those coalitions $L$ such that $(L, L) \in \mathcal{D}(f)$, by the monotonicity of $\mathcal{D}(f)$ we have that for all $y \in X$, $a_t R_{f(\rho)} y$. $\square$

Therefore with single-peaked preferences, while the social preference relation under a voting rule $f$, $R_f$, may differ from the relation under its associated simple rule $f'$, $R_{f'}$, it turns out that the set of core outcomes are exactly the same.

Theorem 4.3 does not extend to weakly single-peaked preferences. To see this, suppose there are three individuals with preferences over $X = \{x, y\}$ such that two of them are indifferent and one strictly prefers $x$ to $y$. Then plurality rule $f_p$ gives:

$$C_{f_p}(\rho) = \{x\}$$

but, writing $f_m$ for majority rule, the simple rule induced by $\mathcal{L}(f_p)$, we have

$$C_{f_{\mathcal{L}(f_p)}}(\rho) = C_{f_m}(\rho) = \{x, y\}.$$

On the other hand, when the preference profile is single-peaked, Theorem 4.3 states that to characterize cores of voting rules, it suffices to characterize cores of simple rules.

**Definition 4.6** *For any simple rule $f$ and single-peaked profile $\rho \in \mathcal{S}$, an alternative $y \in X$ is an $f$-median if and only if $L^+(y) \notin \mathcal{L}(f)$ and $L^-(y) \notin \mathcal{L}(f)$.*

Let $\mu_f(\rho; Q)$denote the set of $f$-medians given $\rho$is single-peaked with respect to $Q$, and note that by the properness of $\mathcal{L}(f)$, $\mu_f(\cdot)$is always non-empty. In fact, we can suppress the dependency of $\mu_f(\cdot)$on $Q$and just write $\mu_f(\rho)$: if $\rho$is single-peaked with respect to $Q$and $Q'$, then $\mu_f(\rho; Q) = \mu_f(\rho; Q')$[Exercise].

**Theorem 4.4** *Let $f$ be a simple rule; then for all $\rho \in \mathcal{S}$, $C_f(\rho) = \mu_f(\rho)$.*

**Proof.** Let $Q$ denote any strict ordering of $X$ with respect to which $\rho$ is single-peaked and label $X$ so that, $\forall t \geq 1$, $a_{t+1} Q a_t$. We first show $C_f(\rho) \subseteq \mu_f(\rho)$. To do this, let $a_t \in C_f(\rho)$ and suppose $a_t \notin \mu_f(\rho)$. So, by definition, either $L^-(a_t) \in \mathcal{L}(f)$ or $L^+(a_t) \in \mathcal{L}(f)$; without loss of generality assume the former. Then by single-peaked preferences, $\forall i \in L^-(a_t)$, $a_{t-1} P_i a_t$ and, since this set of individuals is decisive, we have $a_{t-1} P_{f(\rho)} a_t$. But this contradicts $a_t \in C_f(\rho)$.

We now show $\mu_f(\rho) \subseteq C_f(\rho)$. Let $a_t \in \mu_f(\rho)$ and suppose $a_t \notin C_f(\rho)$. Then there must exist some $a_\tau \in X$ such that $a_\tau P_{f(\rho)} a_t$, or equivalently there exists some $L \in \mathcal{L}(f)$ such that $P(a_\tau, a_t; \rho) = L$. If $a_t Q a_\tau$ then by single-peaked preferences we have that $P(a_\tau, a_t; \rho) \subseteq L^-(a_t)$; but by $a_t \in \mu_f(\rho)$, $L^-(a_t) \notin \mathcal{L}(f)$ and therefore (by the monotonicity of $\mathcal{L}(f)$) for no subset $L$ of $L^-(a_t)$ can it be the case that $L \in \mathcal{L}(f)$, contradicting the presumption that $a_\tau P_{f(\rho)} a_t$. A similar argument holds for $a_\tau Q a_t$.$\square$

If $f$ is a $q$-rule, then $y$ is an $f$-median if and only if $|L^-(y)| < q$ and $|L^+(y)| < q$. In particular, if $f$ is majority rule and $n$ is odd, Theorem 4.4 gives the *Median Voter Theorem* of Black [8]: there is a unique core outcome, equal to the ideal point of the individual whose ideal point constitutes the median (with respect to the single-peaked ordering $Q$) of the set of ideal points; if on the other hand $n$ is even, then the set of best outcomes will consist of an interval between the ideal points of the two "middle" individuals. In general, Theorem 4.4 provides a simple characterization of the set of "best" outcomes under any simple rule $f$ and, by Theorem 4.3, any voting rule as well.

It is worth observing here that Theorem 4.4, like Theorem 4.3, does not extend to the domain of weakly single-peaked preferences, $\mathcal{S}_w$. Example 4.4 illustrates this fact.

**Example 4.4** Let $X = \{w, x, y, z\}$; $N = \{1, 2, 3\}$ and consider the following profile, $\rho$:

$$xP_1yP_1wI_1z$$
$$wP_2xI_2yP_2z$$
$$zP_3yP_3xP_3w.$$

Then $\rho \in \mathcal{S}_w$ relative to the ordering $zQyQxQw$: see Figure 4.3.

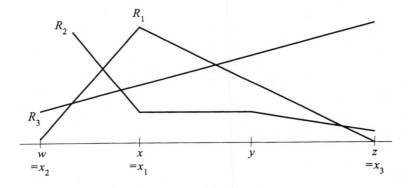

Figure 4.3: Preference profile for Example 4.4

Assume simple majority rule, $f_m$, with $\mathcal{L}(f_m) = \{S \subseteq N : |S| \geq 2\}$. Since $n$ is odd, $f_m$ is a strong simple rule and $C_{f_m}(\rho) = \{x, y\}$. However, because $L^-(x) = \{2\}$, $L^+(x) = \{3\}$ but $L^-(y) = \{1, 2\} \in \mathcal{L}(f_m)$, we have $\mu_{f_m}(\rho) = \{x\}.\square$

## 4.3   One-dimensional outcome space

As noted above, when preferences are single-peaked we can think of assigning each alternative to one of the natural numbers 1,2,3,..., with the property that moves down an individual's preference ordering correspond to moves away from the individual's (unique) best alternative. Now in identifying core outcomes the *finiteness* of the set of alternatives was immaterial; all that was relevant was whether there existed a decisive coalition which preferred to move to the left or the right when considering some alternative as a core outcome. This suggests that if the set of alternatives $X$ is not required to be finite, but is instead *any* subset of the real line, a suitably modified version of Theorem 4.4 will continue to hold.

So let $X$ denote some arbitrary subset of the real line $\Re$, where now the strict ordering $Q$ employed in the previous sections is simply taken to be the strict inequality ordering " $>$ ".

**Definition 4.7** *Given $X \subseteq \Re$, a preference profile $\rho \in \mathcal{R}^n$ is single-peaked on $X$ if for all $i \in N$, there exists $x_i \in X$ such that (1) $x_i P_i y$ for all $y \in X \backslash \{x_i\}$, (2) $y < z < x_i$ implies $z P_i y$, and (3) $x_i < z < y$ implies $z P_i y$.*

Note that in contrast to the definition of single-peaked preferences in Section 4.1, the current definition *does* generate a "rectangular" restriction on preferences, since now the ordering of alternatives is held fixed.

As before, let $\mathcal{S} \subset \mathcal{R}^n$ denote the set of single-peaked preferences profiles on $X$, and for all $x \in X$ let $L^-(x) = \{i \in N : x_i < x\}$, $L^+(x) = \{i \in N : x_i > x\}$. For any simple rule $f$ and single-peaked profile $\rho$, let $\mu_f(\rho) = \{x \in X : L^-(x) \notin \mathcal{L}(f) \ \& \ L^+(x) \notin \mathcal{L}(f)\}$ be the set of $f$-medians.

**Theorem 4.5** *Let $f$ be a simple rule and $X \subseteq \Re$; then for all $\rho \in \mathcal{S}$, $C_f(\rho)$ is nonempty and is equal to the set of $f$-medians $\mu_f(\rho)$. Moreover, if $f \equiv f_{\mathcal{L}(f')}$ for some voting rule $f'$, then $\rho \in \mathcal{S}$ implies $C_f(\rho) = C_{f'}(\rho)$.*

**Proof.** [Exercise].□

A set $Y$ is *convex* if $x, y \in Y$ implies $[\lambda x + (1 - \lambda)y] \in Y$, all $\lambda \in [0, 1]$. Therefore, if the set of alternatives $X$ is a one-dimensional convex set in the real line $\Re$, then $X$ is an interval. Under such circumstances, we have the following useful property of the core.

**Corollary 4.2** *Let $f$ be a voting rule and let $X \subseteq \Re$ be convex; then for all $\rho \in \mathcal{S}$, $C_f(\rho)$ is a convex set.*

**Proof.** [Exercise].□

Finally, when the set of alternatives is not finite, as is the case assumed in this section, it is oftentimes convenient to describe individuals' preferences, not in terms of their primitive binary relations, but rather by a numerical function. Formally, for any binary preference relation $R$ on $X$, say that a function $u : X \to \Re$ *represents* $R$ if and only if, for all $x, y \in X$,

$$xRy \Leftrightarrow u(x) \geq u(y).$$

In other words, $u$ represents $R$ if and only if it assigns higher numbers to strictly more preferred alternatives and assigns the same number to any pair of alternatives that are indifferent to each other. It is important to note that only the ordinal relationship between any two numbers, say $u(x)$ and $u(y)$, matters here; their particular cardinal values have no meaning whatsoever. The function $u$ is called a *utility function*.

When $X \subseteq \Re$ is convex, the analogous property of a utility function $u$ to single-peakedness of $R$, is that $u$ is *strictly quasi-concave*: $u(x) > u(y)$ implies that for all $\lambda \in (0,1)$, $u(\lambda x + (1-\lambda)y) > u(y)$. Strict quasi-concavity is weaker than the more familiar property of *strict concavity*: for all distinct $x, y \in X$ and all $\lambda \in (0,1)$, $u(\lambda x + (1-\lambda)y) > \lambda u(x) + (1-\lambda)u(y)$. Thus all strictly concave functions are strictly quasi-concave but not the converse. Figure 4.4(a) illustrates a strictly quasi-concave (but not concave) function and Figure 4.4(b) illustrates a strictly concave (and therefore quasi-concave) function.

## 4.4    Application: Public goods provision

Suppose the collective choice problem faced by a group of individuals is to decide on the level of some public good, say, national defense. Let $[0, \bar{x}] \subset \Re_+$ denote the set of possible levels, with common element $x$. Individual preferences are defined over two parameters, the level of the public good $x$ and money income $y$, where in this problem the latter will reflect any payments an individual has to make toward the financing of the public good. Suppose individual $i$'s preference $R_i$ over $x$ and $y$ can be represented by a utility function of the form

$$u_i(x, y) = v_i(x) + y,$$

where the function $v_i(\cdot)$ is strictly concave (preferences that are additively separable and linear in income are called *quasi-linear* preferences). If $v_i(\cdot)$ is increasing, then the concavity of the function implies that the marginal gain to $i$ from increasing the level of the public good is decreasing; if $v_i(\cdot)$ is decreasing, it says that the marginal loss to $i$ is increasing.

The cost associated with the level of the public good $x$ is equal to $c(x)$, where $c(\cdot)$ is increasing and convex; thus the marginal cost is increasing in the level of the public good. The project is financed by a uniform tax: if the level $x$ is selected each of the $n$ individuals pays $c(x)/n$.

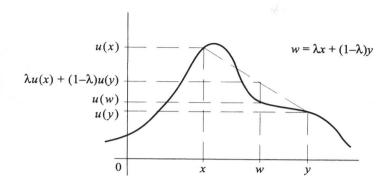

(a) $u$ strictly quasi-concave

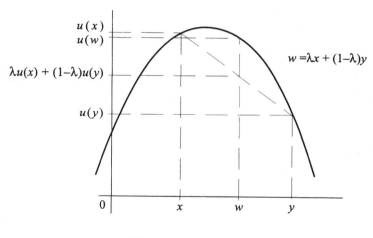

(b) $u$ strictly concave

Figure 4.4: Strictly quasi-concave and concave functions

Given this financing scheme, individual $i$ has *induced* preferences over the level of the public good $x$ represented by

$$u_i^*(x) = v_i(x) - \frac{c(x)}{n}.$$

Because a strictly concave function minus a convex function generates a strictly concave function, $u_i^*(\cdot)$ is strictly concave. And since strictly concave utility functions imply single-peaked preferences, for *any* voting rule $f$ used to determine the collective choice, there will exist a core outcome. Furthermore, letting $x_i^*$ be the (unique) level of $x$ that maximizes $u_i^*(x)$ on $[0, \bar{x}]$ and labeling $N$ so that $x_1^* \leq x_2^* \leq \ldots \leq x_n^*$, Theorem 4.5 implies that any such core outcome is an $f$-median alternative in the interval $[x_1^*, x_n^*]$.

## 4.5   Order-restricted preferences

Assuming single-peaked preference profiles is not always reasonable. For example, toward the end of the Vietnam war, three aggregate alternatives were prominent choices for the USA: $x =$ "pull out immediately"; $y =$ "carry on as before"; and $z =$ "escalate to insure rapid victory". Although there is a "natural" ordering of the set $\{x, y, z\}$, $xQyQz$, it is not unreasonable to rank $y$ last. Thus it is plausible to assume (as in fact was the case) that every possible ordering of the triple could be found in the population. So the preference profile over $\{x, y, z\}$ is not single-peaked. Similarly, while induced preferences might often be single-peaked, as in the example of Section 4.4 above, this is by no means assured. Suppose, in that example, the public good production cost schedule is strictly concave (because the technology is subject to increasing returns to scale) as opposed to convex; then the induced preferences $u_i^*(x)$ need not be single-peaked in $x$. However, single-peakedness is sufficient, not necessary, for acyclic social choice and therefore the absence of single-peakedness does not imply the absence of consistent collective decision making. For example, the following three-person profile over $\{x, y, z\}$ is not single-peaked but nevertheless supports a nonempty majority core, $\{x\}$:

$$xP_1yP_1z$$
$$xP_2zP_2y$$
$$zP_3yP_3x.$$

An alternative restriction is that of *order-restricted* preferences. Unlike single-peakedness, defined with respect to a strict ordering of alternatives, order-restriction is defined with respect to a strict ordering of individuals.

And in many circumstances, ordering people is more natural than ordering alternatives. For example, in redistributive politics policy makers are concerned with reallocating resources from rich to poor people, subject to the constraint (typically) that such redistributions do not reverse the rank-order of individuals' wealth. So while there does not exist an obvious ordering of alternative distributions of wealth, there does exist a natural ordering of individuals in terms of individual wealth.

We now return to the assumption that the set of alternatives $X$ is finite. For any two nonempty finite sets of integers $I, J$, define the binary relation $\succeq$ as $I \succeq J$ if $\min\{i \in I\} > \max\{j \in J\}$, i.e. if the smallest element in $I$ is greater than the greatest element in $J$. If either set is empty let $I \succeq J$ and $J \succeq I$.

**Definition 4.8** *A profile $\rho \in \mathcal{R}^n$ is order-restricted on $X$ if and only if there is a permutation $\sigma$ on $N$ such that, for all distinct pairs $\{x, y\} \subseteq X$, either*

    *(a) $\{\sigma(i) \in N : xP_iy\} \succeq \{\sigma(i) \in N : xI_iy\} \succeq \{\sigma(i) \in N : yP_ix\}$, or*
    *(b) $\{\sigma(i) \in N : xP_iy\} \preceq \{\sigma(i) \in N : xI_iy\} \preceq \{\sigma(i) \in N : yP_ix\}$.*

Thus a profile is order-restricted on $X$ if we can order individuals in such a way that for any pair of alternatives $x$ and $y$, the first $j(xy) \geq 0$ individuals in the ordering strictly prefer $x$ to $y$ (respectively, $y$ to $x$), the final $k(xy) \geq 0$ individuals in the ordering strictly prefer $y$ to $x$ (respectively, $x$ to $y$), and the middle group of individuals, if any, are indifferent between the two. It is important to emphasize that the ordering of individuals is *not* conditional on the pair of alternatives under consideration; however, as indicated by the notation, the "cut-offs", $j(\cdot)$ and $k(\cdot)$ above, *can* depend on the pair. Example 4.5 illustrates the concept.

**Example 4.5** Let $X = \{w, x, y, z\}$ and $N = \{1, 2, 3\}$. Suppose $\rho \in \mathcal{R}^n$ is as follows:

$$xP_1zP_1yI_1w$$
$$xP_2yP_2wI_2z$$
$$zP_3yI_3wP_3x.$$

The profile $\rho$ is *not* order-restricted with respect to the ordering $(1,2,3)$: under this ordering, we have $(yI_1w, yP_2w, yI_3w)$ and so both $(a)$ and $(b)$ fail with respect to $\{y, w\}$. However, consider the permutation $\sigma(1) = 2$, $\sigma(2) = 1$, and $\sigma(3) = 3$. Then the profile $\rho$ *is* order-restricted with respect to the ordering $(\sigma(1), \sigma(2), \sigma(3)) = (2, 1, 3)$. To see this, consider the following table.

| | $\sigma(1) = 2$ | $\sigma(2) = 1$ | $\sigma(3) = 3$ |
|---|---|---|---|
| {w,x} | $xw$ | $xw$ | $wx$ |
| {w,y} | $yw$ | $[wy]$ | $[wy]$ |
| {w,z} | $[wz]$ | $zw$ | $zw$ |
| {x,y} | $xy$ | $xy$ | $yx$ |
| {x,z} | $xz$ | $xz$ | $zx$ |
| {y,z} | $yz$ | $zy$ | $zy$ |

The rows of the table list the six (unordered) pairs of alternatives in $X$ and the columns identify the individuals $\{1, 2, 3\}$ under the permutation $\sigma$. An entry $ab$ (respectively, $[ab]$) in row {a,b} and column $\sigma(j) = i$ indicates that individual $i$ strictly prefers $a$ to $b$ (respectively, is indifferent between $a$ and $b$) under the profile $\rho$. Inspection of the table confirms that $\rho$ is order-restricted.□

Let $\mathcal{O} \subset \mathcal{R}^n$ be the set of order-restricted profiles on $X$.

The following example shows that order-restriction and single-peakedness are independent properties (and in so doing gives an example of a profile that is not order-restricted).

**Example 4.6** We first show there exist single-peaked profiles that are not order-restricted. Let $N = \{1, 2, 3\}$ and $X = \{w, x, y, z\}$. Define $\rho \in \mathcal{R}^n$ by:

$$xP_1yP_1zP_1w$$
$$yP_2xP_2wP_2z$$
$$zP_3yP_3xP_3w.$$

Let $Q$ be the strict ordering of $X$ whereby, $zQyQxQw$. Then $\rho$ is single-peaked on $X$ relative to $Q$; so $\rho \in \mathcal{S}$. However, $\rho$ is not order-restricted. To see this, note that it suffices, by symmetry, to consider only the orderings of $N$, $\{(1, 2, 3), (1, 3, 2), (3, 1, 2)\}$. If the ordering is $(1, 2, 3)$, order-restriction fails on $\{w, z\}$; if the ordering is $(1, 3, 2)$, order-restriction fails on $\{y, z\}$; and if the ordering is $(3, 1, 2)$, order-restriction fails on $\{x, y\}$. Hence, $\sim [\mathcal{S} \subseteq \mathcal{O}]$.

We now check that there are order-restricted profiles that are not single-peaked. Let $N = \{1, 2, 3\}$ and $X = \{x, y, z\}$. Define $\rho' \in \mathcal{R}^n$ by:

$$xP_1zP_1y$$
$$xP_2yP_2z$$
$$yP_3zP_3x.$$

Then $\rho'$ is order-restricted relative to the ordering of $N$, $(1,2,3)$. However, since each alternative is ranked uniquely worst by at least one individual, $\rho'$ cannot be single-peaked. Hence, $\sim [\mathcal{O} \subseteq \mathcal{S}]$.□

The following result is the analogue to Theorem 4.1.

**Theorem 4.6** *Let $f$ be a voting rule; then for all $\rho \in \mathcal{O}$, $f(\rho)$ is quasi-transitive.*

**Proof.**  Let $f$ be a voting rule and $\rho \in \mathcal{O}$. Without loss of generality, suppose $\rho$ is order-restricted with respect to the ordering of $N$, $(1,2,...,n)$. Let $xPy$ and $yPz$ for some $\{x,y,z\} \subseteq X$; we wish to show $xPz$. Since $f$ is a voting rule, $(P(x,y;\rho), R(x,y;\rho)) \in \mathcal{D}(f)$ and $(P(y,z;\rho), R(y,z;\rho)) \in \mathcal{D}(f)$. By order-restriction, either $P(x,y;\rho) = \{1,...,i_1\}$ or $P(x,y;\rho) = \{j,...,n\}$; without loss of generality, assume $P(x,y;\rho) = \{1,...,i_1\}$. Then again by order-restriction, $R(x,y;\rho) = \{1,...,i_2\}$ for some $i_2 \geq i_1$. There are three cases: Figure 4.5 illustrates each in turn.

(1) $P(y,z;\rho) \subseteq N\backslash R(x,y;\rho) = \{i_2+1,...,n\}$. In this case, $\mathcal{D}(f)$ proper implies $R(y,z;\rho) \cap P(x,y;\rho) \neq \emptyset$; let $i^* = \min[i \in R(y,z;\rho) \cap P(x,y;\rho)] \leq i_1$, so $R(y,z;\rho) = \{i^*,...,i_1,...,n\}$.

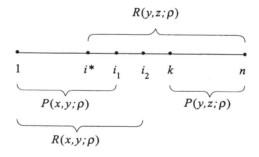

Figure 4.5(a): Case (1)

Since $R_{i*} \in \mathcal{R}$, $xP_{i*}z$. Therefore, by order-restriction, either $\forall j < i^*$, $xP_jz$, or $\forall j > i^*$, $xP_jz$. If $\forall j > i^*$, $xP_jz$ then $yPz$ and $\mathcal{D}(f)$ monotonic imply $xPz$. Assume $\forall j < i^*$, $xP_jz$. Then $\rho \in \mathcal{O}$, $yI_{i*}z$ and $P(y,z;\rho) \subseteq N\backslash R(x,y;\rho)$ imply $xP_jz \ \forall j \in P(x,y;\rho) = \{1,...,i_1\}$ and $xR_jz \ \forall j \in \{i_1,...,i_2\}$. Hence $(P(x,z;\rho), R(x,z;\rho)) \in \mathcal{D}(f)$ and $xPz$.

(2) $P(y,z;\rho) \cap R(x,y;\rho) \neq \emptyset$. Let $P(y,z;\rho) \cap R(x,y;\rho) = \{j_1,...,j_2\}$; then $xP_jz \ \forall j \in \{j_1,...,j_2\}$. By order-restriction, $xP_jz \ \forall j < j_2$ or $xP_jz$ $\forall j > j_1$. There are, again by order-restriction, two subcases.

(2a) $yP_jz \ \forall j \leq j_2$. Then $j_1 = 1$ and, since $xR_jy \ \forall j \leq j_2$, $xP_jz \ \forall j \leq j_2$.

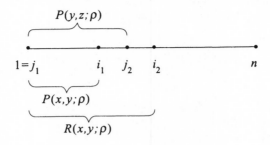

Figure 4.5(b):  Case (2a)

If $R(y, z; \rho) \subseteq R(x, y; \rho)$ then both $P(y, z; \rho) \subseteq P(x, z; \rho)$ and $R(y, z; \rho) \subseteq R(x, z; \rho)$; hence, $yPz$ and $\mathcal{D}(f)$ monotonic imply $xPz$. If $R(x, y; \rho) \subseteq R(y, z; \rho)$ then $P(x, y; \rho) \subseteq P(x, z; \rho)$ and $R(x, y; \rho) \subseteq R(x, z; \rho)$; hence, $xPy$ and $\mathcal{D}(f)$ monotonic again yield $xPz$. And by order-restriction, these are the only two possibilities for (2a).

(2b) $yP_jz \ \forall j \geq j_1$. Then $j_2 = i_2 = n$ and $xP_jz \ \forall j \in \{j_1, ..., i_2\}$.

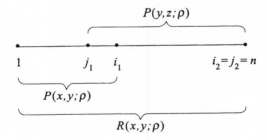

Figure 4.5(c):  Case (2b)

If $xP_jz \ \forall j \leq i_2$ then $\mathcal{D}(f)$ monotonic and $xPy$ imply $xPz$. Suppose $xP_jz$ $\forall j \geq j_1$. Then by order-restriction and definition of $R(x, y; \rho)$, $xR_jz \ \forall j < j_1$ such that $yR_jz$. Hence, $P(y, z; \rho) \subseteq P(x, z; \rho)$ and $R(y, z; \rho) \subseteq R(x, z; \rho)$, in which case $yPz$ and $\mathcal{D}(f)$ monotonic imply $xPz$. This completes the proof of the Theorem.□

Theorem 4.6 implies that the core of any voting rule $f$ is nonempty for all $\rho \in \mathcal{O}$. Furthermore, there is a partial analogue to the core characterization results on single-peaked domains. Fix a voting rule $f$. For any $\rho \in \mathcal{O}$ let $(i_1, ..., i_n)$ be the ordering of $N$ with respect to which $\rho$ is order-restricted and, for any $i_j$, let $L^-(i_j) = \{i_1, ..., i_{j-1}\}$ and $L^+(i_j) = \{i_{j+1}, ..., i_n\}$. Now define

$$
\begin{aligned}
\ell &= \min[i_j : (L^+(i_j), L^+(i_j)) \notin \mathcal{D}(f)]; \\
r &= \max[i_j : (L^-(i_j), L^-(i_j)) \notin \mathcal{D}(f)]; \\
L(\rho) &= \{\ell, ..., r\}.
\end{aligned}
$$

Because $\mathcal{D}(f)$ is monotonic and proper, $\ell$ and $r$ are well-defined with $\ell \leq r$. For example, for simple majority rule with an odd number of people, the set $L(\rho)$ consists of the median individual in the ordering with respect to which $\rho$ is order-restricted.

**Theorem 4.7** *Let $f$ be a voting rule. Then, for all $\rho \in \mathcal{O}$, each $i \in L(\rho)$ has a veto; i.e. for all $x, y \in X$,*

$$[P(x, y; \rho) \cap L(\rho) \neq \emptyset] \Rightarrow x R_{f(\rho)} y.$$

**Proof.** Without loss of generality assume, $\forall j = 1, ..., n, i_j = j$. Let $x, y \in X$ and suppose $x P_i y$ for some $i \in L(\rho)$. By order-restriction, *either* $x P_j y$ $\forall j = 1, ..., i$ *or* $x P_j y$ $\forall j = i, ..., n$. In either case, $x R_{f(\rho)} y$ by definition of $i \in L(\rho)$.□

As a characterization result, Theorem 4.7 is clearly much weaker than Theorem 4.4 for single-peaked profiles. The reason is that, relative to single-peakedness, order-restriction admits a great deal more indifference. To see this, it is useful to introduce an important concept.

**Definition 4.9** *For any coalition $L \subseteq N$ and preference profile $\rho$, the Pareto set for $L$ at $\rho$ is*

$$PS_L(\rho) = \{x \in X : \forall y \neq x, \ P(y, x; \rho) \cap L \neq \emptyset \Rightarrow P(x, y; \rho) \cap L \neq \emptyset\}.$$

Thus if $x \in PS_L(\rho)$ then any alternative $y$ which is strictly preferred to $x$ by a member of $L$ is such that another member of $L$ strictly prefers $x$ to $y$. Equivalently, an alternative $y$ is *not* in the Pareto set for $L$ if there exists another feasible alternative $x$ such that, for all $i \in L$, $x R_i y$ and, for some $j \in L$, $x P_j y$. It is immediate that the Pareto set for all $L$ at any profile is nonempty (by the transitivity of individual preferences and finiteness of $X$).

Note that at all profiles $\rho$ in $\mathcal{R}^n$, the core of $f$ is precisely $PS_N(\rho)$ when $f$ is the Pareto extension rule. However, for an arbitrary voting rule $f$, the core may not even be a subset of the Pareto set for $N$: let $f$ be majority rule, $X = \{x, y\}$, $N = \{1, 2, 3\}$ and let $\rho$ be given by $x I_i y$ for $i = 1, 2$, and $y P_3 x$; then $x \in C_f(\rho)$ but $x \notin PS_N(\rho)$. On the other hand, Theorems 4.6 and 4.7 imply the following relationship between the core and the Pareto set for the coalition $L(\rho)$ at any order-restricted profile.

**Corollary 4.3** *Let $f$ be a voting rule. Then for all $\rho \in \mathcal{O}$,*

$$C_f(\rho) \cap PS_{L(\rho)}(\rho) \neq \emptyset.$$

**Proof.**  Let $y \in PS_{L(\rho)}(\rho)$ and suppose $y \notin C_f(\rho)$. Then there is an alternative in $X$ that is strictly preferred to $y$ at $\rho$. Hence, by Theorem 4.6, there exists $x \in C_f(\rho)$ such that $x P_{f(\rho)} y$ in which case, by Theorem 4.7, $x R_i y$ for all $i \in L(\rho)$. Moreover, if $x \notin PS_{L(\rho)}(\rho)$ there must exist $z \in X$ such that $L(\rho) \subseteq R(z, x; \rho)$ and $z P_j x$ for some $j \in L(\rho)$; but then, by transitivity of individual preferences, $L(\rho) \subseteq R(z, y; \rho)$ and $z P_j y$, contradicting $y \in PS_{L(\rho)}(\rho)$. Therefore, $y \in PS_{L(\rho)}(\rho)$ implies $x \in PS_{L(\rho)}(\rho)$.$\square$

Thus, if $\rho$ is order-restricted and $f$ is a voting rule, then the core $C_f(\rho)$ and the Pareto set $PS_{L(\rho)}(\rho)$ must have at least some elements in common. However, Corollary 4.3 cannot be tightened beyond this, as the following example, resting on the presence of a suitable amount of indifference among individuals, illustrates.

**Example 4.7** Let $f$ be a voting rule and $X = \{x, y\}$.
   (1) Let $N = \{1, ..., 6\}$ and suppose $\mathcal{D}(f)$ equals

$$\{((\{1, ..., 4\}, \{1, ..., 4\}), (\{2, ..., 6\}, \{2, ..., 6\}), (\{1, 6\}, \{1, 6\}))\}$$

together with the appropriate supersets (i.e. respecting the monotonicity of decisive structures). Let $\rho$ be such that $P(x, y; \rho) = \{1, 2, 3\}$, $I(x, y; \rho) = \{4, 5\}$ and $P(y, x; \rho) = \{6\}$. Then $\rho$ is order-restricted relative to $(1, ..., 6)$ with $L(\rho) = \{2, 3, 4\}$. Hence $PS_{L(\rho)}(\rho) = \{x\}$ but $C_f(\rho) = \{x, y\}$.
   (2) Let $N = \{1, ..., 7\}$ and suppose $\mathcal{D}(f)$ equals

$$\{((\{1, 2\}, \{1, ..., 5\}), (\{3, ..., 7\}, \{3, ..., 7\}), (\{2, 6, 7\}, \{2, 6, 7\}))\}$$

together with the appropriate supersets. Let $\rho$ be such that $P(x, y; \rho) = \{1, 2\}$, $I(x, y; \rho) = \{3, 4, 5\}$ and $P(y, x; \rho) = \{6, 7\}$. Then $\rho$ is order-restricted relative to $(1, ..., 7)$ with $L(\rho) = \{3, 4, 5\}$. Hence $PS_{L(\rho)}(\rho) = \{x, y\}$ but $C_f(\rho) = \{x\}$.$\square$

On the other hand, if preferences are everywhere strict on $X$, the argument for Corollary 4.3 immediately yields the following result.

**Corollary 4.4** *Let $f$ be a voting rule and assume all individuals have strict preferences over $X$; i.e. $\rho \in \mathcal{P}^n$. Then if $\rho$ is order-restricted, $C_f(\rho) = PS_{L(\rho)}(\rho)$.*

For instance, if $f$ is simple majority rule and $n$ is odd, the core is the set of ideal points of the median person in the ordering of *individuals* with respect to which $\rho$ is order-restricted. Contrast this with the earlier result on single-peaked preferences under majority rule, where the core consists of the median ideal points in the ordering of *alternatives* with respect to which $\rho$ is single-peaked.

## 4.6 Application: Collective choice of tax-rates

The application of Section 4.4 illustrated how single-peaked preference profiles over a set of collective alternatives might arise as induced preferences from some underlying set of primitive preferences and technologies. As suggested above, however, even when the underlying preferences and technologies exhibit strong regularity properties, single-peaked induced preferences cannot always be guaranteed.

To see when order-restricted preferences can arise in the absence of single-peakedness, consider the following situation: there are $n$ individuals, with preferences defined over two goods, a consumption good and leisure; let $c \in \Re_+$ denote units of the former and $l \in \Re_+$ those of the latter. Individual $i$'s preferences over $(c, l)$ are represented by a utility function of the Cobb-Douglas form

$$u_i(c, l) = c^{\alpha_i} l^{1-\alpha_i}$$

where $\alpha_i \in (0, 1)$. Thus individual preferences over $(c, l)$-pairs differ only to the extent that the parameter $\alpha_i$ differs across individuals. Suppose each individual has an endowment of 1 unit of time that can be allocated to leisure and work ($h = 1 - l$) at a wage-rate $w > 0$, with the price of the consumption good normalized to 1. Assume further that the collective decision to be made is over a set of proportional tax/transfer schemes on earned income. Specifically, the set of possible tax/transfer schemes is $X \subseteq [0, 1] \times \Re$ with typical element $(t, T)$; the interpretation is that $t \in [0, 1]$ is a proportional tax on labor income and $T \in \Re$ is a lump-sum transfer payment. Hence, given any $(t, T)$, and given $h \in [0, 1]$ hours worked an individual can purchase $(1 - t)wh + T$ units of the consumption good. Thus $i$'s indirect utility over labor supply $h \in [0, 1]$ is of the form

$$u_i((1 - t)wh + T, 1 - h) = [(1 - t)wh + T]^{\alpha_i} [1 - h]^{1-\alpha_i}.$$

Individual $i$ maximizes the above expression with respect to the choice variable $h$, generating the first-order condition

$$\frac{\alpha_i(1-t)w}{(1-t)wh+T} - \frac{1-\alpha_i}{1-h} = 0,$$

and note that the second-order condition holds (throughout we assume an interior solution). Solving for the optimal $h$, we get

$$h^* = \frac{\alpha_i[(1-t)w+T] - T}{(1-t)w};$$

in particular, $h^*$ is an increasing function of the preference parameter $\alpha_i$.

It turns out that this monotonicity of $h^*$ in $\alpha_i$ implies individuals' induced preferences over tax-transfer schemes $(t, T)$ are order-restricted. Write individual $i$'s indirect utility over such schemes as

$$v_i(t,T) = [(1-t)wh^* + T]^{\alpha_i}[1 - h^*]^{1-\alpha_i}.$$

Imagine the space of all possible $(t, T)$ as $[0,1] \times \Re$ and consider the indifferences curves of $i$'s indirect utility function in this space (note that $v_i(\cdot)$ is increasing in $T$ and decreasing in $t$). The slope of this indifference curve at $(t, T)$ is given by $-[\partial v_i/\partial t]/[\partial v_i/\partial T]$. By the Envelope Theorem (see, for example, Sundaram [87]) the numerator is

$$\partial v_i/\partial t = \alpha_i[(1-t)wh^* + T]^{\alpha_i-1}[1-h^*]^{1-\alpha_i}[-wh^*]$$

and the denominator is

$$\partial v_i/\partial T = \alpha_i[(1-t)wh^* + T]^{\alpha_i-1}[1-h^*]^{1-\alpha_i}.$$

Thus the slope of the indifference curve of $v_i(\cdot)$ at $(t, T)$ is simply $wh^*$, which as mentioned above is increasing in $\alpha_i$. Hence at each $(t, T)$ the slopes of the individuals' indifference curves are ordered according to the preferences parameter $\alpha$, with lower $\alpha$'s having less steep indifference curves; see Figure 4.6.

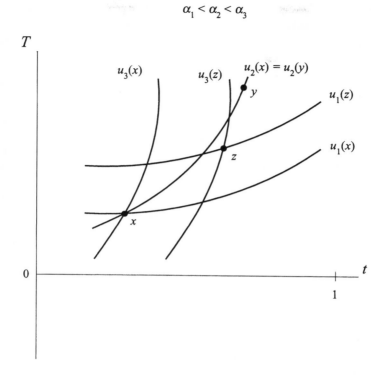

$$\alpha_1 < \alpha_2 < \alpha_3$$

Figure 4.6: Induced preferences over $(t, T)$ pairs

Comparing any two tax-transfer schemes $(t, T) = x$, $(t', T') = y$, we see that if individual $i$ is indifferent between $x$ and $y$, and $x << y$, then all those individuals with $\alpha_j < \alpha_i$ prefer $y$ to $x$ and all those with $\alpha_j > \alpha_i$ prefer $x$ to $y$ (if $t < t'$ and $T > T'$ everyone would prefer $x$ to $y$). Therefore preferences over any finite set $X \subseteq [0, 1] \times \Re_+$ are order-restricted, implying by Theorem 4.6 that a core outcome exists for any voting rule. Finally, note in Figure 4.6 that the three individuals' preferences are not single-peaked over the set $\{x, y, z\}$. The profile over this triple is: $y P_1 z P_1 x$, $x I_2 y P_2 z$, and $x P_3 z P_3 y$.

## 4.7 Discussion

Complementing Chapter 3, where we studied collective rationality under restrictions on the set of alternatives, this chapter has explored collective rationality under restrictions on preferences (Theorems 4.1, 4.2, and 4.6). Although each type of restriction is a restriction on the domain of preference aggregation rules, the character of the results in each case is somewhat different. Under restrictions on sets of alternatives but not on preferences, we are able to provide both *necessary and sufficient* conditions for the acyclicity of aggregation rules; but under restrictions on preferences alone, we only provide *sufficient* conditions for acyclicity. However, restrictions on preference profiles sufficient for acyclicity are the best we can do. This is obvious for collegial rules by Theorem 2.4. To see that it is also the case for non-collegial (and weakly Paretian) rules, note that to say a given restriction on profiles, say to a set $\mathcal{R}^* \subset \mathcal{R}^n$, is necessary for an aggregation rule $f$ to be acyclic, is equivalent to claiming that if $\mathcal{R}^*$ is augmented by a profile that does not satisfy the restriction, then $f$ fails to be acyclic. Now for any such restricted class, we can always add a profile $\rho' \in \mathcal{R}^n$ under which the preferences of all members of some minimal decisive coalition are identical and those of individuals not in the coalition are arbitrary; in particular, because $f$ is noncollegial, there exists a minimal decisive coalition strictly smaller than $N$ and we can choose $\rho' \notin \mathcal{R}^*$. But by definition of a decisive coalition, $f(\rho')$ is acyclic and, therefore, $f$ is acyclic for all profiles $\rho \in \mathcal{R}^* \cup \{\rho'\}$, thus contradicting the claim that $\mathcal{R}^*$ captures a necessary condition for acyclicity of $f$. On the other hand, for each restriction on profiles studied here, we can always find a profile $\rho^\circ \in \mathcal{R} \backslash \mathcal{R}^*$ such that $f$ is not acyclic on $\mathcal{R}^* \cup \{\rho^\circ\}$.

The two classes of restrictions on preference profiles analyzed are single-peaked profiles, defined with respect to an ordering of the set of *alternatives*, and order-restricted profiles, defined with respect to an ordering of the set of *individuals*. Such restricted classes of profiles are not the only ones that can lead to collective rationality (see the exercises below); however, in some important cases (e.g. choosing between candidates for office on ideological grounds), they carry a strong intuitive appeal and, as the applications demonstrate, they can arise naturally in many political and economic settings. Furthermore, in contrast to restrictions on alternative sets, the restrictions on preference profiles examined here also provide a powerful characterization of the set of best elements or core outcomes under any voting rule (Theorems 4.3 and 4.4; Corollaries 4.3 and 4.4). For example the Median Voter Theorem tells us that under single-peaked preferences and simple majority rule (with an odd number of individuals), it is sufficient to identify the median of the most preferred alternatives to identify which alternative constitutes the core. Likewise under order-restricted preferences with simple majority rule it is sufficient to identify which alternative is most preferred by the median individual. This makes empirical analysis much easier, as it reduces collective choice to a particular individual's choice. Specifically, to identify the consequential properties of simple majority rule with an odd number of individuals under single-peaked preferences, it is sufficient to identify the behavior of the individual whose most preferred alternative is the median alternative; and, similarly, under order-restricted preferences it is sufficient to identify the behavior of the median individual.

## 4.8 Exercises

**4.1.** (a) Prove: If $n$ is odd then plurality rule $f_p(\rho)$ is transitive for all $\rho \in \mathcal{S}$ [Hint: use Exercise 1.1 and Theorem 4.1].

(b) Prove: If $\rho$ is single-peaked with respect to $Q$ and $Q'$ then $\mu_f(\rho; Q) = \mu_f(\rho; Q')$.

**4.2.** Prove Theorem 4.5 and Corollary 4.2.

**4.3.** Say that a profile $\rho \in \mathcal{R}^n$ satisfies *limited agreement* on $X$ if for all triples $\{x, y, z\}$ from $X$ there is a subset $\{u, v\} \subset \{x, y, z\}$ such that for all $i \in N$, $u R_i v$. A preference aggregation rule $f$ is *strongly Paretian* iff $\forall x, y \in X$, $\forall \rho \in \mathcal{R}^n$,

$$[R(x, y; \rho) = N \ \& \ P(x, y; \rho) \neq \emptyset] \Rightarrow x P_{f(\rho)} y.$$

Show that if $\rho$ satisfies limited agreement and $f$ is a strongly Paretian voting rule then $f(\rho)$ is quasi-transitive.

**4.4.** Say that a profile $\rho \in \mathcal{R}^n$ satisfies *value restriction* on $X$ if for all triples $\{a, b, c\}$ from $X$, there exists a labeling of these as $\{x, y, z\}$ such that at least one of the following holds:

(V1) $\forall i \in N$ such that $\sim [x I_i y \ \& \ y I_i z]$, $x P_i y$ or $x P_i z$
(V2) $\forall i \in N$ such that $\sim [x I_i y \ \& \ y I_i z]$, $y P_i x$ or $z P_i x$
(V3) $\forall i \in N$ such that $\sim [x I_i y \ \& \ y I_i z]$, $[x P_i y \ \& \ x P_i z]$ or $[y P_i x \ \& \ z P_i x]$

Show that if $\rho$ satisfies value restriction and $f$ is a voting rule, then $f(\rho)$ is quasi-transitive.

**4.5.** Say that a profile $\rho \in \mathcal{R}^n$ satisfies *extremal restriction* on $X$ if for all triples $\{x, y, z\}$ from $X$, $x P_i y P_i z$ for some $i \in N$ implies $\forall j \in N$, $[z P_j x \Rightarrow z P_j y P_j x]$. Show that if $\rho$ satisfies extremal restriction then plurality rule $f_p(\rho)$ is transitive. Prove or provide a counter-example to the claim that this result extends to all voting rules.

**4.6.** What formal relationships, if any, exist between profiles satisfying single-peakedness, limited agreement, value restriction and extremal restriction?

**4.7.** (a) Provide an example to show that a profile can be order-restricted on every triple in some set $X$, but not be order-restricted on $X$ itself.

(b) Prove: If $\rho$ is order-restricted on a triple, then $\rho$ satisfies value restriction on that triple. Prove or provide a counterexample to the converse statement.

(c) Prove: If $\rho$ satisfies (V1) or (V2) on some triple, then $\rho$ is order-restricted on that triple. Prove or provide a counterexample to the converse statement.

**4.8.** Do the preferences in Section 4.6 remain order-restricted when individuals can differ in their wage rates (i.e. individuals are described by a pair $(\alpha_i, w_i) \in (0,1) \times \Re_+$)? Provide a proof or counterexample, as appropriate.

## 4.9   Further reading

Black [8] and Arrow [1][3] were the first to recognize the importance of single-peaked preferences. Inada [40] and Sen and Pattanaik [83] consider alternatives and generalizations. See also Sen [77, ch. 10]. Rothstein [64][65] first identified the class of order-restricted profiles; he further connected it to the class of value restricted profiles and, with a core characterization result, provided a direct proof of the acyclicity of plurality rule on this domain. Gans and Smart [31] provide an alternative characterization of order-restricted profiles in terms of a "single-crossing" property on individuals' preferences over the set of alternatives. The second application, on collective choice of tax-rates, is based on Roberts [62]. Romer and Rosenthal [63] provide a survey of relatively early empirical work based on the Median Voter Theorem.

# Chapter 5

# The Spatial Model

A maintained assumption of almost all of the previous discussion is that the set of alternatives facing society is finite. But there are many situations in which a finiteness assumption is inappropriate: the choice of tax-rates or expenditure levels, the allocation of time to various collective activities, the setting of maximal legal pollution levels or a minimum wage are more naturally considered as continuously variable and thus inappropriately modeled in terms of finite sets. In this chapter, therefore, we consider preference aggregation and collective choice when the set of feasible alternatives is some subset of the multi-dimensional Euclidean space, $\Re^k$. An important special case, introduced in Chapter 4, is $k$ equal to one. In that chapter we saw how the assumption of single-peaked preferences over a one-dimensional set of alternatives, or *policy space*, generated nonempty cores for voting rules. On the other hand, it is a simple exercise to generate two-dimensional examples with individuals having single-peaked preferences over each dimension where the core is empty. Example 5.1 illustrates this for simple majority rule.

**Example 5.1** Let $X = [0,1]^2$; $N = \{1,2,3\}$ and assume $R_i$ is Euclidean; that is, $R_i$ can be represented by the utility function $u_i(x) = -\|x - x_i\|^2$, where $x_i$ is $i$'s most preferred alternative. Set $x_1 = (1,0)$, $x_2 = (0,0)$ and $x_3 = (0,1)$: see Figure 5.1. Then for any $x \in X$, there exists $y \in X$ such that $|P(y,x;\rho)| \geq 2$. To see this, let $x = (a,b)$, and construct $y$ as follows.

(1) If $b \neq 0$, set $y = (a,0)$; then 1 and 2 will strictly prefer $y$ to $x$.

(2) If $a \neq 0$ and $b = 0$, set $y = (0,0)$; then 2 and 3 strictly prefer $y$ to $x$.

(3) If $a = b = 0$, set $y = (\frac{1}{2}, \frac{1}{2})$; then 1 and 3 strictly prefer $y$ to $x$.□

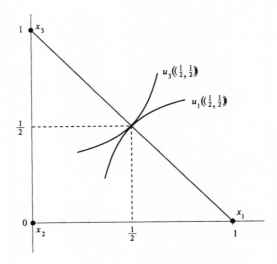

Figure 5.1: Preference distribution for Example 1

Therefore as long as the number of dimensions is sufficiently low (in this case $k = 1$), a majority rule core will exist, whereas for higher number of dimensions a core is no longer assured. In Section 5.2 below we will see that this type of result holds true for *any* voting rule; specifically, for a given voting rule we can identify a number such that as long as the dimension of the issue space is less than this number a core is certain to exist, while for higher dimensions this is no longer true. Further, this critical number is precisely equal to the voting rule's Nakamura number minus one, and hence we have an exact analogue to Theorem 3.4 with respect to the number of *dimensions* of the choice problem (as opposed to the number of *alternatives* in the finite case).

On the other hand majority rule core points are not ruled out in higher dimensions, as seen by the following:

**Example 5.2** $X = [0,1]^2$; $N = \{1,2,3\}$; $u_i(x) = -\|x - x_i\|^2$ with $x_1 = (1,0)$, $x_2 = (\frac{1}{2}, \frac{1}{2})$ and $x_3 = (0,1)$.$\square$

Here it is easily seen that individual 2's most preferred alternative, $x_2 = (\frac{1}{2}, \frac{1}{2})$ is a majority rule core point, and from this we can conclude that nonexistence is not guaranteed in higher dimensions. As well, it is evident that this core point satisfies a certain symmetry property with respect to the voters' preferences. In Section 5.3 below we provide general properties

for core points associated with voting rules, properties which are a generalization of the core characterization in Chapter 4 for the one-dimensional
case.

Finally, note that the existence of a core point in Example 5.2 is sensitive
to the exact specification of the voters' preferences: if voter 1's ideal point
is changed to $(1 - \epsilon, 0)$, $\epsilon > 0$, then a core no longer exists; see Figure 5.2.

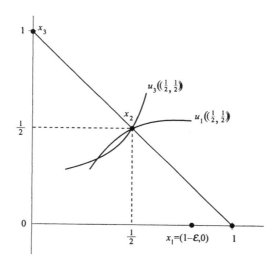

Figure 5.2: Existence of the core in Example 5.2 is fragile

This sensitivity is a topic addressed in Chapter 6, where we also take up the
issue of what can be said about collective preference when the core is empty.

In proving some of these results, a different sort of technology will be
used from that previously. In particular, recall that the principle approach
for guaranteeing the existence of core outcomes in Chapters 3 and 4 (where
the set of outcomes $X$ is assumed finite) was to identify conditions under
which the social preference relation under the relevant aggregation rule was
necessarily acyclic for any preference profile and then appeal to Theorem 1.1.
In the spatial context, on the other hand, it will be shown that some amount
of convexity of preferences can take the place of the acyclicity requirement in
Theorem 1.1. Therefore we begin this chapter with some results on sufficient
conditions for the existence of maximal elements in a spatial setting.

## 5.1   Choosing from a continuum

Let the set of alternatives, $X$, be a $k$-dimensional subset of $\Re^k$ and let $R$ be a binary relation on $X$. Although the set of alternatives is no longer finite, the various possible properties of $R$, e.g. completeness and transitivity, remain as before; in particular, $R$ is acyclic on $X$ if, for all finite subsets $\{x, y, z, \ldots, u, v\}$ of $X$, $xPy, yPz, \ldots, uPv$ implies $xRv$.

As in Chapter 1, our first question concerns conditions on $R$ that insure the nonemptiness of the maximal set $M(R, X)$. So as before let $R$ be reflexive and complete. Is acyclicity enough, as in the finite case? In general, the answer is "no", as the following example demonstrates.

**Example 5.3** Let $X = [0, 1]$ and define $R$ as follows: for all $x, y \in [0, 1)$, $xPy$ if and only if $x > y$; and if $z = 1$ then $xPz$, all $x \in [0, 1)$. Then $R$ is transitive on $X$ yet $M(R, X) = \emptyset$. See Figure 5.3.□

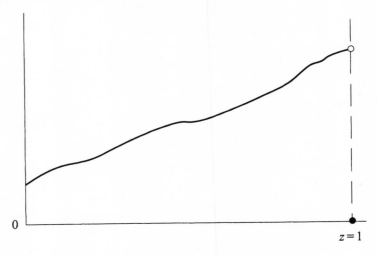

$$z = 1$$

Figure 5.3:  $M(R, [0, 1]) = \emptyset$

Inspection of Figure 5.3 suggests that the problem revealed in the example is due to a lack of continuity in $R$ on $X$. And although this is the case, it turns out to be a little more subtle than the observation of a "jump" in $R$ at $z = 1$.

For all $x \in X$, define the sets

$$P(x) \;\; = \;\; \{y \in X : yPx\}$$

$$P^{-1}(x) \;=\; \{y \in X : xPy\}.$$

Thus elements of $P(x)$ are all those alternatives that are strictly preferred to $x$ and elements of $P^{-1}(x)$ are all those alternatives to which $x$ is strictly preferred (these are sometimes referred to as the (strict) *upper* and *lower* *contour sets*, respectively, associated with the relation $R$). A set $Y$ is *open* in $\Re^k$ if, for all points $x$ in $Y$, there is some $\epsilon > 0$ such that all points within $\epsilon$ of $x$ are in $Y$ (the complement of an open set is *closed*). Say that $Z$ is *open relative to* $X$ if $Z$ can be written as $Z = Y \cap X$, where $Y$ is open in $\Re^k$. For example, if $X = [0,1]$ then $Z = [0, \frac{1}{2})$ is open relative to $X$ as it can be written as $X \cap (-\frac{1}{2}, \frac{1}{2})$, even though $Z$ is not open in $\Re$. In all of what follows, we use the term "open" to mean "open relative to $X$".

**Definition 5.1** *A binary relation $R$ is*
    *(1) lower continuous if for all $x \in X$, $P^{-1}(x)$ is open;*
    *(2) upper continuous if for all $x \in X$, $P(x)$ is open;*
    *(3) continuous if $R$ is both lower and upper continuous.*

In Example 5.3, the relation $R$ is not lower continuous at any $x < z = 1$. If $x = 0$ then $P^{-1}(x) = \{z\}$ and if $x \in (0,1)$ then $P^{-1}(x) = [0, x) \cup \{z\}$; none of these sets is open. On the other hand, $P^{-1}(1) = \emptyset$ is open and so $R$ is in fact lower continuous at $z = 1$. It is the lack of lower continuity in $R$ that causes problems in Example 5.3; as we shall see below, any relation that is both lower continuous and transitive has maximal elements.

Consider now the following requirement for the relation $R$.

**Definition 5.2** *A binary relation $R$ on $X$ satisfies condition F if, for all finite subsets $Y \subset X$, there exists some $x \in X$ such that $xRy$ for all $y \in Y$.*

Note that this condition does not require the alternative $x$ which is preferred to all elements of the finite set $Y$ itself to be *in* $Y$, only that we can find such an $x$ somewhere in the larger set $X$. And clearly, if $R$ is acyclic on $X$ then $R$ necessarily satisfies condition $F$ since, by Theorem 1.1, for each finite set $Y$ there exists an element $y$ of $Y$ *itself* such that, for all $z$ in $Y$, $yRz$.

Unlike properties of binary preference relations such as completeness or transitivity, condition $F$ has no obvious or natural substantive interpretation. It is, however, useful in deriving more primitive and intuitive properties of a binary relation $R$ that are sufficient for a nonempty maximal set, $M(R, X)$. In particular, in the presence of lower continuity, we show that condition $F$ is both necessary and sufficient for there to exist a best element in $X$. It then follows that any properties of $R$ that imply condition $F$ are, with lower continuity, sufficient for $M(R, X)$ nonempty.

A set $B \subset \Re^k$ is *compact* if and only if every open cover $\mathcal{C}$ of $B$ contains a finite subcover of $B$; in other words, $B$ is compact if, for every family of open sets $\mathcal{C}$ such that, for all $A \in \mathcal{C}$, $A \subset \Re^k$ and $\cup_{\mathcal{C}} A \supseteq B$, there is a finite subfamily $\mathcal{A} = \{A_1, \ldots, A_s\} \subseteq \mathcal{C}$ such that $\cup_{i=1}^{s} A_i \supseteq B$. Since we are restricting attention to Euclidean space $\Re^k$, it turns out that a set $B \subset \Re^k$ is compact if and only if it is closed and bounded (see, e.g., Sundaram [87, ch. 1]).

**Lemma 5.1** *Assume $X$ is compact and $R$ lower continuous. Then $M(R, X)$ is nonempty if and only if $R$ satisfies condition $F$.*

**Proof.** Necessity is immediate: if $x \in M(R, X)$ then, by definition, for *any* subset $Y \subseteq X$ and for all $y \in Y$, $xRy$. To see sufficiency, suppose condition $F$ holds but $M(R, X) = \emptyset$. Then $\forall x \in X$, $\exists y \in X$ with $x \in P^{-1}(y)$. Therefore $\{P^{-1}(z) : z \in X\}$ is an open cover of $X$. Since $X$ is compact there exists a finite set $Y \subset X$ such that $\{P^{-1}(y) : y \in Y\}$ is an open cover of $X$. But this implies that for every $x \in X$ there exists some $y \in Y$ such that $yPx$, a contradiction of condition $F$.□

As remarked above, if $R$ is acyclic on $X$ then $R$ satisfies condition $F$. Consequently, Lemma 5.1 implies that if $R$ is lower continuous and acyclic, $M(R, X)$ is nonempty. In contrast to the finite case, however, the spatial model allows us to replace acyclicity with convexity assumptions on $X$ and $R$ and preserve the existence of maximal elements.

**Definition 5.3** *Given a convex set $X \subseteq \Re^k$, a preference ordering $R$ on $X$ is strictly convex if $xRy$ and $x \neq y$ imply $[\lambda x + (1-\lambda)y]Py$ for all $\lambda \in (0,1)$.*

In particular, if $x$ and $y$ are judged indifferent by $R$, then any (strict) convex combination of the two alternatives is strictly preferred to both $x$ and $y$. This suggests a close connection between strictly convex preferences and single-peaked preferences when $X$ is one-dimensional [Exercise]. Furthermore, $R$ strictly convex implies that the upper contour set, $P(x)$, is itself a convex set for any alternative $x$. (Note that the definition does not make sense when the set $X$ is *not* convex, as is the case when $X$ is finite, since in that instance $[\lambda x + (1-\lambda)y]$ might not be an element of $X$ and hence might not be a feasible alternative.)

For some of the results in later sections, individuals' preferences are assumed to be strictly convex. However, for the existence of maximal elements,

strict convexity of $R$ is stronger than we require. For any set $Y \subseteq X$, let
$ConY$ denote the *convex hull* associated with $Y$:

$$ConY = \{z \in X : z = \sum_{i=1}^{m} \lambda_i y_i \text{ for some } \{y_1, \ldots, y_m\} \subset Y$$

$$\text{and } (\lambda_1, \ldots, \lambda_m) \in [0,1]^m \text{ such that } \sum_{i=1}^{m} \lambda_i = 1\}.$$

That is, the convex hull of a set $Y$ consists of all the points which can be
written as convex combinations of points in $Y$. Note that if the set $Y$ is
convex, then $Y = ConY$.

**Definition 5.4** *A binary relation $R$ on $X$ is semi-convex if, for all $x \in X$,
$x \notin ConP(x)$.*

In one dimension, semi-convexity says the following: for any $x$, the set $P(x)$
of alternatives strictly preferred to $x$ must lie either to the right, or to the
left, of $x$, but cannot have some elements to the right and some to the left.
So, for example, single-peaked preferences are semi-convex, but multiple-
peaked preferences are not. More generally, if the set $P(x)$ is a convex set
for all $x \in X$, as for example when $R$ is a strictly convex preference order,
then $R$ is necessarily semi-convex since in this case $P(x) = ConP(x)$ and
$R$ reflexive implies $x$ is not in $P(x)$. Moreover, if $R$ is semi-convex but not
strictly convex, then $R$ is not transitive. Example 5.4 provides an illustration
of this for $X \subset \Re$; establishing the claim more generally is left as an exercise.

**Example 5.4** Let $X = [0,1]$ and partition $X$ into $A = [0, \frac{1}{3}]$, $B = (\frac{1}{3}, \frac{2}{3})$,
$C = [\frac{2}{3}, 1]$. Now define the preference relation $R$ by

$$\forall a \in A, P(a) = B \text{ and } P^{-1}(a) = C;$$
$$\forall b \in B, P(b) = C \text{ and } P^{-1}(b) = A;$$
$$\forall c \in C, P(c) = A \text{ and } P^{-1}(c) = B.$$

Then $R$ is semi-convex but not strictly convex. Consider, for example, any
distinct $a, a' \in A$; we have $aIa'$ but for all $\lambda \in (0,1)$ $[\lambda a + (1 - \lambda)a']$ is
indifferent to both $a$ and $a'$.$\square$

**Lemma 5.2** *Assume $X$ is convex. Then $R$ lower continuous and semi-
convex on $X$ implies $R$ satisfies condition F.*

**Proof.** We first need a technical result, a corollary of the Knaster, Kuratowski, Mazurkiewicz Lemma; proofs for both can be found in Border [14, ch. 5].

(KKM corollary) Let $A = \{a_0, a_1, \ldots, a_m\}$ be any set of $m+1$ points in $\Re^k$, let $\{S_0, S_1, \ldots, S_m\}$ be a collection of closed sets, and let $M = \{0, 1, \ldots, m\}$. If, for all $L \subseteq M$, $Con(\{a_i\}_{i \in L}) \subseteq \cup_{i \in L} S_i$, then $\cap_{j \in M} S_j \neq \emptyset$.

We now prove the lemma. Let $Y = \{y_0, y_1, \ldots, y_m\}$ denote some finite subset of $X$, $M = \{0, 1, \ldots, m\}$, and define $R(x) = X \backslash P^{-1}(x)$; note that by definition $R(x)$ is closed since, by $R$ lower continuous, $P^{-1}(x)$ is open. We wish to show that $\cap_{i \in M} R(y_i) \neq \emptyset$; in fact, we will show that $\cap_{i \in M}(R(y_i) \cap ConY) \neq \emptyset$, i.e. for any finite set of points $Y$ there exists a point $x$ in the convex hull of $Y$ such that, $\forall y \in Y$, $xRy$. To see this, let $\tilde{R}(y_i) = R(y_i) \cap ConY$. If for all $L \subseteq M$ we have that

$$Con(\{y_i\}_{i \in L}) \subseteq \bigcup_{i \in L} \tilde{R}(y_i) \qquad (*)$$

then by KKM corollary we are done. So suppose (*) fails to hold for some $L \subseteq M$. Then there exists $z \in Con(\{y_i\}_{i \in L})$ such that for all $i$ in $L$, $z \notin \tilde{R}(y_i)$, which in turn implies that for all $i \in L$, $y_i \in P(z)$. But then $z \in ConP(z)$, contradicting the assumption of $R$ semi-convex. Therefore (*) holds for all $L \subseteq M$, and hence, by KKM corollary, $\cap_{i \in M} \tilde{R}(y_i) \neq \emptyset$. And since $Y$ is an arbitrary finite subset of $X$, we have that condition $F$ holds.□

Combining Lemmas 5.1 and 5.2 immediately gives a set of primitive sufficient conditions on $R$ for the maximal set $M(R, X)$ to be nonempty.

**Theorem 5.1** *Assume $X$ is compact and convex. If $R$ is lower continuous and semi-convex on $X$, then $M(R, X) \neq \emptyset$.*

As we shall see, it is Theorem 5.1 that will be employed for the general statement concerning the existence of core points. That is, we will identify conditions under which the social preference relation associated with a voting rule $f$ is lower continuous and semi-convex; by Theorem 5.1, such conditions are sufficient for the existence of core points.

## 5.2   Core existence

In this section we state and prove results on the existence and nonexistence of core outcomes for voting rules. Throughout, we assume the set of alternatives $X \subset \Re^k$ to be convex and compact. We begin with an analogous result to Theorem 4.3 above: if individual preferences are strictly convex then the core outcomes associated with a particular voting rule $f$ will be equivalent to the core outcomes of the induced simple rule $f' \equiv f_{\mathcal{L}(f)}$, i.e. the simple rule derived from $f$. Consequently, under convexity, studying the cores of voting rules is equivalent to studying the cores of simple rules. And, as Chapter 3 makes clear, since the structure of simple rules is considerably more straightforward than that of voting rules, this equivalence property is extremely useful from a purely technical perspective. On the other hand, it is important to bear in mind that the equivalence does not extend to all properties of voting and simple rules, even under the convexity assumption [Exercise].

Say that a preference profile $\rho = (R_1, \ldots, R_n)$ satisfies a certain property if each component $R_i$ satisfies the property.

**Theorem 5.2** *Let $f$ be a voting rule and $f' \equiv f_{\mathcal{L}(f)}$. If $\rho \in \mathcal{R}^n$ is strictly convex, then $C_f(\rho) = C_{f'}(\rho)$.*

**Proof.** Since $f$ is in general more resolute than $f'$, it must be that $C_f(\rho) \subseteq C_{f'}(\rho)$. To see that the converse inclusion holds, let $x \in C_{f'}(\rho)$ and suppose $x \notin C_f(\rho)$. Then by definition there exists $y \in X$ such that $yP_fx$, implying by Theorem 3.3 that $(P(y, x; \rho), R(y, x; \rho)) \in \mathcal{D}(f)$. By strict convexity, then, for all $i \in R(y, x; \rho)$, $zP_ix$, where $z = \lambda x + (1 - \lambda)y$ for some $\lambda \in (0, 1)$. But since the coalition $R(y, x; \rho)$ is a decisive coalition, i.e. $R(y, x; \rho) \in \mathcal{L}(f)$, $zP_{f'}x$ as well, implying $x \notin C_{f'}(\rho)$; contradiction.$\square$

Therefore, if we assume strictly convex individual preferences, we can without loss of generality confine attention to the existence of core points for simple rules, as these will coincide with the set of core points for the relevant voting rules as well. In what follows we will prove an existence result for simple rules under a weaker notion of convexity (namely, semi-convexity). Hence the extension of this existence result to voting rules will hold true under the stronger assumption of strict convexity.

For any individual $i$'s preference relation $R_i$ and any $x \in X$, let $P_i(x) = \{y \in X : yP_ix\}$ and $P_i^{-1}(x) = \{y \in X : xP_iy\}$. For any coalition $L \subseteq N$, define

$$P_L(x) = \bigcap_{i \in L} P_i(x) \quad \text{and} \quad P_L^{-1}(x) = \bigcap_{i \in L} P_i^{-1}(x).$$

That is, for the coalition $L$, $P_L(x)$ denotes all the alternatives that are strictly preferred to $x$ by all members of $L$, while $P_L^{-1}(x)$ gives those to which $x$ is strictly preferred by all members of $L$. $P_L(\cdot)$ and $P_L^{-1}(\cdot)$ thus capture the coalitional preferences associated with $L$.

For any simple rule $f$ define

$$P_f(x) = \bigcup_{L \in \mathcal{L}(f)} P_L(x) \text{ and } P_f^{-1}(x) = \bigcup_{L \in \mathcal{L}(f)} P_L^{-1}(x).$$

We can think of $P_f(x)$ and $P_f^{-1}(x)$ as the upper and lower contour sets associated with the collective preference relation $f(\rho)$: any element $y$ of $P_f(x)$ is such that $y$ is strictly preferred to $x$ by some decisive coalition $L \in \mathcal{L}(f)$, while any element $z$ of $P_f^{-1}(x)$ is such that $x$ is strictly preferred to $z$ by some decisive coalition $L' \in \mathcal{L}(f)$. In particular, since core points under a simple rule $f$ are defined to be those outcomes for which no decisive coalition can find a strictly preferred alternative, $x \in C_f(\rho)$ if and only if $P_f(x) = \emptyset$ and, therefore, if and only if $P_L(x) = \emptyset$ for all $L \in \mathcal{L}(f)$.

**Lemma 5.3** *If $\rho \in \mathcal{R}^n$ is lower continuous, then for all simple rules $f$, $f(\rho)$ is lower continuous.*

**Proof.** For all $x \in X$ and $L \in \mathcal{L}(f)$, $P_L^{-1}(x)$ is a finite intersection of open sets and hence is open. Therefore $P_f^{-1}(x)$ is a finite union of open sets and hence is open.$\square$

Therefore lower continuity of individual preferences is inherited by the social preference relation $f(\rho)$. To use Theorem 5.1 for a core existence result, it remains to find conditions under which $f(\rho)$ is also semi-convex. Unlike lower continuity, however, it turns out that more is needed here than simply having the profile $\rho$ be semi-convex.

Recall that $k$ denotes the dimension of the policy space and, for any simple rule $f$, $s(f)$ is the Nakamura number of $f$.

**Lemma 5.4** *Let $f$ be a simple rule and assume $\rho \in \mathcal{R}^n$ is semi-convex. Then $k \leq s(f) - 2$ implies $f(\rho)$ is semi-convex.*

**Proof.** The argument uses Caratheodory's Theorem, a proof of which can be found in Border [14, ch. 2].

(Caratheodory's Theorem) Let $Y$ be any set in $\Re^k$ and let $z \in ConY$; then $z$ can be written as a convex combination of $k + 1$ points in $Y$. That is, if $z$ is in the convex hull of $Y$, there exists a set $\{y_1, \ldots, y_{k+1}\} \subset Y$ and a vector $\lambda \in [0,1]^{k+1}$ such that $\sum_{j=1}^{j=k+1} \lambda_j = 1$ and $z = \sum_{j=1}^{j=k+1} \lambda_j y_j$.

Now suppose, contrary to the lemma, that $f(\rho)$ is not semi-convex. Then there exists some alternative $z \in X$ such that $z \in ConP_f(z)$. By Caratheodory's Theorem there exists $\{y_1, \ldots, y_{k+1}\} \subset P_f(z)$ such that $z \in Con\{y_1, \ldots, y_{k+1}\}$. Since, for all $j = 1, \ldots, k+1$, $y_j \in P_f(z)$ and $f$ is simple there exist decisive coalitions $L_1, \ldots, L_{k+1}$ such that $y_j \in P_{Lj}(z)$, $j = 1, \ldots, k+1$. Let $\mathcal{L} = \{L_j\}$. By assumption, $k \leq s(f) - 2$; hence $|\mathcal{L}| \leq k+1 \leq s(f) - 1$. By the definition of $s(\cdot)$, therefore, $K(\mathcal{L}) \neq \emptyset$, and hence there exists some $i \in N$ such that, for all $j = 1, \ldots, k+1$, $i \in L_j$. But then $y_j \in P_i(z)$, all $j = 1, \ldots, k+1$, which implies $z \in Con\{y_1, \ldots, y_{k+1}\} \subset ConP_i(z)$, a contradiction of $R_i$ semi-convex.$\square$

Figure 5.4 illustrates Lemma 5.4 by showing how it can fail when there are too many dimensions relative to the Nakamura number of the aggregation rule. Figure 5.4 describes the set $P_f(z)$ when there are three individuals with strictly convex, and hence semi-convex, preferences over $\Re^2$ and the simple rule is majority rule, $f_m$. Hence $s(f_m) = 3 < k+2$ and $z \in ConP_{f_m}(z)$ with no contradiction of $\rho$ semi-convex.

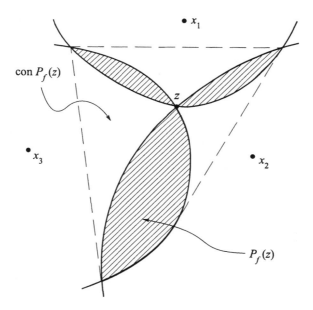

Figure 5.4: $f(\rho)$ is not semi-convex at $z$

Combining Lemma 5.3, Lemma 5.4, and Theorem 5.1 yields the desired core existence theorem for simple rules and, by Theorem 5.2, for voting rules also.

**Theorem 5.3** *Let $f$ be a simple rule and assume $\rho \in \mathcal{R}^n$ is lower continuous and semi-convex. Then $k \leq s(f) - 2$ implies $C_f(\rho) \neq \emptyset$.*

Theorem 5.3 thus gives a sufficient condition analogous to that identified in Theorem 3.2 for finite sets of alternatives: as long as the dimension of the policy space is below some critical number, there will exist a core outcome. Further, this critical number is again identified by the Nakamura number, $s(f)$, associated with the rule. And since by Lemma 3.2 we know that the Nakamura number is greater than or equal to 3 for *any* simple rule, a core always exists when the policy space is of one dimension; therefore we get the existence result found in Theorem 4.5 as a corollary to the above result (although in Theorem 5.3 the continuity assumption is somewhat stronger, and the convexity assumption somewhat weaker).

Theorem 5.3 can also be viewed as providing a prescription of what sorts of simple rules should be used if one is concerned about the existence of core outcomes. For instance, as in the finite model, any collegial rule (i.e. one for which the Nakamura number is infinite) possesses a core but clearly has some questionable normative properties. On the other hand, among noncollegial rules, cores can be assured in higher dimensional spaces by using rules with appropriately larger Nakamura numbers. And as in the finite case, here too there is a trade-off between existence and resoluteness; for example, in the class of $q$-rules with a given set of individuals, the larger is $q$ the higher is the Nakamura number but the less resolute the rule becomes. Furthermore, since the largest Nakamura number for any noncollegial simple rule is $n$ (Lemma 3.1), Theorem 5.3 (and the example of Figure 5.4) suggests that cores cannot be guaranteed for any noncollegial rule whenever the alternative set has at least $n - 1$ dimensions. That is, if $k > n - 2$ then for any simple rule we can find a lower continuous and semi-convex profile $\rho$ such that the core is empty. Indeed, not only is the dimensionality condition in Theorem 5.3 necessary for the result, an even stronger claim holds.

A preference relation $R$ on $X$ is said to be *continuously differentiable* if it can be represented by a utility function possessing continuous partial derivatives at every point $x$ in the interior (defined later) of $X$.

**Theorem 5.4** *For any noncollegial simple rule $f$, if $k \geq s(f) - 1$ then there exists a continuously differentiable, strictly convex preference profile $\rho$ such that $C_f(\rho) = \emptyset$.*

**Proof.** The proof is by construction (illustrated in Figure 5.5 for $X \subset \Re^3$). For the simple rule $f$ let $s = s(f)$ and let $\mathcal{L} = (L_1, \ldots, L_s) \subseteq \mathcal{L}(f)$ be such that $K(\mathcal{L}) = \emptyset$ (such a set exists by the definition of the Nakamura number). Let

$$\Delta = \{(x_1, \ldots, x_s) \in [0,1]^s : \sum_{j=1}^{s} x_j = 1\}$$

be a simplex of dimension $s - 1$. By suitably rescaling if necessary, the simplex $\Delta$ can always be embedded in the space $X$. So without loss of generality let $X = \Delta$.

Since $\Delta$ has precisely $s$ faces, we associate with each face a single coalition in $\mathcal{L}$. For each $L_j \in \mathcal{L}$, denote $\mathcal{M}_j = \mathcal{L}\backslash\{L_j\}$. Hence $|\mathcal{M}_j| = s - 1$, $K(\mathcal{M}_j) \neq \emptyset$ and $t \neq j$ implies $K(\mathcal{M}_t) \cap K(\mathcal{M}_j) = \emptyset$ (since otherwise we would have $K(\mathcal{L}) \neq \emptyset$). Assume, $\forall i \in N$, $R_i$ is Euclidean; that is, $u_i(x) = -\|x - x_i\|^2$ where $x_i$ is $i$'s most preferred alternative. Such preferences are clearly continuously differentiable. Now, $\forall i \in K(\mathcal{M}_j)$, set $x_i$ equal to the vertex opposite the face associated with $L_j$; otherwise (i.e. if $i$ is not a member of any $K(\mathcal{M}_j)$) $x_i$ is set on an edge or face of $\Delta$ to match $i$'s membership in the coalitions of $\mathcal{L}$. See Figure 5.5 for an example of the construction in which $n > 4$, $k = 3$, $s(f) = 4$, $\mathcal{L} = \{L_1, \ldots, L_4\} \subseteq \mathcal{L}(f)$, $K(\mathcal{M}_4) = \{1\}$, $L_1 \cap L_2 = \{1, 2\}$, and $3 \in L_2$.

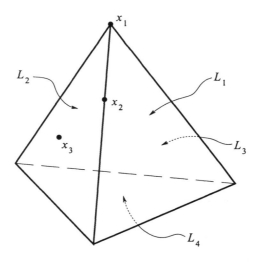

Figure 5.5: Construction for the proof to Theorem 5.4

Under this construction, then, the ideal point of each member of coalition $L_j$ belongs to the face of $\Delta$ associated with $L_j$, and therefore $P_{L_j}(x) = \emptyset$ only if $x$ belongs to this face. But since the faces do not intersect, there does not exist an alternative $x$ such that $P_{L_j}(x) = \emptyset$ for all $L_j \in \mathcal{L}$. Therefore, $\mathcal{L} \subseteq \mathcal{L}(f)$ implies $P_f(x) \neq \emptyset$ for all $x \in X$ and hence $C_f(\rho) = \emptyset.\square$

Thus for policy spaces of dimension $s(f) - 2$ or less, continuous differentiability and strict convexity of individual preferences is not required to guarantee existence of socially maximal elements (Theorem 5.3) and, for policy spaces of dimension $s(f) - 1$ or more, continuous differentiability and strict convexity of individual preferences is not enough to guarantee existence of socially maximal elements (Theorem 5.4). It is worth noting the parallel between these results for the spatial model and those on acyclicity of simple rules for the finite model. Theorem 3.2 proves that, in the finite setting, a simple rule $f$ is acyclic if and only if the number of alternatives is less than or equal to the Nakamura number of $f$ less one. In view of Theorem 1.1, therefore, this result says that if $|X| \leq s(f) - 1$ the core of $f$ is nonempty at every profile $\rho \in \mathcal{R}^n$ and if $|X| \geq s(f)$ there exists some profile $\rho \in \mathcal{R}^n$ at which the core of $f$ is empty.

Theorem 5.4 also provides a corollary for nonsimple rules analogous to a result for the finite model. Recall Theorem 2.4, which states that if $|X| \geq n$ then, for any noncollegial aggregation rule $f$, there exists a profile $\rho$ such that $f(\rho)$ is cyclic on $X$ and the core is empty. Since the set of decisive coalitions is monotonic (Lemma 2.2), any noncollegial aggregation rule is such that, for all individuals $i$ in $N$, $N\backslash\{i\}$ is decisive. Consequently, if $x$ in $X$ is a core point under such a rule it is necessarily a core point under the simple $q$-rule with $q = n - 1$. That is, the core of any noncollegial aggregation rule is a subset of the core of the simple $q = n - 1$ rule; hence conditions implying the emptiness of the latter also imply the emptiness of the former. By Theorem 5.4 and Lemma 3.3(2), if $k \geq n - 1$ there exists a preference profile $\rho$ such that the core of the simple $q = n - 1$ rule is empty. Therefore, the corollary for nonsimple rules, analogous to Theorem 2.4, is that for any noncollegial aggregation rule $f$, if $k \geq n - 1$ there exists a continuously differentiable, strictly convex, preference profile $\rho$ such that the core of $f$ at $\rho$ is empty.

## 5.3  Application: Distributive politics

The canonical distributive politics problem is "divide the dollar", whereby one dollar is to be allocated by collective choice among the $n$ members of the polity. For this problem the set of alternatives is the $(n-1)$-dimensional simplex,

$$X = \{(x_1, \ldots, x_n) \in [0,1]^n : \sum_{i \in N} x_i = 1\}$$

which is clearly compact and convex. In view of Theorems 5.3 and 5.4, the only simple rules for which core outcomes are certain to exist are collegial rules.

It is worth emphasizing that while the emptiness of the core for "divide the dollar" is well-known under an assumption of selfish preferences – that is, for all $i \in N$, all $x \in X$, $u_i(x) = x_i$ – Theorem 5.4 is proved using Euclidean preferences that give weight to all components of the allocation vector. Moreover, it should be clear from the construction that the theorem can as readily, if not quite so concisely, be established using more general classes of convex preferences than Euclidean. Consequently, we argue that the absence of core outcomes in the distributive politics problem is *not* due to selfishness on the part of individuals, but rather to the inherent complexity of the choice problem, exemplified by the dimensionality $k = n - 1$ of the alternative set.

## 5.4 Characterizing core points

Theorem 5.3 demonstrates how core outcomes will necessarily exist for policy spaces of sufficiently low dimension (relative to the simple rule $f$ aggregating preferences); and while Theorem 5.4 tells us that core outcomes are not guaranteed to exist in high dimensions, Example 5.2 shows how *non*existence is not guaranteed either. Leaving aside for the moment the relationship between core existence and the dimensionality of the policy space, this section considers general properties of core points associated with a simple rule independent of the rule's Nakamura number. So this section can be thought of as generalizing the results of Section 4.2 above, in that the focus is on locating core points in the multidimensional model. In addition, the results here can be used to provide further insight into the properties of preference profiles that are necessary or sufficient for the existence of core points. That is, identifying properties of preferences that are implied by, or imply, the existence of core alternatives also tells us a great deal about whether such alternatives are likely to be robust when they exist, or even if existence is a likely event in the relevant space of profiles.

Throughout this section we assume individual preference orders are continuous and strictly convex; let $\mathcal{R}_{cs} \subset \mathcal{R}$ denote the set of such preference orders and $\mathcal{R}^n_{cs} \subset \mathcal{R}^n$ the set of such preference profiles. Recall from Chapter 4 that, for any $L \subseteq N$, the Pareto set for $L$ is:

$$PS_L(\rho) = \{x \in X : \forall y \neq x, \ P(y,x;\rho) \cap L \neq \emptyset \Rightarrow P(x,y;\rho) \cap L \neq \emptyset\}.$$

Alternatives in $PS_L(\rho)$ are said to be *Pareto efficient* for $L$. So if $x$ is Pareto efficient for $L$, any move away from $x$ will be strictly opposed by at least one member of the coalition $L$. In particular, if $L$ is a decisive coalition under $f$ and if $x \in PS_L(\rho)$ is *not* in the core, then necessarily $x$ is overturned by some decisive coalition $L' \neq L$. With this observation in mind, we have

**Lemma 5.5** *Let $f$ be a simple rule and assume $\rho \in \mathcal{R}^n_{cs}$. Then $C_f(\rho) = \cap_{L \in \mathcal{L}(f)} PS_L(\rho)$.*

**Proof.** [Exercise].$\square$

Identifying the core for any simple rule, $f$, therefore, is equivalent to identifying those points common to the Pareto sets of all the decisive coalitions under $f$. It follows, for example, that the majority core, $C_{f_m}(\rho)$, is nonempty if and only if there exists a point, $x$, such that $x$ is an element of the Pareto set, $PS_L(\rho)$, for every coalition $L$ with more than $n/2$ members: see Example 5.5.

**Example 5.5** Let $N = \{1,2,3,4\}$ and assume each $i \in N$ has Euclidean preferences on $X = \Re^2$ with ideal points $\{x_i\}_{i \in N}$ as illustrated in Figure 5.6.

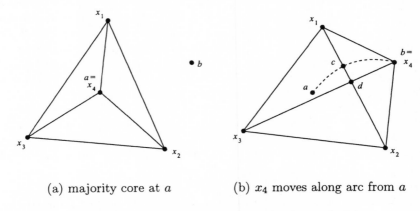

(a) majority core at $a$          (b) $x_4$ moves along arc from $a$

Figure 5.6: Preference distributions for Example 5.5

With Euclidean preferences (but not in general), the Pareto set for any coalition $L$ is simply the convex hull of the members' ideal points: $PS_L(\rho) = Con\{x_i\}_{i \in L}$. Therefore, as is easily seen in Figure 5.6(a), the intersection of the Pareto sets of all the decisive coalitions under majority rule is $\{a\}$, and thus the core is $\{x_4\}$. Now leave $x_1$, $x_2$, and $x_3$ fixed but move $x_4$ along the arc from $a$ through $c$ to $b$: see Figure 5.6(b). Between $a$ and $c$, the core continues to coincide with individual 4's ideal point, $x_4$. However, once $x_4$ moves beyond $c$ the core no longer coincides with $x_4$ but moves down the line from $c$ to $d$. $\square$

Our next result provides an alternative characterization of the core, analogous to that found in Theorem 4.4. For any $x \in X$ and $y \in \Re^k$, let:

$$\gamma_x(y) = \{z \in \Re^k : z = tx + (1-t)y \text{ for some } t \in \Re\};$$
$$\Gamma(x) = \{\gamma_x(y) : y \in X\}.$$

In words, $\gamma_x(y)$ is the (one-dimensional) line through $x$ and $y$, and $\Gamma(x)$ is the set of all lines through $x$. To save on notation, where there is no ambiguity we write $\gamma_x$ for a generic element of $\Gamma(x)$.

**Definition 5.5** *For any $x \in X$, $i$'s induced ideal points on $\gamma_x \in \Gamma(x)$ are*

$$b_i(\gamma_x) = \{z \in \gamma_x \cap X : \forall y \in X \cap \gamma_x, \ zR_iy\}.$$

So $i$'s induced ideal points on the line $\gamma_x(y)$ are $i$'s most preferred alternatives given that only points in $\gamma_x(y)$ are available. When $R_i \in \mathcal{R}_{cs}$ and $X$ is compact and convex, such induced ideal points are uniquely defined for every line $\gamma_x \in \Gamma(x)$. Furthermore, $i$'s preferences over $\gamma_x$ are single-peaked about this point.

For any point $y \in \gamma_x$, partition $\gamma_x$ into $\{y\}$ and two open halflines denoted $h_y^+(\gamma_x)$ and $h_y^-(\gamma_x)$. Assume $\rho \in \mathcal{R}_{cs}^n$, and let

$$L^+(y) = \{i \in N : b_i(\gamma_x) \in h_y^+(\gamma_x)\}$$

and

$$L^-(y) = \{i \in N : b_i(\gamma_x) \in h_y^-(\gamma_x)\}.$$

See Figure 5.7 for an illustration. The sets $L^-(y)$ and $L^+(y)$ thus correspond to those of Chapter 4 for the line $\gamma_x(y)$.

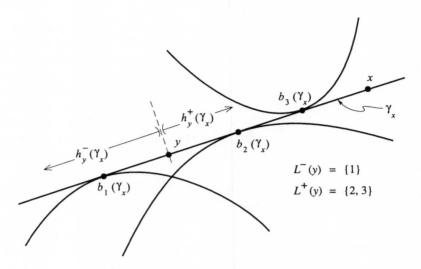

Figure 5.7: Partitioning the line $\gamma_x$

**Definition 5.6** *Let $f$ be a simple rule and $\rho \in \mathcal{R}_{cs}^n$. For any $x \in X$, $\gamma_x \in \Gamma(x)$, the set of induced $f$-medians in $X$ on $\gamma_x$ is,*

$$\mu_f(\rho|_{\gamma_x}) = \{z \in \gamma_x \cap X : L^+(z) \notin \mathcal{L}(f) \ \& \ L^-(z) \notin \mathcal{L}(f)\}.$$

(Recall that $L \subset L'$ and $L \in \mathcal{L}(f)$ imply $L' \in \mathcal{L}(f)$.) Because $R_i \in \mathcal{R}_{cs}$ for all $i \in N$ and $X$ is compact and convex, $\mu_f(\rho|_{\gamma_x})$ is nonempty. For example, suppose $f$ is simple majority rule; then $L^+(z) \in \mathcal{L}(f)$ if and only if $|L^+(z)| > n/2$ and $\mu_{f_m}(\rho|_{\gamma_x})$ is the set of induced median points along the line $\gamma_x$ in $X$.

**Theorem 5.5** *Let $f$ be a simple rule and assume $\rho \in \mathcal{R}_{cs}^n$. Then $x \in C_f(\rho)$ if and only if $x \in \mu_f(\rho|_{\gamma_x})$ for all $\gamma_x \in \Gamma(x)$.*

**Proof.** (Necessity) Let $x \in C_f(\rho)$ and suppose, to the contrary, that there exists $\gamma_x \in \Gamma(x)$ such that $x \notin \mu_f(\rho|_{\gamma_x})$. Therefore, either $L^+(x) \in \mathcal{L}(f)$ or $L^-(x) \in \mathcal{L}(f)$; without loss of generality, assume $L^+(x) \in \mathcal{L}(f)$. By $\rho \in \mathcal{R}_{cs}^n$, each individual $i$'s preferences over $\gamma_x$ are single-peaked about $b_i(\gamma_x)$. Since $X$ is convex, therefore, there exists $w \in \gamma_x \cap X$ such that, $\forall i \in L^+(x)$, $wP_ix$. But $L^+(x) \in \mathcal{L}(f)$ and so $x \in C_f(\rho)$ is impossible.

(Sufficiency) If $x \in \mu_f(\rho|_{\gamma_x})$ then, $\forall w \in \gamma_x \cap X$, $[wP_ix, \ \forall i \in L] \Rightarrow L \notin \mathcal{L}(f)$. Thus, $x \in \mu_f(\rho|_{\gamma_x})$ for all $\gamma_x \in \Gamma(x)$, which implies $x \in C_f(\rho)$.$\Box$

In effect, the result says that for an alternative $x$ to belong to the core of a simple rule $f$, $x$ must constitute an induced $f$-median point on every line passing through $x$. Since in one-dimensional issue spaces there is only one line passing through a point, Theorem 5.5 yields Theorem 4.4, and hence Black's Median Voter Theorem for majority rule, as a special case. When individual $i$'s preferences are Euclidean, $i$'s induced ideal point on any line $\gamma_x$, $b_i(\gamma_x)$, is simply the point on $\gamma_x$ closest to $i$'s ideal point, $x_i$. So in Figure 5.6(a), it is easily seen that for all $x_4$ on the arc segment $[a, c]$, $x_4$ is a median on all lines through $x_4$; moreover, no other point satisfies this condition. And, as in Figure 5.6(b), when $x_4$ equals $b$ the point $d$ is the only alternative that is a median on all lines through $d$.

Lemma 5.5 and Theorem 5.5 are global characterization results, describing core points in terms of individuals' preferences over the entire set of alternatives $X$. If, as is often the case, individual preferences are further assumed to have differentiable utility representations, then more subtle core-characterization results are available. Assume, as for Theorem 5.4 above, that for all individuals $i \in N$, $R_i$ can be represented by a continuously differentiable utility function, $u_i : X \to \Re$. For any $x \in X$, let $\nabla u_i(x) = (\partial u_i(x)/\partial x_1, \ldots, \partial u_i(x)/\partial x_k)$ be the *gradient vector* of $u_i$ at $x$. Geometrically, the gradient vector $\nabla u_i(x)$ is normal to the tangent of the indifference surface at $x$ and its substantive interpretation is that it points in the direction of greatest marginal increase in $u_i(\cdot)$. In other words, if, starting at a policy $x$, one wished to increase individual $i$'s utility as much as possible with an infinitessimal move away from $x$, the direction in which to make such a move is given by the gradient vector. In particular, if $x$ is $i$'s ideal point then there are *no* utility-increasing moves away from $x$ for $i$, and $\nabla u_i(x) = (0, \ldots, 0)$.

**Definition 5.7** *A differentiable function $u : \Re^k \to \Re$ is pseudo-concave at $x$ if and only if $u(y) > u(x)$ implies $\nabla u(x) \cdot (y - x) > 0$.*

Suppose $u$ represents a strictly convex preference order $R \in \mathcal{R}_{cs}$. Then pseudo-concavity of $u$ insures that there is at most one point, say $x^* \in \Re^k$ at which the derivative vanishes; intuitively, if $x^*$ exists then $x^*$ is the most preferred alternative under $R$. Strictly convex weak orders representable by differentiable utility functions may not be pseudo-concave. For example, suppose $k = 1$ and that $R \in \mathcal{R}_{cs}$ is representable by the utility function, $u(x) = x^3$; then for all $y > 0$, $u(y) > u(0)$ but $u'(0) \cdot y = 0$.

For any $x \in X \subseteq \Re^k$ and any $\epsilon > 0$, let $B(x, \epsilon)$ denote the ball in $\Re^k$ with center $x$ and radius $\epsilon$: $B(x, \epsilon) = \{w \in \Re^k : \|x - w\| < \epsilon\}$. The *interior* of $X$, denoted $X°$, is the set

$$X° = \{x \in X : \text{ for some } \epsilon > 0, \ B(x, \epsilon) \subset X\}.$$

Now let $\mathcal{R}_{ds} \subset \mathcal{R}_{cs}$ denote the set of strictly convex weak orders representable by continuously differentiable and pseudo-concave utility functions, and fix a profile $\rho \in \mathcal{R}_{ds}^n$. Then for any $L \subseteq N\backslash\emptyset$ and $x \in X°$, define the convex cone generated by the gradient vectors $\{\nabla u_i(x)\}_L$ as

$$p_L(x) = \{y \in \Re^k : y = \sum_{i \in L} \lambda_i \nabla u_i(x) \text{ where, } \forall i \in L, \ \lambda_i \geq 0 \text{ and } \sum_{i \in L} \lambda_i > 0\}.$$

When $L = \emptyset$, set $p_\emptyset(x) = \emptyset$. Figure 5.8 illustrates $p_L(x)$ for $L = \{1, 2\}$ in $\Re^2$.

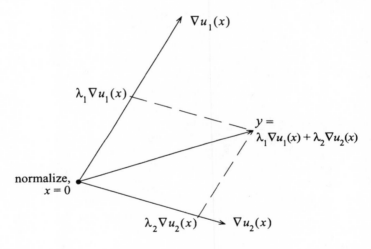

Figure 5.8: The set $p_{\{1,2\}}(x)$

Then we have

**Lemma 5.6** *Let $\rho \in \mathcal{R}_{ds}^n$ and $x \in X°$. Then $x \in PS_L(\rho)$ if and only if $0 \in p_L(x)$.*

**Proof.** (Necessity) The argument uses the Separating Hyperplane Theorem, a proof of which may be found in Border [14, ch. 2].

(Separating Hyperplane Theorem) Let $A$ and $B$ be disjoint nonempty convex subsets of $\Re^k$; let $A$ be closed and $B$ be compact. Then $A$ and $B$ can be strictly separated by a hyperplane: i.e. there exists a vector $r$, normal to the hyperplane, such that, for all $a \in A$ and all $b \in B$, $r \cdot a > 0$ and $r \cdot b \le 0$.

Fix $\rho$ and $x \in X^\circ$. Let $x \in PS_L$ and suppose the claim is false. Then for every set of scalars $\{\lambda_i\}_{i \in L}$ with $\sum_L \lambda_i > 0$, $\sum_L \lambda_i \nabla u_i(x) \ne 0$. Let

$$\Lambda = \{\lambda \in [0,1]^{|L|} : \sum_L \lambda_i = 1\},$$

$$Y = \{y \in \Re^k : y = \sum_L \lambda_i \nabla u_i(x) \text{ for some } \lambda \in \Lambda\}.$$

The following argument is illustrated in Figure 5.9 for $L = \{1, 2\}$ in $\Re^2$.

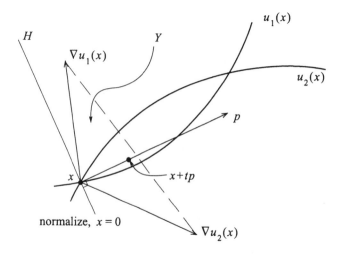

Figure 5.9: The necessity argument of Lemma 5.6

By supposition $0 \notin Y$, $\{0\}$ is convex and compact and, by definition, $Y$ is convex and closed. Hence, the Separating Hyperplane Theorem implies there exists $p \in \Re^k$ such that, $\forall y \in Y$, $p \cdot y > 0$. Since, $\forall i \in L$, $e_i \in \Lambda$ (where $e_i$ is the $i^{th}$ element of the usual basis for $\Re^{|L|}$), we have $\nabla u_i(x) \in Y$. Hence $\forall i \in L$, $p \cdot \nabla u_i(x) > 0$. By assumption, $x \in X^\circ$ and, $\forall i \in L$, $u_i$ is differentiable. Therefore, for sufficiently small $t > 0$, $x + tp \in X$ and, setting $tp \equiv h$,

$$\lim_{t \to 0} \frac{u_i(x + tp) - u_i(x)}{t} \equiv p \cdot \lim_{h \to 0} \frac{u_i(x + h) - u_i(x)}{h} = p \cdot \nabla u_i(x).$$

So for sufficiently small $t > 0$, $p \cdot \nabla u_i(x) > 0$ implies $u_i(x+tp) > u_i(x)$. But since $p \cdot \nabla u_i(x) > 0$ for all $i \in L$, this contradicts $x \in PS_L$.

(Sufficiency) Suppose for some $\lambda \in \Lambda$ and $x \in X^\circ$, $\sum_L \lambda_i \nabla u_i(x) = 0$ and assume, to the contrary, that there exists some $y \in X$ such that $P(x,y;\rho) \cap L = \emptyset$. Then $\forall i \in L$, $u_i(y) \geq u_i(x)$. Let $z = tx + (1-t)y$, $t \in (0,1)$, and let $H$ denote the hyperplane in $\Re^k$ containing $x$, normal to the vector $(z-x)$. By strict convexity, $\forall i \in L$, $u_i(z) > u_i(x)$. So by pseudo-concavity, $\forall i \in L$, $\nabla u_i(x) \cdot (z-x) > 0$. Hence, $\forall i,j \in L$, $i \neq j$, $\nabla u_i(x)$ and $\nabla u_j(x)$ must lie in the same halfspace defined by $H$. See Figure 5.10.

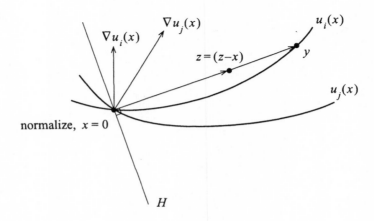

Figure 5.10: The sufficiency argument for Lemma 5.6

Therefore, there is no $\lambda \in \Lambda$ for which $\sum_L \lambda_i \nabla u_i(x) = 0$: contradiction.$\square$

To see the intuition for Lemma 5.6, assume $X$ is a two-dimensional policy space and assume no two individuals share the same preferences; we consider a two-person (Figure 11) and a three-person example (Figure 12). So suppose, first, that $L = \{1,2\}$. Then in Figure 11(a) the Pareto set for $L$, $PS_L(\rho)$, is the familiar "contract curve" in $\Re^2$ defined by points of tangency between the indifference curves of individuals 1 and 2; Figure 5.11(b) describes exactly the same situation as Figure 5.11(a), save that the indifference curves through the points $x$ and $y$ are replaced by the individuals' respective gradient vectors at these points.

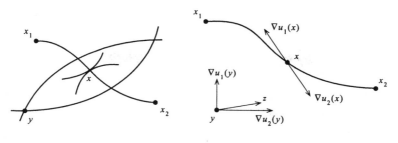

(a) indifference curves at $x, y$      (b) gradient vectors at $x, y$

Figure 11: Intuition for Lemma 5.6 for $L = \{1, 2\}$

As illustrated, since $y$ is not in $PS_L(\rho)$ both gradient vectors, $\nabla u_1(y)$ and $\nabla u_2(y)$, point into the same halfspace and so there exists a utility-improving move for both individuals, toward the point $z$ for instance. On the other hand, at $x \in PS_L(\rho)$ the two gradient vectors $\nabla u_1(x)$ and $\nabla u_2(x)$ point in diametrically opposite directions, reflecting the fact that, at any Pareto efficient point $x$ for $L$, any strict utility-improving move away from $x$ for one individual must be a strict utility-worsening move for the other. And since $\nabla u_1(x)$ and $\nabla u_2(x)$ point in diametrically opposing directions they must, component by component, have opposing signs; therefore, we can find a non-negative scalar, say $\lambda_1$, such that $\lambda_1 \nabla u_1(x) + \nabla u_2(x) = 0$.

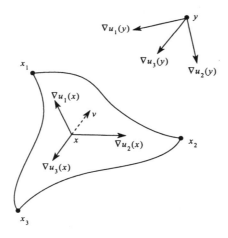

Figure 5.12: Intuition for Lemma 5.6 for $L = \{1, 2, 3\}$

Second, suppose that $L = \{1, 2, 3\}$ and, for each $i \in L$, let $x_i$ denote $i$'s most preferred policy. In this case, the Pareto set for $L$ is a two-dimensional subset of $X$, and the gradient vectors at typical Pareto efficient and Pareto inefficient points for $L$ are as illustrated in Figure 5.12. Again, $y$ is not Pareto efficient for $L$ and all three gradient vectors at $y$ point into the same halfspace. And just as for the two-person example, at any Pareto efficient point for $L$ such as $x$, it is impossible to find a common halfspace into which all the gradient vectors point. Any utility-improving move away from $x$ for any pair of individuals is necessarily a utility-worsening move for the third. Consequently, we can find some positive linear combination of any two of the gradient vectors at $x$, say $v = \lambda_1 \nabla u_1(x) + \lambda_2 \nabla u_2(x)$ with $\lambda_1 > 0$ and $\lambda_2 > 0$, such that $v + \lambda_3 \nabla u_3(x) = 0$ for some $\lambda_3 > 0$.

Although Lemma 5.6 is of independent interest, its value lies in the core characterization theorem it yields when combined with Lemma 5.5.

**Theorem 5.6** *Let $f$ be a simple rule, $\rho \in \mathcal{R}_{ds}^n$ and $x \in X^\circ$. Then $x \in C_f(\rho)$ if and only if*

$$0 \in \bigcap_{L \in \mathcal{L}(f)} p_L(x).$$

Note that the necessity half of Lemma 5.6 does not require any convexity assumption on preferences, only that $\nabla u_i(x)$ exists for all individuals $i$ in $N$. And it is only the necessity part of Lemma 5.6 that is needed to prove necessity for Theorem 5.6. Consequently, the assumption of pseudo-concave preferences is essential only for the sufficiency half of this result.

There are additional necessary restrictions on sets of gradient vectors at a point $x$ for $x$ to be in the core and in some cases these restrictions are easier to check. Such restrictions include the well-known Plott conditions for majority rule core points introduced in the next result, a sufficiency theorem for a policy to be in the majority rule core. For any nonempty set $L \subseteq N$, say that a function $\pi : L \to L$ is a *pairing* if $\pi$ is one-one and if, for all $i \in L$, $\pi(\pi(i)) = i$.

**Definition 5.8** *Let $L \subseteq N$, $x \in X$. The set of gradient vectors $\{\nabla u_i(x)\}_{i \in L}$ satisfies the Plott conditions at $x$ if there exists a pairing $\pi : L \to L$ such that,*

$$\forall i \in L, \ \nabla u_i(x) = -\lambda_i \nabla u_{\pi(i)}(x) \ \text{for some } \lambda_i \in \Re_{++}.$$

So the Plott conditions are satisfied at an alternative for a coalition, if each member of the coalition can be paired with another in such a way that their gradient vectors at that alternative point in exactly opposite directions.

**Theorem 5.7** *Let $\rho \in \mathcal{R}_{ds}^n$, $x \in X^\circ$ and $L = \{i \in N : \nabla u_i(x) \neq 0\}$. If $\{\nabla u_i(x)\}_{i \in L}$ satisfies the Plott conditions at $x$ then $x \in C_{f_m}(\rho)$.*

**Proof.** $L \subseteq N$ is decisive if and only if $|L| > n/2$; hence, by the hypothesis, for any decisive coalition $L$ there must exist $j, \ell \in L$ such that $\nabla u_j(x) = -t \nabla u_\ell(x)$, $t > 0$. For all $i \in L \backslash \{j, \ell\}$, let $\lambda_i = 0$ and set $\lambda_j = 1$ and $\lambda_\ell = t$; then $0 = \sum_L \lambda_i \nabla u_i(x)$. Since $L$ is an arbitrary decisive coalition, the result follows from Theorem 5.6.$\square$

Given $\rho \in \mathcal{R}_{ds}^n$ and $n$ odd, the converse of Theorem 5.7, perhaps surprisingly, also turns out to be true; that is, if $x$ is a majority core point then the gradient vectors for the members of $L$ satisfy the Plott conditions. A direct proof of this claim is somewhat involved, but the claim itself follows as a corollary to a more general core characterization result established below. The Plott conditions, however, are not in general (i.e. for arbitrary $n$) necessary for a core point as Figure 5.6, from Example 5.5, illustrates. In Figure 5.6(b) the set of individuals with nonzero gradient vectors at the point $d$, the set $L$ above, is $N = \{1, 2, 3, 4\}$, the individuals can be paired $\{1, 2\}$ and $\{3, 4\}$ and, within each pair, the gradient vectors at $d$ are pointed in opposite directions. On the other hand, in Figure 5.6(a) the set $L$ is now given by $\{1, 2, 3\}$ and since this is an odd number there is obviously no possible pairing yet a core point exists at $a = x_4$.

When the Plott conditions hold at a policy $x$, every decisive coalition (i.e. every coalition capable of overturning $x$) is "blocked" in that no such coalition can unanimously agree to a better alternative to $x$. As an illustration of the result, recall Black's Median Voter Theorem for $k = 1$. At the median voter's most preferred policy, every individual whose most preferred policy is to the left of the median is paired with a distinct individual whose most preferred policy is to the right of the median; i.e. the distribution of preferences is such that the Plott conditions hold at the median point.

The intuitive notion of blocking underlying the Median Voter Theorem is illustrated in Figure 5.13 for a six person, two-dimensional example in which all six individuals have Euclidean preferences on $\Re^2$, $x_6 \in C_{f_m}(\rho)$ but the Plott conditions fail on $\{\nabla u_1(x_6), \dots, \nabla u_5(x_6)\}$. It is clear from the illustration that every decisive coalition is blocked in that there is no coalition of four or more individuals that can agree on a change away from $x_6$. And it is this observation that suggests looking for a general characterization of core points for arbitrary voting rules in terms of the more general concept of blocking.

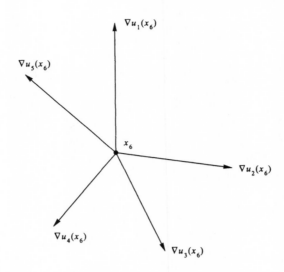

Figure 5.13: Plott conditions do not hold at a core point

Let $f$ be any simple rule, with associated family of decisive coalitions $\mathcal{L}(f)$.

**Definition 5.9** *For any $L \subseteq N$, the set of pivotal coalitions for $\mathcal{L}(f)$ in $L$, $E_L(\mathcal{L}(f))$, is the set of all coalitions $M \subseteq L$ such that, for every binary partition $\{C, D\}$ of $L \backslash M$, $C \cup M \in \mathcal{L}(f)$ or $D \cup M \in \mathcal{L}(f)$.*

For example, if (as in Figure 5.13) $f = f_m$ and $n = 6$, then:

$$
\begin{aligned}
|L| &< 4 \text{ implies } E_L(\mathcal{L}(f_m)) \text{ is empty} \\
|L| &= 4 \text{ implies } E_L(\cdot) = \{M \subseteq L : |M| \geq 3\} \\
|L| &= 5 \text{ implies } E_L(\cdot) = \{M \subseteq L : |M| \geq 2\} \\
|L| &= 6 \text{ implies } E_L(\cdot) = \{M \subseteq L : |M| \geq 1\}.
\end{aligned}
$$

This example illustrates two fundamental properties of $E_L(\cdot)$ for simple rules: (1) for any $L$, $E_L(\cdot)$ is monotonic ($M \in E_L(\cdot)$ and $M \subset M' \subseteq L$ implies $M' \in E_L(\cdot)$); and (2) $E_L(\cdot)$ is nonempty if and only if $L \in \mathcal{L}(f)$.

The definition of "pivotal coalitions" is not immediately intuitive; indeed, for some $f$ it allows the empty set to be a pivotal coalition for $\mathcal{L}(f)$ in some $L$. To see this, suppose $n$ is odd and recall $\mathcal{L}(f_m) = \{L \subseteq N : |L| > n/2\}$; then $\emptyset$ is a pivotal coalition of $\mathcal{L}(f_m)$ in $N$ since, for every binary partition $\{C, D\}$ of $N \backslash \emptyset = N$, $\max\{|C|, |D|\} > n/2$.

One way to think about the definition is the following: fix some $L \subseteq N$ and an $M \subseteq L$; now consider any arbitrary division of $L \backslash M$ into two mutually exclusive subgroups, $\{C, D\}$, and for each $K \in \{C, D\}$ ask the question, "If $K$ and $M$ merge, will they constitute a decisive coalition?" If, for *every* such division of $L \backslash M$, the answer to this question is "Yes" for at least one $K$, then $M$ is a pivotal coalition in $L$. In other words, however the individuals in $L \backslash M$ sort themselves into two disjoint groups $\{C, D\}$, one of these groups can be decisive if it is expanded to include $M$ as an "ally". So, in the example above with the empty set being pivotal for $N$ under $f_m$, the answer is vacuously "Yes" since, for every binary partition, there is necessarily one coalition that is decisive on its own and, therefore, that is decisive if no one is added.

Fix a profile $\rho \in \mathcal{R}_{ds}^n$. For any nonempty set $L \subseteq N$ and $x \in X^\circ$, define the subspace spanned by $\{\nabla u_i(x)\}_{i \in L}$ as,

$$sp_L(x) = \{y \in \Re^k : y = \sum_{i \in L} \lambda_i \nabla u_i(x) \text{ where, } \forall i \in L, \ \lambda_i \in \Re\}.$$

If $L = \emptyset$, set $sp_L(x) = \{0\}$. Note the difference between $sp_L(x)$ and $p_L(x)$, the convex cone generated by $\{\nabla u_i(x)\}_{i \in L}$: in the latter the coefficients $\{\lambda_i\}$ are required to be nonnegative with at least one strictly positive, whereas in the former these coefficients can take on any real value. Thus in Figure 5.8 above, $sp_{\{1,2\}}(x)$ is the whole of $\Re^2$ and $p_{\{1,2\}}(x)$ is a strict subset of $\Re^2$. Figure 5.14 below describes an example in which $sp_{\{1,2\}}(x)$ is a plane through $\Re^3$.

We are now in a position to introduce the appropriate concept of blocking.

**Definition 5.10** *For any $x \in X^\circ$ and $M \in E_L(\mathcal{L}(f))$, say that $M$ is blocked in $L$ at $x$ if $0 \in p_{M^*}(x)$, where $M^* = \{i \in L : \nabla u_i(x) \in sp_M(x)\}$.*

To understand this definition, consider any $C \subseteq N$ and note that Lemma 5.6 implies:

$$0 \notin p_C(x) \Leftrightarrow \exists y \in p_C(x) \text{ such that, } \forall i \in C, \ \nabla u_i(x) \cdot y > 0.$$

So if $0 \notin p_C(x)$ there is a point, $z = \lambda x + (1 - \lambda) y$ for some $\lambda \in (0, 1)$, that every member of $C$ strictly prefers to $x$: $u_i(z) > u_i(x)$ for every $i \in C$. And conversely, if $0 \in p_C(x)$ then there exists no such point. Thus $M \in E_L(\cdot)$ is blocked in $L$ at $x$ if, when the set $M$ is augmented by all those individuals in $L \backslash M$ whose gradient vectors lie in the same subspace

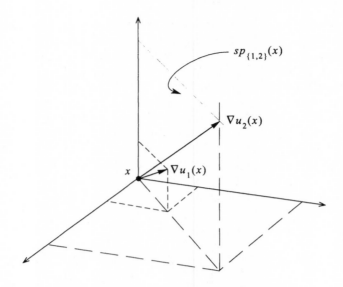

Figure 5.14: The set $sp_{\{1,2\}}(x)$

spanned by $\{\nabla u_i(x)\}_{i \in M}$, the resulting coalition, $M^*$, would be unable to find an alternative to $x$ that they all strictly prefer to $x$ itself. For example, if $M = \{i\}$ the subspace $sp_{\{i\}}(x)$ is simply the line containing the gradient vector $\nabla u_i(x)$; therefore, $\{i\}$ is blocked in $L$ at $x$ only if there is some other individual $j \in L$ whose gradient vector lies on the same line and points in the opposite direction. In other words, the set of gradient vectors $\{\nabla u_i(x), \nabla u_j(x)\}$ satisfies the Plott conditions at $x$.

Thus Definition 5.10 generalizes the notion of blocking that underlies the Plott conditions, Definition 5.8. And, with this observation in mind, the following result is easily seen to be a generalization of Theorem 5.7.

**Theorem 5.8** *Assume* $\rho \in \mathcal{R}_{ds}^n$ *and* $x \in X^\circ$. *Then for any simple rule* $f$, $x \in C_f(\rho)$ *if and only if for every* $L \subseteq N$ *and every* $M \in E_L(\mathcal{L}(f))$, $M$ *is blocked in* $L$ *at* $x$.

The proof of the theorem uses the following lemma.

**Lemma 5.7** *Let* $f$ *be a simple rule,* $\rho \in \mathcal{R}_{ds}^n$ *and* $x \in X^\circ$. *If, for all* $D \in \mathcal{L}(f)$, $D$ *is blocked in* $D$ *at* $x$ *then, for every* $L \subseteq N$ *and every* $M \in E_L(\mathcal{L}(f))$, $M$ *is blocked in* $L$ *at* $x$.

**Proof.** Suppose $L \subseteq N$ and $0 \notin p_{M^*}(x)$ for some $M \in E_L(\cdot)$. There are two cases. (1) If $\dim[sp_M(x)] = k$ then $M^* = L$. Since $M \in E_L(\cdot)$, $L \in \mathcal{L}(f)$; hence $0 \notin p_{M^*}(x)$ implies $0 \notin p_L(x)$, contradicting the assumption that all $D \in \mathcal{L}(f)$ are blocked in $D$ at $x$. (2) If $\dim[sp_M(x)] < k$ then $\exists \beta \in \Re^k$ such that, $\forall v \in sp_M(x)$, $\beta \cdot v = 0$. Let

$$A = \{i \in L : \beta \cdot \nabla u_i(x) > 0\} \text{ and } B = \{i \in L : \beta \cdot \nabla u_i(x) < 0\}.$$

By $L$ finite, we can choose such a $\beta$ for which $A \cup B = L \backslash M^*$ and, clearly, $A \cap B = \emptyset$. Figure 5.15 illustrates the argument to follow for simple majority rule on $\Re^2$ and $n = 3$: here, $M = M^* = \{1\}$, $A = \{2\}$, and $B = \{3\}$.

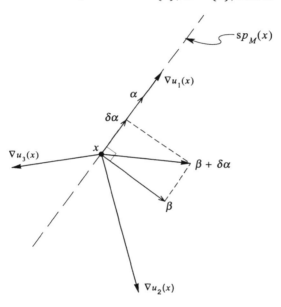

Figure 5.15: Argument for Lemma 5.7

Since $M \in E_L(\cdot)$ and $M^* \supseteq M$, either $M^* \cup A \in \mathcal{L}(f)$ or $M^* \cup B \in \mathcal{L}(f)$; assume $M^* \cup A \equiv D \in \mathcal{L}(f)$. By supposition, $\exists \alpha \in sp_M(x)$ with $\alpha \cdot \nabla u_i(x) > 0$, all $i \in M^*$. Choose $\delta > 0$ such that, $\forall i \in A$, $(\beta + \delta\alpha) \cdot \nabla u_i(x) > 0$. Let $\zeta = \beta + \delta\alpha \in \Re^k$. Then $\forall i \in D$, $\zeta \cdot \nabla u_i(x) > 0$, in which case $0 \notin p_D(x)$ : contradiction.$\square$

**Proof of Theorem 5.8** Necessity is immediate from Theorem 5.6 and Lemma 5.7. To check sufficiency, simply note that, by definition, $L \in E_L(\cdot)$

implies $L \in \mathcal{L}(f)$. Therefore, since $L^* = L$, we have $0 \in \cap_{L \in \mathcal{L}(f)} p_L(x)$ and the result follows from Theorem 5.6.$\square$

The gain that Theorem 5.8 offers beyond the characterization of core points given by Theorem 5.6 lies entirely in the necessity part of the result in that it is in principle easier to check in any given instance whether some alternative $x$ is in the core. To illustrate this, recall the example of Figure 5.13 above. First note that any coalition involving $i = 6$ will satisfy the blocking condition. So to check the blocking condition here, it suffices (by monotonicity of $E_L(\cdot)$) to consider only minimal pivotal coalitions; in the example this amounts to setting $L = \{1, 2, 3, 4, 5\}$, since any $M \subset L$ with $|M| = 2$ is in $E_L(\cdot)$. From Figure 5.13 we see $0 \notin p_M(x_6)$; however, $M^* = N \backslash \{6\}$ for every $M$ and so $0 \in p_{M^*}(x)$. Thus there is no decisive coalition $C$ excluding $i = 6$ for which $0 \notin p_C(x_6)$; i.e. every decisive coalition is blocked in the intuitive sense discussed earlier. The example is easily generalized, as the following two corollaries to Theorem 5.8 make clear.

**Corollary 5.1** Let $\rho \in \mathcal{R}_{ds}^n$ and $n$ odd. Assume no two individuals have the same ideal point. If $x \in C_{f_m}(\rho)$ then $\nabla u_j(x) = 0$ for some $j \in N$ and $\{\nabla u_i(x)\}_{i \in N \backslash \{j\}}$ satisfies the Plott conditions at $x$.

**Proof.** Let $L = \{i \in N : \nabla u_i(x) \neq 0\}$. (1) $L = N$ : then $\emptyset \in E_L(\mathcal{L}(f_m))$. Since $sp_\emptyset(x) = \{0\}$, $\emptyset = \emptyset^*$. But $p_\emptyset(x) = \emptyset$, so $0 \notin p_{\emptyset^*}(x)$. Hence, $x \notin C_{f_m}(\rho)$ by Theorem 5.8. Therefore, $x \in C_{f_m}(\rho)$ implies $\exists j \in N$ with $\nabla u_j(x) = 0$. (2) $|L| = n - 1$: then $\exists j \in N \backslash L$ and, by $n$ odd, $E_L(\mathcal{L}(f_m)) = \{C \subseteq L : |C| \geq 1\}$. Therefore, $\forall i \in N \backslash \{j\}$, $\{i\} \in E_L(\cdot)$. By Theorem 5.8, if $x \in C_m(\rho, X)$ and $0 \in p_{\{i\}^*}(x)$ then, $\forall i \neq j$, $\exists \pi(i) \in N \backslash \{i, j\}$ such that $\nabla u_i(x) = -\lambda_i \nabla u_{\pi(i)}(x)$, $\lambda_i > 0$. So the claim is proved if $\pi : N \backslash \{j\} \to N \backslash \{j\}$ is a pairing. Suppose not. Then there exist two disjoint coalitions in $L$, $A$, and $B$, such that (i) $\forall i, k \in A$, $\nabla u_i(x) = t_i \nabla u_k(x)$, $t_i > 0$; (ii) $B = \{h \in L : \forall i \in A, \nabla u_i(x) = -\lambda_i \nabla u_h(x), \lambda_i > 0\}$; and (iii) $|A| > |B|$. See Figure 5.16 for an example in which $N = \{1, \ldots, 7\}$ and we can take $A = \{1, 2\}$ and $B = \{3\}$. Now, for any sets $K \subseteq M \subseteq N$, to check whether $K$ is pivotal in $M$ under majority rule it suffices to check whether a coalition of size $|K| + \lceil \frac{1}{2} |M \backslash K| \rceil$ is decisive. So let $M = L \backslash B$ and let $K$ be any set in $M$ with $|K| \geq |B| + 1$; then

$$|K| + \lceil \frac{1}{2} |M \backslash K| \rceil \geq |K| + \frac{|L| - |B| - |K|}{2}$$
$$\geq \frac{|L| + 1}{2}$$
$$= n/2.$$

Hence, by $n$ odd, any such set $K \subseteq M$ is a pivotal coalition in $M$ and, therefore, $A \in E_M(\cdot)$ by $(iii)$ and definition of $M$. But since $B \cap M = \emptyset$, $(i)$ and $(ii)$ imply that $A$ is not blocked in $M$: contradiction.$\square$

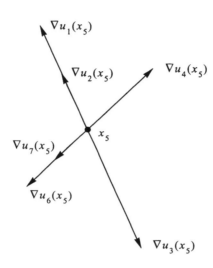

Figure 5.16: Example of $\pi$ not being a pairing

Thus, as claimed above, when $n$ is odd the Plott conditions are necessary as well as sufficient for an alternative to be a majority rule core point. Under these circumstances, the Plott conditions amount to requiring that every individual with nonzero gradient vector at a core point is blocked by some other individual at that point. Figure 5.17 illustrates the corollary for $N = \{1, 2, 3, 4, 5\}$ and $X$ in $\Re^2$. In Figure 5.17(a) the Plott conditions are satisfied at $w$, which coincides with individual 5's ideal point, $x_5$. In Figure 5.17(b) differs from Figure 5.17(a) only in that individual 5's ideal point is at $z$, where we can choose $z$ arbitrarily close to $w$. The Plott conditions are no longer satisfied at $w$, since no individual has that as their ideal point (a necessary condition from Corollary 5.1). Furthermore, $z$ is not a core point either since the gradient vectors cannot be paired to satisfy the Plott conditions. This illustration makes clear how fragile is the existence of a majority rule core point when $n$ is odd and the dimension of the space exceeds one.

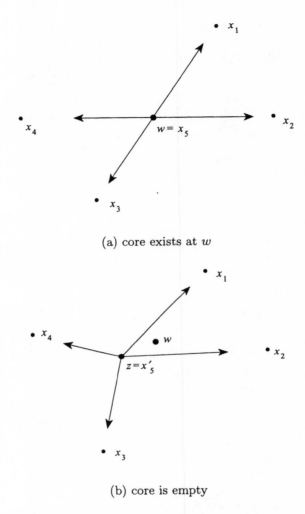

(a) core exists at $w$

(b) core is empty

Figure 5.17: Fragility of the majority rule core

Now majority rule is simply a $q$-rule with $q = (n+1)/2$ when the number of individuals is odd, and $q = (n+2)/2$ when the number of individuals is even. In view of Corollary 5.1, therefore, we might expect that, for arbitrary $q$-rules, some appropriately generalized Plott conditions also have to hold at a core point. The final result of the chapter confirms that this is indeed the case.

**Corollary 5.2** *Let $\rho \in \mathcal{R}^n_{ds}$ and let $f$ be a q-rule. Assume no two individuals have the same ideal point and, for any $x \in X^\circ$, let $L = \{i \in N : \nabla u_i(x) \neq 0\}$. If $x \in C_f(\rho)$ then either (i) $|L| = n$ and all coalitions of size at least $(2q-n-1)$ are blocked in $L$ at $x$, or (ii) $|L| = n-1$ and all coalitions of size at least $2q - n$ are blocked in $L$ at $x$.*

**Proof.** If $L = N$, then $E_L(\mathcal{L}(f)) = \{C \subseteq L : |C| \geq 2q - n - 1\}$; and if $|L| = n - 1$, then $E_L(\mathcal{L}(f)) = \{C \subseteq L : |C| \geq 2q - n\}$. So the result follows directly from Theorem 5.8 and the monotonicity of $E_L(\cdot)$.$\square$

## 5.5 Discussion

For many applications it is natural to think of the feasible set of alternatives as representable by some subset of Euclidean space. Indeed, a spatial metaphor is common in the everyday language of politics: political parties are discussed as being "centrist", "leftist", "extreme right-wing"; candidates for office are described as "moving to the left" or attempting to "capture the middle ground"; and so on and so forth. In many collective choice environments, therefore, the spatial model is both intuitively appealing and technically convenient.

As in previous chapters, our main concern here is with the existence of socially optimal or core alternatives with respect to some underlying method of preference aggregation. The fundamental result in this regard is that such alternatives are guaranteed if the dimensionality of the choice space is below a critical number (Theorem 5.3). Moreover, this bound on the dimensionality of the space is shown to be tight (Theorem 5.4). Comparing these results with those found in Chapter 3, we see that the dimensionality of the choice space plays essentially the same role in insuring nonempty cores for the spatial model as does the number of alternatives in the finite model. Specifically, a nonempty core for $f$ is assured in the finite model if and only if the number of alternatives is no more than the Nakamura number less one, $s(f) - 1$; whereas it is assured for $f$ in the spatial model if and only if the number of dimensions is no more than the Nakamura number less two, $s(f) - 2$. In view of this relationship between the two settings in terms of the Nakamura number, it follows that the discussion in Chapter 3 on the trade-off across rules between their resoluteness, equality and the extent to which choices are well-defined, applies directly to the spatial model.

Where the spatial model allows us to say more is in regard to characterizing core outcomes. We are able to extend the median voter-type results of Chapter 4 to the multi-dimensional spatial model, showing that when a

core exists then it must be centrally located with respect to the distribution
of individual preferences (Theorems 5.5 and 5.6). An alternative characterization theorem, one based on the well-known Plott conditions for majority
rule, suggests just how fragile is the existence of a nonempty core in sufficiently high dimensional spaces: what is required is that critical sets of
individuals are "balanced" across a core point in such a way that no group
that agrees on a better point is decisive (Theorem 5.8). In the next chapter
we take up the issue of core stability and go on to study what is true of
collective preference relations when cores do not exist.

## 5.6   Exercises

**5.1** Identify the relationships between strictly convex preferences, single-
peaked preferences, and strictly quasi-concave utility functions when $X$ is
one-dimensional.

**5.2** Prove that if $R$ is a complete, non-convex preference relation on a convex
set $X \subset \Re^k$, then $R$ semi-convex implies $R$ is not transitive. Discuss whether
this result extends to situations in which $X$ is not convex.

**5.3** Suppose $\rho \in \mathcal{R}_s^n$ is a convex profile on $X \subset \Re^k$, $X$ compact and convex.
Let $f$ be a voting rule and $f' = f_{\mathcal{L}(f)}$. Construct an example to show that
the equivalence relation between $C_f(\rho)$ and $C_{f'}(\rho)$ does not extend to all
properties of these rules.

**5.4** Prove Lemma 5.5. Is the assumption that $\rho \in \mathcal{R}_{cs}^n$ needed for the result?

**5.5** Suppose $f$ is a strong simple rule and $\rho \in \mathcal{R}_{cs}^n$. Prove that $C_f(\rho) \neq \emptyset$
implies $|C_f(\rho)| = 1$ whenever $X$ is a convex set in $\Re^k$.

**5.6** Suppose each $i \in N$ has Euclidean preferences with ideal point $x_i \in X$.
Provide examples to show that there is no equivalence relation between any
pair from $\{(a), (b), (c)\}$, where:

(a) $z \in X$ is a *multidimensional median* iff, $\forall r = 1, \dots, k$,

$$|\{i \in N : z_r < x_{ir}\}| \leq n/2 \text{ and } |\{i \in N : z_r > x_{ir}\}| \leq n/2;$$

(b) $z \in X$ is a *partial median* iff $z$ is a multidimensional median for some
set of orthogonal basis vectors;

(c) $z \in X$ is a *total median* iff $\forall y \in \Re^k$, $|\{i \in N : (x_i - z) \cdot y > 0\}| \leq n/2$.

**5.7** Suppose each $i \in N$, $|N|$ odd, has preferences described by a differentiable and pseudo-concave utility representation $u_i(\cdot)$. Let $X = \Re^k$. Prove or provide a counterexample to the claims that: *(i)* $x \in C_{f_m}(\rho)$ if $x$ is a total median; and *(ii)* $x \in C_{f_m}(\rho)$ only if $x$ is a total median.

**5.8** For any $z \in \Re^k$ and $J \subseteq \{0,1,2,\ldots,k\}$, let $z^J \in \Re^k$ be defined by: $z_r^J = z_r$ if $r \in J$ and $z_r^J = 0$ otherwise. Then $R_i$ is *separable* on $\Re^k$ if, for all $x, y \in X$, all $J \subseteq \{0, 1, 2, \ldots, k\}$ and $j \in J$,

$$[x + (y - x)^J] R_i [x + (y - x)^{J \setminus \{j\}}] \Leftrightarrow [x + (y - x)^{\{j\}}] R_i x.$$

(a) Interpret the concept of separable preferences. Assuming $R_i$ is representable by a differentiable utility function, what does $R_i$ separable imply for the shapes of $i$'s indifference curves in $\Re^k$?

(b) Answer 5.7 with the additional assumption that, for all $i \in N$, $R_i \in \mathcal{R}_{cs}$ is separable.

## 5.7  Further reading

The fundamental existence theorem, Theorem 5.1, is due to Bergstrom [7] and Sonnenschein [85], who generalize a result of Fan [26]. Our development follows Schofield [76]; see also Schofield [74]. Schofield [73] and Strnad [86] exploit the theorem to yield a general core-existence result for simple rules; see also Grandmont [34] and Greenberg [35]. Schofield [75] proves Theorem 5.4. Cueing off Downs [25, ch. 8], Davis and Hinich [22] and Davis, DeGroot, and Hinich [23] introduced the basic multidimensional spatial model for simple majority rule. Plott [56] provided local conditions for the existence of a majority core when preferences were smooth; McKelvey and Wendell [52] review subsequent work on this issue and provide several new global characterization results; Matthews [45] extends Plott to more general rules. Lemma 5.6 was first proved by Smale [84]. McKelvey and Schofield [51] give the most general core-characterization theorem, Theorem 5.8. (In [51], McKelvey and Schofield refer to the condition on gradient vectors introduced in Definition 5.10 by saying that a point $x$ satisfies the *pivotal gradient restrictions* whenever, for all $L \subseteq N$ and all $M \in E_L(\cdot)$, $M$ is blocked in $L$ at $x$.) Cox [21] proves Theorem 5.5 for simple majority rule.

# Chapter 6

# Instability and Chaos

The core characterization results of the previous chapter suggest that cores are quite fragile in high-dimensional spaces, in the sense that they simply may not exist for relatively large sets of preferences. This intuition is especially transparent for the case of majority rule: Corollary 5.1 states that with an odd number of individuals, each with a distinct ideal point, preferences must be distributed in a very special way to support a nonempty core. So, for example, if all individuals have Euclidean preferences on a two-dimensional issue space and the profile $\rho \in \mathcal{R}_{cs}^n$ supports a majority core at $x_j$ for some $j \in N$, then virtually any perturbation of $x_j$ will lead to the core being empty. Furthermore, for *any* noncollegial rule, Theorem 5.4 tells us that core points need not exist if the dimension of the policy space $k$ is sufficiently large.

The preceding observations prompt the following question: Given a noncollegial simple rule $f$ and an arbitrary preference profile $\rho$, how likely is it that the core of $f$ is nonempty? The answer to this question, the subject of Section 6.1 below, is that for issue spaces of sufficiently large dimension the likelihood of the core being nonempty is negligible. Thus for relatively complex social problems, where "complexity" is here identified with the number of dimensions of the issue space, it is almost surely the case that there does not exist any one alternative which is judged to be at least as good as all the others according to the social preference relation.

A second question, then, is: How badly behaved is the preference relation in an environment where the core fails to exist? In other words, what constraints if any does the aggregation rule *per se* impose on collective preferences when its maximal set is empty? This question is addressed in Section 6.2, where it is shown that when social preference breaks down, in the sense of not admitting a core alternative, it breaks down completely: social preference cycles fill the space, and one can get from any alternative to any other via the social preference relation. Taken together, the results of Sections 6.1 and 6.2 generate a pessimistic view concerning the extent to which "collective preferences" can be seen as the primary determinant behind many observed collective decisions.

## 6.1   Generic nonexistence of core points

Although the underlying intuition for the common lack of a core point is exactly that offered for the majority rule example above, stating the question and a solution formally requires a mathematical technology peculiar to this section of the text. The central concept is that of *genericity*. Loosely speaking, a set is generic if its defining property is a common property, identifying the typical situation. Conversely, a set is *not* generic if the defining property of the set is a knife-edge property and so cannot typically be expected to obtain. When studying whether the existence of a nonempty core is a rare event, the relevant sets whose genericity is of concern are sets of preference profiles, especially those for which no core points exist. However, to develop some formal intuition for the idea of a set being generic or non-generic, it is useful first to consider a set of points rather than a set of profiles. Formally, a set $T \subset \Re^k$ is *generic* if $T$ is *open* in $\Re^k$ (for all $x \in T$, there is some $\epsilon > 0$ such that $B(x, \epsilon) = \{y \in \Re^k : \|x - y\| < \epsilon\} \subset T$) and *dense* in $\Re^k$ (for all $y \notin T$, for all $\epsilon > 0$, $B(y, \epsilon)$ contains points in $T$). Example 6.1 illustrates the concept.

**Example 6.1** Let $M$ be the unit circle in $\Re^2$ centered at zero: $M = \{(x_1, x_2) \in \Re^2 : x_1^2 + x_2^2 = 1\}$. The set $M$ is a one-dimensional *manifold* in $\Re^2$, i.e. a subset of $\Re^2$ which locally "looks like" the real line $\Re$. See Figure 6.1. Then the set of points not in $M$, $\Re^2 \backslash M$, is both open (for any $x \in \Re^2 \backslash M$ there exists $\epsilon > 0$ such that, for all $y \in \Re^2$ for which $\|x - y\| < \epsilon$, $y \in \Re^2 \backslash M$) and dense (for all $w \in M$ and $\epsilon > 0$ there exists $y \in \Re^2$ such that $\|w - y\| < \epsilon$ and $y \in \Re^2 \backslash M$). Thus, $\Re^2 \backslash M$ is generic and, generically, points in $\Re^2$ are not on the unit circle $M$.□

We are interested in finding conditions under which the set of preference profiles for which core points fail to exist is generic. The idea is to restrict attention just to those preference profiles $\rho$ that have smooth utility representations, i.e. $R_i$ is representable by a utility function, $u_i : X \to \Re$, possessing continuous partial derivatives of all orders. To save on notation,

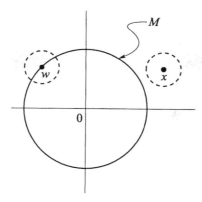

Figure 6.1: The circle $M$ is nongeneric in $\Re^2$

we describe profiles hereon by their utility representation; so $C_f(\rho) \equiv C_f(u)$ when $u = (u_1, \ldots, u_n)$ represents $\rho \in \mathcal{R}^n$. Let $\mathcal{U}$ denote the family of all smooth utility profiles on $X$ and let $f$ be a simple rule. Next, we define a particular superset of the core of $f$ defined by points $x \in X$ at which the differential $du(x)$ satisfies a specific restriction; then we look for a sufficient condition for the restriction to fail for "almost all" smooth profiles $u \in \mathcal{U}$ at every point $x \in X$, that is, to fail *generically*. This implies that the superset must generically be empty, which in turn implies that the core must generically be empty.

Example 6.1 illustrated the concept of genericity in terms of sets of points in $\Re^k$. Here, we need to extend the concept to sets of utility profiles in $\mathcal{U}$, and this requires specifying when it is that two utility profiles $u, u' \in \mathcal{U}$ are "close". Loosely speaking, we shall say $u$ is *within* $\epsilon$ *of* $u'$, where $\epsilon > 0$, if for all $x \in X$ and all $i \in N$, $|u_i(x) - u_i'(x)| < \epsilon$ and, for partial derivatives of all orders $t$, $|\partial^t u_i(x)/\partial x^t - \partial^t u_i'(x)/\partial x^t| < \epsilon$; that is the values of the functions $u_i$ and $u_i'$ are everywhere within $\epsilon$, as are the values of all the partial derivatives. Now, say that the set of utility profiles with empty cores is *dense* in $\mathcal{U}$ if, whenever $C_f(u)$ is not empty, for any $\epsilon > 0$ there exists a profile $u'$ within $\epsilon$ of $u$ for which the core $C_f(u')$ is empty; and say that this set of profiles is *open* in $\mathcal{U}$ if, whenever $C_f(u)$ is empty, there exists $\epsilon > 0$ such that, for all $u'$ within $\epsilon$ of $u$, $C_f(u')$ is empty as well. Then if it turns out that the set of utility profiles with empty cores is indeed dense and open in $\mathcal{U}$, we infer the existence of the core at $u$ is a non-generic property and, therefore, cannot be expected to constitute the typical situation; that is, the core is generically empty.

It is important to note here that the denseness condition does not require *all* utility profiles within a given $\epsilon$ to have nonempty cores, only that there is one such profile. To see why, recall Example 5.2 in the previous chapter in which a core point existed with Euclidean preferences. Moving the ideal points of individuals' 1 and 3 "out" a little while keeping 2's ideal point along the line connecting 1 and 3's, still supports a core point. So while there are a huge number of perturbations to the ideal points in that example that result in the core being empty, not every perturbation has this consequence.

Our first genericity result is not the strongest in that it identifies a bound for generic emptiness of the core that is not as low as possible. However, it provides a useful introduction to the logic underlying the general problem. Recall that $k$ is the dimension of the alternative space $X$ and, to save on notation, write the core of a $q$-rule as $C_q(\cdot)$.

**Theorem 6.1** *For any noncollegial $q$-rule, the core $C_q(\cdot)$ is generically empty on $\mathcal{U}$ if*

$$k > \sigma(n, q) \equiv \frac{(n - q + 1)(q - 1)}{(n - q)}.$$

So, for example, if $f$ is simple majority rule and $n$ is odd, $q = (n + 1)/2$ and the Theorem implies that $C_{f_m}(u)$ is almost always empty when the dimension of the issue space $k$ exceeds $(n + 1)/2$. And note that $\sigma(n, q)$ is increasing in $q$, implying that for a fixed value of $k$, lower values of $q$ are more likely to be associated with generic emptiness of the core.

Theorem 6.1 only addresses the question of core existence with respect to $q$-rules. However, we can generate an upper bound for the generic existence of the core for an arbitrary noncollegial rule $f$ using exactly the same arguments. If $f$ is noncollegial, the collection of decisive coalitions $\mathcal{L}(f)$ is such that, for every $i \in N$, there exists some coalition $L \in \mathcal{L}(f)$ with $i \notin L$. By monotonicity it must be that the coalition $N \setminus \{i\} \in \mathcal{L}(f)$ as well. Hence, if $x \in C_f(u)$ then necessarily $x$ is a core point for the $q$-rule with $q = n - 1$ as well. Therefore a sufficient condition for $C_f(u)$ to be empty is that $C_{n-1}(u)$ be empty and Theorem 6.1 yields,

**Corollary 6.1** *For any noncollegial rule $f$, the core $C_f(\cdot)$ is generically empty on $\mathcal{U}$ if $k > 2(n - 2)$.*

That is, if the dimension of $X$ exceeds $2n - 4$ the core of *any* noncollegial rule is generically empty.

We now turn to a formal justification of Theorem 6.1. The starting point is found in the necessity half of Lemma 5.6, which states that a necessary condition for a point $x$ to be Pareto efficient with respect to the coalition $L$ is that the gradient vectors of the members of $L$ are *semi-positively dependent* at $x$; that is, there exist $|L|$ nonnegative scalars $\{\lambda_i\}$ such that $\sum_L \lambda_i > 0$ and $0 = \sum_L \lambda_i \nabla u_i(x)$. This semi-positive dependence guarantees there is no direction away from $x$ that all members of the coalition $L$ prefer to move; further, since this half of Lemma 5.6 does not require voter preferences to be convex, in all of what follows preferences are only required to be representable by smooth utility functions. For any coalition $L \subseteq N$ and profile $u \in \mathcal{U}$ let

$$\mathcal{I}(L, u) = \{x \in X : \{\nabla u_i(x)\}_{i \in L} \text{ are semi-positively dependent}\}$$

and, for the simple rule $f$, define the *infinitessimal core* of $f$ under $u$ as

$$\mathcal{I}_f(u) = \bigcap_{L \in \mathcal{L}(f)} \mathcal{I}(L, u).$$

By Theorem 5.6,

$$C_f(u) \subseteq \mathcal{I}_f(u). \tag{a}$$

Therefore, if the infinitessimal core is empty then necessarily the core is empty.

Suppose now that instead of requiring semi-positive dependence of the gradient vectors $\{\nabla u_i(x)\}_{i \in L}$ at $x$, only *linear* dependence is required (i.e. $\forall i \in L$, $\lambda_i \in \Re$ and $\lambda_j \neq 0$ some $j$). For all coalitions $L \subseteq N$ and utility profiles $u$, define

$$\Lambda(L, u) = \{x \in X : \{\nabla u_i(x)\}_{i \in L} \text{ are linearly dependent}\}.$$

Thus for all $L \subseteq N$, $\mathcal{I}(L, u) \subseteq \Lambda(L, u)$. Finally, define

$$\Lambda_f(u) = \bigcap_{L \in \mathcal{L}(f)} \Lambda(L, u).$$

Then,

$$\mathcal{I}_f(u) \subseteq \Lambda_f(u). \tag{b}$$

Therefore if $\Lambda_f(u)$ is empty then, by (a) and (b), the core is empty.

Let $f$ be an arbitrary $q$-rule and write $\Lambda_q(u) = \Lambda_f(u)$. It turns out that determining whether a point $x$ is in $\Lambda_q(u)$ is equivalent to verifying a relatively simple property of the differential of the utility profile $u : X \to \Re^n$.

The map defined by this differential, $du(x) : \Re^k \to \Re^n$, is linear and therefore can be represented by the $(n \times k)$ Jacobian matrix

$$J_u(x) = \begin{bmatrix} \nabla u_1(x) \\ \nabla u_2(x) \\ \vdots \\ \nabla u_n(x) \end{bmatrix}.$$

The rank of $du(x)$ is given by the rank of the matrix $J_u(x)$, i.e. the maximum number of linearly independent rows or columns. Let $z = \min\{k, n\}$ and, for all $p = 0, \ldots, z$, define

$$S_p(u) = \{x \in X : \text{rank } J_u(x) = p\}$$

and let

$$S(u) = \bigcup_{p=0}^{z-1} S_p(u).$$

The set $S(u)$ consists of the *singularities* of the mapping $u : X \to \Re^n$; that is, points where the rank of the Jacobian $J_u(\cdot)$ is less than maximal. The set $\Lambda_q(u)$ will then be a subset of $S(u)$.

**Lemma 6.1** *Let $f$ be a $q$-rule. For all $u \in \mathcal{U}$, $\Lambda_q(u) = \bigcup_{p=0}^{q-1} S_p(u)$.*

**Proof.** $x \in \Lambda_q(u) \Leftrightarrow \forall L \in \mathcal{L}(f), \ x \in \Lambda(L, u)$
$\quad \Leftrightarrow \forall L \in \mathcal{L}(f), \ \{\nabla u_i(x)\}_{i \in L}$ are linearly dependent
$\quad \Leftrightarrow$ any set of $m \geq q$ gradient vectors are linearly dependent
$\quad \Leftrightarrow$ any set of $m \geq q$ rows in $J_u(x)$ are linearly dependent
$\quad \Leftrightarrow$ rank $J_u(x) \leq q - 1$
$\quad \Leftrightarrow x \in S_p(u)$ for some $p = 0, \ldots, q - 1$
$\quad \Leftrightarrow x \in \bigcup_{p=0}^{q-1} S_p(u).\square$

Therefore elements of $\Lambda_q(u)$ are precisely those points in $X$ where the rank of the Jacobian matrix $J_u(\cdot)$ is at most $q - 1$.

Let $\ell(k, n)$ denote the space of linear maps from $\Re^k$ to $\Re^n$; in particular for all $x \in X$ we have that $du(x) \in \ell(k, n)$. The space $\ell(k, n)$ can be identified with the set of all real $(n \times k)$ matrices, which is equivalent to $\Re^{n \times k}$ (with each coordinate in the latter giving one of the $n \times k$ entries in the matrix). For any $p = 0, \ldots, z$ let $\ell_p(k, n)$ be the elements in $\ell(k, n)$ of rank $p$; the collection $\{\ell_p(k, n)\}_{p=0}^z$ then partitions the space of real $n \times k$ matrices.

Next let $du : X \to \ell(k, n)$ be the mapping which assigns to every point $x$ in $X$ the linear map $du(x)$ and let

$$du^{-1}(\ell_p(k, n)) = \{x \in X : du(x) \in \ell_p(k, n)\};$$

that is, an alternative $x \in X$ is in $du^{-1}(\ell_p(k, n))$ if the differential of $u$ at $x$ is a linear map of rank $p$. Then $x \in X$ is an element of the set $S_p(u)$ if and only if $du(x) \in \ell_p(k, n)$:

$$S_p(u) = du^{-1}(\ell_p(k, n)). \qquad (c)$$

That is, a singularity point of the utility profile $u$ is an element of $X$ where the mapping $du$ intersects the set $\ell_p(k, n)$ for some integer $p < z$.

A certain class of these intersections have the attractive properties that, first, they are the "generic" form of intersection (in the sense of genericity described above) and, second, when such intersections occur the sets $S_p(u)$ are nicely behaved; these are the *transversal* intersections. While the formal definition of transversality is quite technical, the underlying intuition is fairly straightforward and enough for our purposes. To develop this intuition, consider the following simple examples.

**Example 6.2** Let $f : \Re \to \Re^2$ be the function, $f(x) = (x, x^2)$, i.e. the graph of $x^2$, and let $M = \{(x_1, x_2) \in \Re^2 : x_1^2 + x_2^2 = 1\}$ be the unit circle in $\Re^2$ centered at zero; see Figure 6.2(a). The function $f$ intersects the set $M$ at exactly two points, and so the inverse image of the set $M$ under the function $f$, $f^{-1}(M)$, consists of exactly 2 points in the domain of the function $f$. Hence, $f^{-1}(M)$ is a zero-dimensional set in $\Re$. Further, note that any function $\hat{f}$ sufficiently close to $f$ must also intersect the set $M$, and do so a finite number of times. Next, suppose we have a function $g : \Re \to \Re^2$ as in Figure 6.2(b); here the function $g$ intersects the set $M$ in more than a finite number of places, and so $g^{-1}(M)$ is not zero-dimensional, but rather one-dimensional. However, we can always find functions $\hat{g}$ close to $g$ such that either $\hat{g}$ does not intersect $M$ ($\hat{g}_1$ in Figure 6.2(b)), or else intersects $M$ a finite number of times ($\hat{g}_2$ in Figure 6.2(b)). We wish to distinguish between the "crosswise" intersection of $f$ with $M$ found in Figure 6.2(a) with the "tangential" intersection of $g$ with $M$ found in Figure 6.2(b): the former are stable under perturbations of the function while the latter are not, and it is precisely these "crosswise" intersections that are transversal. As a final example in $\Re^2$, consider Figure 6.2(c) in which the function $h : \Re \to \Re^2$ does not intersect the unit circle $M$ at all. Clearly, any function $\hat{h}$ close to $h$ also fails to intersect $M$. In this case, then, the inverse image of $M$ is empty.□

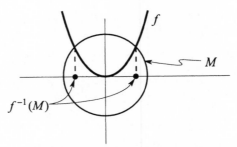

(a) inverse image $f^{-1}(M)$ nonempty, zero-dimensional

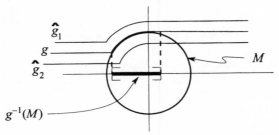

(b) inverse image $g^{-1}(M)$ nonempty, one-dimensional

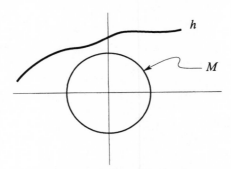

(c) inverse image $h^{-1}(M)$ empty

Figure 6.2: Inverse images for Example 6.2

Generalizing from Example 6.2, the set of smooth functions from $\Re$ into $\Re^2$ which either do not intersect the set $M$ or else intersect it transversally constitutes an open and dense set. Furthermore, the transversal intersections are such that the inverse image of $M$ is zero-dimensional. The next example illustrates possibilities for higher dimensional spaces.

**Example 6.3** Define $f : \Re \to \Re^3$ by $f(x) = (x, x^2, 0)$ and let $M \subset \Re^3$ be defined by $M = \{(x_1, x_2, x_3) : x_1^2 + x_2^2 = 1, x_3 = 0\}$, i.e. there is a third dimension in Figure 6.2(a) coming out from the page. As before $f$ intersects $M$ at two points and so $f^{-1}(M)$ is zero-dimensional. However, unlike the two-dimensional situation of Example 6.2(a), now we can find a function $\hat{f}$ close to $f$ which does not intersect $M$ at all; for example $\hat{f}(x) = (x, x^2, \delta)$ where $\delta > 0$. In fact, for *any* function which intersects $M$ we can find a nearby function which does not intersect $M$, simply by using this third dimension as an extra degree of freedom. Therefore, not all intersections are stable under perturbations and so are not transversal. Moreover, the set of smooth functions from $\Re$ into $\Re^3$ which do not intersect $M$ is open and dense.□

Thus, when mapping into $\Re^2$, the dimension of the domain of the functions is 1, the dimension of the set $M$ is 1, and the dimension of the space in which $M$ and the image of $f$ lives is 2; and the conclusion is that "generically" functions either do not intersect $M$ at all or else are transversal and generate a zero-dimensional inverse image of $M$ (Example 6.2). But when mapping into $\Re^3$, although it is still the case that the first two identified dimensions are still 1, the set $M$ and the image of the functions live in 3 dimensions, with the conclusion being that "generically" functions do not intersect $M$ at all (Example 6.3). What happens if instead of increasing the dimensionality of the space, the dimensionality of the relevant manifold (the set $M$ in the preceding examples) is increased? Example 6.4 provides an illustration.

**Example 6.4** Let $M$ be the unit disk in $\Re^2$: $M = \{(x_1, x_2) : x_1^2 + x_2^2 \leq 1\}$. Then $M$ is a two-dimensional, rather than a one-dimensional, manifold. Again defining $f : \Re \to \Re^2$ by $f(x) = (x, x^2)$, the inverse image of $M$ under $f$ is now one-dimensional, as it is for functions close to $f$; see Figure 6.3(a). Thus the intersection of $f$ with $M$ is again transversal or "crosswise". On the other hand, Figure 6.3(b) illustrates a non-transversal or "tangential" intersection of a function $g : \Re \to \Re^2$ with $M$ so that, in particular, nearby functions do not intersect $M$ at all. And as before, if a function $h : \Re \to \Re^2$ does not intersect $M$ then functions near to $h$ do not intersect $M$ either; see Figure 6.3(c). In this example, therefore, the dimension of the domain of functions is 1, the dimension of the set $M$ is 2, and $M$ and the image of $f$ live in 2 dimensions, with the conclusion being that generically functions either do not intersect $M$ at all and so have empty inverse images, or else are transversal and have one-dimensional inverse images. On the other hand,

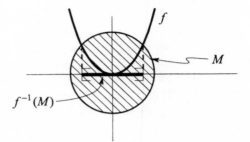

(a) inverse image $f^{-1}(M)$ one-dimensional

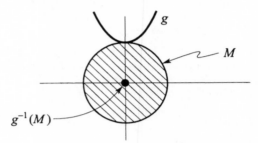

(b) inverse image $g^{-1}(M)$ zero-dimensional

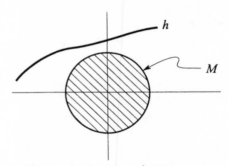

(c) inverse image $h^{-1}(M)$ empty

Figure 6.3: Inverse images for Example 6.4

if we again embed $f$ and $M$ in $\Re^3$, then $f^{-1}(M)$ remains one-dimensional but there exist nearby functions for which this is no longer true (e.g. use $\hat{f}$ above). Yet in this three-dimensional setup we can imagine functions going "through" $M$ and having nearby functions which go "through" $M$ as well.

Thus in general functions from $\Re$ to $\Re^3$ either do not intersect $M$ at all or else are transversal and generate *zero*-dimensional inverse images.□

Intuitively, then, transversal intersections of a smooth function and a manifold are those that are stable under arbitrary perturbations of the function. The examples make apparent that whether an intersection is transversal, and what the dimension of the inverse image of the manifold might be, depend critically on the dimensionalities of the domain and range of the function and of the manifold. More formally, let $h : \Re^s \to \Re^t$ be an arbitrary smooth function and let $M$ be an $m$-dimensional manifold in $\Re^t$. The mapping $h$ is *transversal to* $M$ if at every point $x$ in $\Re^s$ either (i) $h(x) \notin M$, or (ii) $h$ intersects $M$ transversally at $x$. Equivalently, $h$ is transversal to $M$ if all intersections are transversal. Next, define the *codimension* of an $m$-dimensional manifold $M \subset \Re^t$ to be $c \equiv t - m$, i.e. the number of additional or "free" dimensions in the space $\Re^t$. The following result, a proof of which is in Levine [43], generalizes the earlier examples.

**Lemma 6.2** *Suppose $h : \Re^s \to \Re^t$ is transversal to a manifold $M$ in $\Re^t$ of codimension $c$; then $h^{-1}(M)$ is either empty or a manifold in $\Re^s$ of codimension $c$.*

Of particular importance here is this: if $h$ is transversal to $M$, and if $c = (t - m)$ is strictly greater than $s$, then the dimension of $h^{-1}(M)$ is less than zero implying $h^{-1}(M)$ is empty. That is, if $c > s$ then the only way $h$ can be transversal to $M$ is if $h$ *never* intersects $M$.

Returning to the argument for Theorem 6.1, we have a mapping $du : \Re^k \to \Re^{n \times k} \equiv \ell(k,n)$ and a subset $\ell_p(k,n)$ describing the rank-$p$ linear maps, where it can be shown that the set $\ell_p(k,n)$ constitutes a manifold in $\ell(k,n)$ of codimension equal to $(k-p)(n-p)$ (Levine [43]). Further, $S_p(u)$, the set of points $x \in X$ for which the differential $du(x)$ is of rank $p$, is given by the set $du^{-1}(\ell_p(k,n))$, the inverse image of the set $\ell_p(k,n)$ under the mapping $du$. Therefore, by Lemma 6.2, if $du$ is transversal to $\ell_p(k,n)$ then $S_p(u)$ is either empty or else a manifold in $\Re^k$ of codimension $(k-p)(n-p)$; hence

$$\dim S_p(u) = k - (n-p)(k-p). \tag{d}$$

In general, then, whenever the inequality

$$k < (n-p)(k-p) \tag{e}$$

holds we know that if $du$ is transversal to $\ell_p(k,n)$ then $S_p(u)$ is empty.

Next, note that the right-hand side of (e) is decreasing in $p$; therefore if $(k, n, p)$ satisfies (e) then $(k, n, p')$, with $p' < p$, satisfies (e) as well. Thus by Lemma 6.1, if $du$ is transversal to $\ell_p(k, n)$ for all $p$, then to insure that $\Lambda_q(u)$ is empty it suffices to check that $p = q - 1$ satisfies (e). This gives the following inequality guaranteeing the emptiness of $\Lambda_q(u)$ when transversality holds:

$$
\begin{aligned}
k &< (n - q + 1)(k - q + 1) \Leftrightarrow \\
k &> (n - q + 1)(q - 1)/(n - q) \equiv \sigma(n, q)
\end{aligned}
\tag{f}
$$

Thus, by (a), (b), Lemma 6.1 and (f) we have that whenever $k$ is greater than $\sigma(n, q)$ and $du$ is transversal to all $\ell_p(k, n)$ the core $C_q(u)$ is empty.

It remains to establish that, as claimed above, transversality is indeed the "typical" state of affairs; i.e. $C_q(u) \neq \emptyset$ when $k > \sigma(n, q)$ is a knife-edge property. Recall that two profiles $u, u' \in \mathcal{U}$ are close if the values of the functions as well as partial derivatives of all orders are close; a subset $V$ of $\mathcal{U}$ is *dense* if for any $u \in \mathcal{U}$ and any neighborhood $W$ of $u$, it is the case that $W \cap V \neq \emptyset$; and a property $K$ of utility profiles is *generic* if the set $\{u$ satisfies $K\}$ constitutes an open and dense subset of $\mathcal{U}$. Say that a subset $V$ of $\mathcal{U}$ is *residual* if it contains a countable intersection of open dense sets. Then by the Transversality Theorem of Thom (Golubitsky and Guillemin [33]), the set

$$\{u \in \mathcal{U} : du \text{ is transversal to } \ell_p(k, n)\}$$

is residual for any $p < \min\{k, n\}$. Furthermore, under the appropriate structure on $\mathcal{U}$ for which $u, u'$ being close is precisely defined (the Whitney $C^\infty$ topology), $\mathcal{U}$ is a space in which all residual subsets are dense; and since a finite intersection of residual sets is residual, the set

$$S^* = \{u \in \mathcal{U} : \forall p = 0, \ldots, q - 1, du \text{ is transversal to } \ell_p(k, n)\}$$

is residual (given $q - 1 < k$) and therefore dense in $\mathcal{U}$. Finally, using results in Levine [43] and Golubitsky and Guillemin [33], it follows that such subsets are open as well. Therefore $du$ is generically transversal to $\ell_p(k, n)$ for all $p$, as required. In particular, $S_p(u)$ is generically empty whenever the parameters $(k, n, p)$ are such that (e) holds, or more generally that $\Lambda_q(u)$ is generically empty whenever $k > \sigma(n, q)$. Theorem 6.1 follows.

As remarked earlier, the sufficient condition for generic emptiness of cores in Theorem 6.1 is strong. Using the restrictions on gradient vectors identified in Theorem 5.8, it is possible to derive tighter bounds on the dimensionality of the policy space for which a given $q$-rule generically has an empty core. In particular, a proof for the following result is given by Saari [67].

**Theorem 6.2** *Assume $n \geq 5$. For any noncollegial $q$-rule, the core $C_q(\cdot)$ is generically empty on $\mathcal{U}$ if*

$$k > \bar{\sigma}(q, n) \equiv 2q - n + \max\{\frac{4q - 3n - 1}{2(n - q)}, 0\}.$$

(A version of this theorem holds for $n = 3$ and $n = 4$. However, the precise statements for these cases are a little more involved and we omit them here: see Saari [67].) For example, when $n$ is odd (even), the theorem implies that majority rule core points generically do not exist when the dimensionality of the policy space is at least two (three). And arguing exactly as for Corollary 6.1, Theorem 6.2 implies

**Corollary 6.2** *Asume $n \geq 5$. For any noncollegial rule $f$, the core $C_f(\cdot)$ is generically empty on $\mathcal{U}$ if $k > 3(n - 3)/2$.*

Recall from Lemma 3.2 that the Nakamura number for any noncollegial $q$-rule is $s(q, n) = \lceil n/(n - q) \rceil$. And by Theorem 5.3, the core of such a $q$-rule is nonempty *for all $u \in \mathcal{U}$* only if $k \leq s(q, n) - 2$. On the other hand, Theorem 6.2 says that for $n \geq 5$ and dimensions $k > \bar{\sigma}(q, n)$, the core of the $q$-rule is generically empty. Consequently, for many $(q, n)$ pairs, there exist integers $k$ such that, for $s(q, n) - 2 < k \leq \bar{\sigma}(q, n)$, there may exist *some* profiles $u \in \mathcal{U}$ for which the $q$-rule core is nonempty and for which arbitrary perturbations of such profiles do *not* lead to empty cores. Once the dimensionality of the space exceeds $\bar{\sigma}(q, n)$, however, *no* profile $u \in \mathcal{U}$ for which core points exist is robust to arbitrary perturbations; in other words, core points generically fail to exist.

## 6.2 Application: Distributive politics revisited

The genericity results above are, like their predecessors in earlier chapters, stated and proved at a fairly high level of abstraction. To provide some context for the results, consider the following example: suppose we think of the set $N = \{1, .., n\}$ of individuals as being representatives to a legislature from districts, each with two members or more, so that the overall population size, $s$, is at least $2n$. Let the issue before the legislature be how to divide a fixed amount of monetary benefits $m > 0$, not between the $n$ districts but rather between the $s$ individuals in the population. Therefore the policy space is $X = \{(x_1, \ldots, x_s) \in \Re^s_+ : \sum x_i = m\}$, and hence has dimension $s - 1 \geq 2n - 1$.

In terms of the preferences on $X$ of any legislator $j \in N$, we might consider that in principle they are intimately related through the electoral process to the underlying preferences in $j$'s constituency. Thus relevant questions become: What are the constituent-level preferences over the distribution of benefits, and how do these preferences get translated into legislator-level preferences? However, even without offering any detailed answers to these questions, Corollary 6.1 (and Corollary 6.2) allows us to say something about the subsequent legislative interaction. Specifically, as long as legislator preferences on $X$ are smooth it is almost always the case that a core point fails to exist for any noncollegial simple rule. In particular, for any distribution $x \in X$ of benefits across the $s$ individuals, there invariably exists some distinct distribution $y \in X$ and a coalition of at least $n - 1$ legislators who prefer $y$ to $x$. Therefore, unless individual preferences and the mechanism mapping them into legislative preferences generate the knife-edge property of core points identified in Chapter 5, one cannot reasonably explain the complex distributional choices made by a legislature as being the product of a social preference maximization exercise.

## 6.3   Cycles

One of the central results of Chapter 5 is that in sufficiently high dimensional spaces, the existence of a nonempty core for any noncollegial voting rule cannot be guaranteed. Moreover, as Theorem 6.1 and its subsequent corollary indicates, the existence of a core in high dimensions is fragile: perturbing the preference profile slightly typically leads to the core vanishing. *Inter alia*, this suggests that concepts such as the "will of the majority" are frequently vacuous: when the core is empty, there is *always* some alternative and a decisive coalition in favor of changing the status quo to that alternative. Although, from a practical perspective, the existence results are fundamental, questions concerning the structure of a given rule when the core is empty are both natural and normatively relevant. The latter concern derives from the following considerations.

Fix a preference profile $\rho \in \mathcal{R}^n$ and a simple rule $f$. When the core $C_f(\rho)$ is empty, there is no alternative that is unequivocally "at least as good as" every other alternative as measured by the criteria embodied in $f$. And since the social preference relation $R = f(\rho)$ is lower continuous whenever individual preferences are (Lemma 5.1), there must exist a collective preference *cycle* of the form $a_1 P a_2 P \ldots a_r P a_1$ (since from Chapter 5 we know that any lower continuous and acyclic relation will have a maximal element on a compact set).

**Definition 6.1** *For any set $X$, the top cycle set for $(f, \rho)$ in $X$ is given by*

$$T_f(\rho) = \{x \in X : \forall y \in X \backslash \{x\}, \exists \{a_0, a_1, \ldots, a_r\} \subset X \text{ such that } \\ a_0 = x, a_r = y, r < \infty \text{ and}, \forall t \leq r - 1, \ a_t P a_{t+1} \}.$$

In other words, $x$ is in the top cycle set if and only if we can get to $x$ from *any* $y$ via the asymmetric part of $f$ in a finite number of steps. For example, suppose $f$ and $\rho$ are such that $x P y, y P z, z P x$ and, for all $w \notin \{x, y, z\}$, for all $v \in \{x, y, z\}$, $v P w$; then $T_f(\rho) = \{x, y, z\}$. Notice that any finite number of alternatives from the top cycle set $\{x_s\}_{s=1}^t$ is contained in a collective preference cycle, since one can get from $x_1$ to $x_2$ in a finite number of steps, from $x_2$ to $x_3$, ... and from $x_t$ back to $x_1$. Furthermore, no alternative outside of the top cycle set can be socially preferred to any alternative inside the set, since if $z P x$ and $x \in T_f(\rho)$ then $z$ can reach any other alternative via $P$ (through $x$) in a finite number of steps.

When the set of alternatives $X$ is finite and the strict social preference relation is complete (as is the case, for example, with majority rule, $n$ odd and no individual indifference), it is readily checked that the top cycle set is never empty and coincides with the core when $C_f(\rho)$ is not empty [Exercise]. As such it seems an attractive candidate for making collective choices even when the core is empty. This sort of prescription, however, is only persuasive if the top cycle set is in some sense "small" relative to $X$, since otherwise the constraint on social choice is minimal. For instance, we might like $T_f(\cdot)$ to contain only Pareto undominated alternatives; i.e. $T_f(\rho) \subseteq PS_N(\rho)$. Unfortunately this is not a general property even in the finite world.

**Example 6.5** Let $N = \{1, 2, 3\}$, $X = \{w, x, y, z\}$, $f$ be majority rule, and $\rho$ given by

$$z P_1 x P_1 y P_1 w$$
$$w P_2 z P_2 x P_2 y$$
$$y P_3 w P_3 z P_3 x.$$

Then $x \in T_f(\rho)$, since $x P y, y P w$ and $w P z$; but, $\forall i \in N$, $z P_i x$. $\square$

In this example the top cycle set $T_f(\rho)$ is the whole of $X$, calling its prescriptive qualities for collective choice into question. In fact, it turns out that in the spatial model the coincidence of the top cycle set with all of $X$ is, in a somewhat analogous sense to what was found in Section 6.1, the "typical" state of affairs for strong simple rules. This section is concerned with making this claim precise, where rather than assuming smooth utility representations and relying on genericity results from differential topology, we will simply assume continuous, convex preferences and argue that the conditions needed for $T_f(\rho)$ *not* to coincide with $X$ are so severe as to make them highly unlikely.

**Definition 6.2** *Let $f$ be a strong simple rule; $x, y \in X$; $\rho \in \mathcal{R}^n$; and $i, j \in N$. Say that, with respect to $\{x, y\}$ :*
   *(1) $i$ is a dummy voter at $\rho$ if, for all $L \subseteq N\backslash\{i\}$,*

$$[P(x, y; \rho)\backslash\{i\} \subseteq L \subseteq N\backslash P(y, x; \rho)]$$

*implies that $L \cup \{i\} \in \mathcal{L}(f)$ only if $L \in \mathcal{L}(f)$.*
   *(2) $i$ is as strong as $j$ at $\rho$ if, for all $L \subseteq N\backslash\{i, j\}$,*

$$[P(x, y; \rho)\backslash\{i, j\} \subseteq L \subseteq N\backslash P(y, x; \rho)]$$

*implies that $L \cup \{j\} \in \mathcal{L}(f)$ only if $L \cup \{i\} \in \mathcal{L}(f)$.*

In other words, if $i$ is a dummy voter at $\rho$ with respect to some pair of alternatives, then $i$ is incapable of influencing the social preference ranking of that pair, however individuals indifferent over the pair are treated. On the other hand, if $i$ is as strong as $j$ at $\rho$ with respect to some pair of alternatives, then for every coalition $L$ that excludes $i$ and $j$, $L \cup \{j\}$ is decisive over the pair only if $L \cup \{i\}$ is decisive over the pair. It is straightforward to check that if the rule $f$ is anonymous then every individual is as strong as every other individual at all pairs of alternatives [Exercise]. Example 6.6 illustrates these definitions.

**Example 6.6** Consider three cases.
   (1) In this case, all individuals are as strong as each other, while certain individuals are dummy voters for some pair of alternatives but not for others. Let $N = \{1, \ldots, 7\}$, let $f$ be simple majority rule and consider the following profile on $\{x, y, z\}$:

$$
\begin{aligned}
i &= 1, 2 & & yP_i z P_i x \\
i &= 3, 4 & & z P_i x I_i y \\
i &= 5 & & x I_i y I_i z \\
i &= 6, 7 & & x P_i z P_i y
\end{aligned}
$$

Since majority rule is anonymous, each individual is as strong as any other. However, we claim that individual 1 is not a dummy voter at $\{x, y\}$ (indeed, no individual is a dummy voter here) but 1 (along with 2 and 5) is a dummy voter at $\{z, y\}$. To check the former, set $L = \{5, 6, 7\}$ and note that $1 \notin L$ and that $P(x, y; \rho) \backslash \{1\} \subseteq L \subseteq N \backslash P(y, x; \rho)$. Then $L \cup \{1\} \in \mathcal{L}(f)$ and $L \notin \mathcal{L}(f)$. To show 1 *is* a dummy voter at $\{z, y\}$, note that $P(z, y; \rho) \backslash \{1\} = \{3, 4, 6, 7\} \in \mathcal{L}(f)$ and therefore any coalition $L$ satisfying the condition above must also be decisive.

(2) In this case, neither of individuals 1 or 2 is a dummy voter at a pair of alternatives, but whereas 1 is as strong as 2, 2 is not as strong as 1 at that pair. Let $N = \{1, \ldots, 5\}$, let $f$ be weighted majority rule with weights $w_1 = 0.4$, $w_2 = \ldots = w_5 = 0.15$. Consider the profile:

$$
\begin{aligned}
i &= 1, 2 & x P_i y \\
i &= 3 & x I_i y \\
i &= 4, 5 & y P_i x
\end{aligned}
$$

We claim neither individual 1 nor 2 is a dummy voter at $\{x, y\}$, however 2 is not as strong as 1. To see the former, let $L = \{2\}$ and note that $L \cup \{1\}$ is decisive but $L$ is not; so 1 is not a dummy voter. And switching the roles of 1 and 2, the same argument gives that 2 is not a dummy voter either. To check the second claim, note first that since $P(x, y; \rho) \backslash \{1, 2\} = \emptyset$ and $N \backslash P(y, x; \rho) = \{1, 2, 3\}$, the only sets we have to consider are $L = \emptyset$ and $L = \{3\}$. When $L$ is empty, adding $i \in \{1, 2\}$ leaves $L \cup \{i\}$ not decisive. However, when $L = \{3\}$, $L \cup \{1\}$ is decisive but $L \cup \{2\}$ is not.

(3) Finally, we give an example in which individual 1 is a dummy voter at a pair and 2 is not, yet 1 is as strong as 2 at that pair. To do this, use the same set $N$ and rule $f$ as in (2). Let the profile be:

$$
\begin{aligned}
i &= 1 & x I_i y \\
i &= 2, \ldots, 5 & x P_i y
\end{aligned}
$$

First note that $P(x, y; \rho) = \{2, \ldots, 5\}$ so that any superset $L$ of this set is decisive, so 1 is a dummy voter at $\{x, y\}$. On the other hand, setting $L = \{3, 4, 5\}$ we have that $L \cup \{2\}$ is decisive but $L$ is not, so 2 is not a dummy voter. To see that 1 is as strong as 2, note that $P(x, y; \rho) \backslash \{1, 2\} = \{3, 4, 5\}$ and so any superset $L$ must be such that both $L \cup \{1\}$ and $L \cup \{2\}$ are decisive. $\square$

Next we introduce a weak heterogeneity property on preferences, which employs the following mathematical concepts. For any set $B \subseteq \Re^k$, the *relative topology of B in* $\Re^k$ is the family of sets, say $\mathcal{J}$, given by the intersection

of $B$ with every open set in $\Re^k$; then, for any set $A \subset B$, say that $A$ has
an *empty interior* in the relative topology of $B$ if the only set $V \in \mathcal{J}$ such
that $V \subseteq A$ is the empty set. For any $i \in N$ and any $w \in X \subseteq \Re^k$, let
$I_i(w) = \{y \in X : yI_iw\}$. Note that for $R_i$ strictly convex and continuous
(i.e. $R_i \in \mathcal{R}_{cs}$), $i$ has a unique ideal point in $X$ and, therefore, for all points
$w$ in the space other than this, $I_i(w)$ will contain a continuum of alternatives
in $X$.

**Definition 6.3** *A profile $\rho \in \mathcal{R}^n_{cs}$ satisfies diversity if, for all $x \in X$ and
for all $i, j \in N$ such that $x$ is neither individual's ideal point, $I_j(x) \cap I_i(x)$
has an empty interior in the relative topology on $I_i(x)$.*

Diversity is a mild requirement on the distribution of preferences, precluding
individuals' indifference surfaces being the same on an open neighborhood
of any point. In $\Re^2$, for example, this means that any pair of individuals' indifference curves through any point coincide only on a discrete set of points;
Figure 6.4 illustrates this for two individuals.

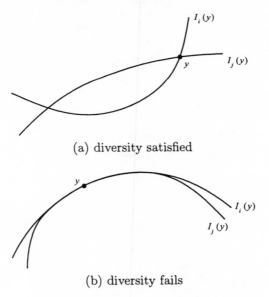

(a) diversity satisfied

(b) diversity fails

Figure 6.4: The diversity condition in $\Re^2$

And in $\Re^k$ the condition is satisfied if preferences are Euclidean and all
individuals' ideal points in $X$ are distinct.

Finally, let $P$ be the strict preference relation defined from a simple rule $f$; for any $\rho \in \mathcal{R}^n$ and $x \in X$, define

$$Q_{f(\rho)}(x) = \{y \in X : \exists \{a_0, a_1, \ldots, a_r\} \subset X \text{ such that}$$
$$a_0 = x, a_r = y, r < \infty \text{ and, } \forall t \leq r - 1, \ a_{t+1} P a_t\}.$$

Thus $Q_{f(\rho)}(x)$ is the set of feasible alternatives reachable from $x$ via the asymmetric part of the social preference relation $f(\rho)$. Note that for all $x \in T_f(\rho)$ and for all $y \in X$, $x \in Q_{f(\rho)}(y)$. Where there is no ambiguity about the rule, the subscript $f(\cdot)$ is dropped and we simply write $Q(x)$.

For any set $Y \subseteq X$, let $Y^c$, $\partial Y$, and $\bar{Y}$, respectively, denote the *complement, boundary*, and the *closure* of $Y$ in $X$:

$$
\begin{aligned}
Y^c &= X \backslash Y, \\
\partial Y &= \{y \in X : \forall \epsilon > 0, \ B(y, \epsilon) \cap Y \neq \emptyset \ \& \ B(y, \epsilon) \cap Y^c \neq \emptyset\}, \\
\bar{Y} &= \cap \{Z \subseteq X : Z \text{ is closed and } Z \supseteq Y\},
\end{aligned}
$$

where, as before, $B(y, \epsilon) = \{w \in X : \|w - y\| < \epsilon\}$. To avoid some technical complications with respect to boundary points of the set $X$, assume hereafter that $X = \Re^k$ (i.e. $X$ remains closed and convex but is no longer bounded). Furthermore we assume preferences are continuous and strictly convex, although this too is stronger than necessary. See McKelvey [49] for a proof of the following result that imposes virtually no restrictions on the set $X$ and assumes preferences are only continuous with thin indifference sets.

**Theorem 6.3** *Let $X = \Re^k$, $f$ be a strong simple rule and suppose $\rho \in \mathcal{R}^n_{cs}$ satisfies diversity. Then for any $x \in X$, either $\partial Q(x) = \emptyset$ or both (1) and (2) obtain:*

*(1) There exists some $j \in N$ such that, for all $y \in \partial Q(x)$, $\partial Q(x) \subseteq I_j(y)$;*

*(2) If $y, z \in \partial Q(x)$ with $z \in I_i(y)$ for some $i \in N \backslash \{j\}$ and either $i$ is not a dummy voter or $i$ is as strong as $j$ with respect to $\{y, z\}$ at $\rho$, then there exists $\ell \in N \backslash \{i, j\}$ such that $z \in I_\ell(y)$.*

**Proof.** Let $x \in X$ and assume $\partial Q(x) \neq \emptyset$; we need to show that both (1) and (2) hold on the boundary $\partial Q(x)$. We do this via a sequence of seven claims.

*Claim 1*: $Q(x)$ is open.

*Proof:* Since individuals' preferences are continuous, $\forall y \in X$ and $\forall i \in N$, $P_i(y)$ is open. Recall $P_L(y) \equiv \cap_{i \in L} P_i(y)$; so $P_L(y)$ is open since it is a finite intersection of open sets. By definition, $zPy$ iff $z \in [\cup_{L\in\mathcal{L}(f)}P_L(y)] \equiv P(y)$; hence $P(y)$ is open since it is a finite union of open sets. Finally, $y \in Q(x)$ iff there exists a finite sequence $(a_0 \equiv x, a_1, \ldots, a_r \equiv y)$ with $a_{t+1} \in P(a_t)$ all $t$; hence $y \in \cup_t P(a_t)$, a finite union of open sets and so open.

*Claim 2*: $y, z \in \partial Q(x)$ implies $yIz$.

*Proof*: By supposition, $\partial Q(x) \neq \emptyset$ and so $Q(x) \neq \emptyset$. Now suppose $y, z \in \partial Q(x)$ and $yPz$; then $yP_Lz$ for some $L \in \mathcal{L}(f)$. Since $P_L(z)$ is open $\exists \epsilon > 0$ such that, $\forall w \in B(z, \epsilon) = \{w \in X : \|w - z\| < \epsilon\}$, $yP_Lw$. Hence, $\forall w \in B(z, \epsilon)$, $yPw$. By hypothesis, $z \in \partial Q(x)$. Since $Q(x)$ is open, $\exists w' \in B(z, \epsilon) \cap Q(x)$. But, by definition of $Q(x)$, $yPw'$ implies $y \in Q(x)$ and, therefore, since $Q(x)$ is open, $y \notin \partial Q(x)$; contradiction.

*Claim 3*: $Q(x)$ is convex.

*Proof*: Let $y, z \in Q(x)$ and consider $b = \lambda y + (1 - \lambda)z$, $\lambda \in (0, 1)$. By $X$ convex, $b \in X$. By $P$ complete, either $yRz$ or $zRy$. Without loss of generality, assume $yRz$; then $P(z, y; \rho) \notin \mathcal{L}(f)$ and so, by $f$ strong, $R(y, z; \rho) \in \mathcal{L}(f)$. Since $P_i$ is strictly convex, $\forall i \in R(y, z; \rho)$, $bP_iz$ implying, $bPz$. Therefore, $z \in Q(x)$ implies $b \in Q(x)$.

*Claim 4*: $\forall y \in \partial Q(x)$, $P(y) = Q(x)$.

*Proof*: Let $y \in \partial Q(x)$, $w \in Q(x)$. By Claims 1 and 3 and the fact that $X = \Re^k$, $\exists z \in Q(x)$ such that $w = \lambda y + (1 - \lambda)z$ for some $\lambda \in (0, 1)$. By $y \notin Q(x)$, $zRy$; hence convex preferences and $f$ strong imply $wPy$. Since $w$ is arbitrary, therefore, $Q(x) \subseteq P(y)$. Now let $z \in X\backslash\overline{Q(x)}$ and suppose $zPy$; then $zP_Ly$ for some $L \in \mathcal{L}(f)$. Since $P_L(y)$ is open $\exists \epsilon > 0$ such that, $\forall w \in B(y, \epsilon) = \{w \in X : \|w - y\| < \epsilon\}$, $zP_Lw$. Hence, $\forall w \in B(y, \epsilon)$, $zPw$. By hypothesis, $y \in \partial Q(x)$. Since $Q(x)$ is nonempty and open, $\exists w' \in B(y, \epsilon) \cap Q(x)$. But by definition of $Q(x)$, $zPw'$ implies $z \in Q(x)$ : contradiction. Hence $P(y) \subseteq \overline{Q(x)}$. Finally, by Claim 2, $\partial Q(x) \cap P(y) = \emptyset$ : therefore, $P(y) = Q(x)$.

*Claim 5*: $\exists j \in N$ such that, $\forall y, z \in \partial Q(x)$, $yI_jz$.

*Proof*: By Claim 4, $\forall w \in \partial Q(x)$,

$$P(w) \equiv \bigcup_{L\in\mathcal{L}(f)} [\bigcap_{i\in L} P_i(w)] = Q(x) \neq \emptyset.$$

Hence, $\forall w \in \partial Q(x)$, $\partial Q(x) \subseteq \cup_{i\in N} I_i(w)$. For all $i \in N$ and all $y \in \partial Q(x)$, let $J_i(y) = I_i(y) \cap \partial Q(x)$. Then $\forall y \in \partial Q(x)$, $\partial Q(x) = \cup_{i\in N} J_i(y)$. Since $N$ is finite and $Q(x)$ is open, $\exists j \in N$ such that the relative interior of $J_j(y_1)$ is not empty for some $y_1 \in \partial Q(x)$; without loss of generality, set $j = 1$. Now define a sequence of points $\{y_i\}_{i=1}^{i=n} \subset J_1(y_1)$ such that, for all $\ell > 1$, for all

$r, s \in \{1, \ldots, n\}$, $\sim [y_r I_\ell y_s]$. That such a sequence exists follows from the diversity assumption and the choice of $J_1(y_1)$ (loosely speaking, there are a lot more points in $J_1(y_1)$ than in $\cup_{\ell \neq 1}[J_1(y_1) \cap J_\ell(y_1)]$): see Figure 6.5.

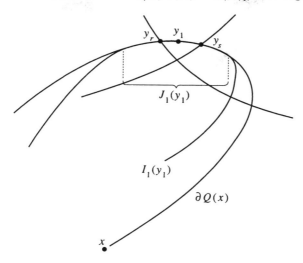

Figure 6.5: Construction for Claim 5

Because $y_i \in \partial Q(x)$ all $i = 1, \ldots, n$ and, for all $w \in \partial Q(x)$, $\cup_{i \in N} J_i(w) = \partial Q(x)$, we have for all $r, s \in N$:

$$\partial Q(x) = \cup_{i \in N} J_i(y_r) = \cup_{i \in N} J_i(y_s). \tag{\dagger}$$

Now suppose $J_1(y_1) \neq \partial Q(x)$. Then $\exists z \in \partial Q(x) \backslash J_1(y_1)$. By construction, $J_1(y_i) = J_1(y_1)$ $\forall i = 1, \ldots, n$; hence, ($\dagger$) implies that, $\forall i = 1, \ldots, n$, $z \in \cup_{\ell=2}^{\ell=n} J_\ell(y_i)$. But then, for some $\ell > 2$ and some $r, s \in N$, we must have $z \in J_\ell(y_r) \cap J_\ell(y_s)$; that is, $y_r I_\ell z$ and $z I_\ell y_s$. By $R_i$ transitive, therefore, $y_r I_\ell y_s$: contradiction. Therefore, $J_1(y_1) = \partial Q(x)$. The claim and statement (1) of the theorem now follow.

*Claim 6*: Let $y, z \in \partial Q(x)$ with $z \in I_i(y)$ for some $i \in N \backslash \{j\}$, $i$ not a dummy voter with respect to $\{y, z\}$ at $\rho$: then $z \in I_\ell(y)$ for some $\ell \in N \backslash \{i, j\}$.

*Proof:* Suppose the claim is false. Then $\exists B(z, \epsilon)$, defined as usual, such that $\forall \ell \neq i, j$, either $B(z, \epsilon) \subseteq P_\ell(y)$ or $B(z, \epsilon) \subseteq P_\ell^{-1}(y)$. Since $z \in I_i(y)$, $\exists v \in \partial Q(x) \cap P_i(y) \cap B(z, \epsilon)$ and $\exists w \in \partial Q(x) \cap P_i^{-1}(y) \cap B(z, \epsilon)$: see Figure 6.6.

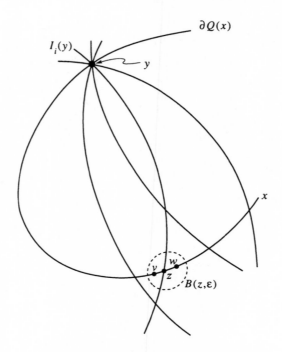

Figure 6.6: Construction for Claim 6

By Claim 2, $vIy$ and $wIy$. Therefore,

$$P(v, y; \rho) = P(y, z; \rho) \cup \{i\} \notin \mathcal{L}(f)$$

and

$$P(y, w; \rho) = P(z, y; \rho) \cup \{i\} \notin \mathcal{L}(f).$$

Therefore, by $f$ strong, $P(z, y; \rho) \cup \{j\} \in \mathcal{L}(f)$ and $P(y, z; \rho) \cup \{j\} \in \mathcal{L}(f)$ (because, by supposition, only $i$ and $j$ are indifferent between $y$ and $z$). Let $L \subseteq N \backslash \{i\}$ be any coalition excluding $i$ such that, $P(y, z; \rho) \backslash \{i\} \subseteq L \subseteq N \backslash P(z, y; \rho)$. Then (since $i$ and $j$ are the only individuals indifferent between $y$ and $z$), $L \in \{P(y, z; \rho),\ P(y, z; \rho) \cup \{j\}\}$. By the preceding argument, $P(y, z; \rho) \cup \{i\} \notin \mathcal{L}(f)$ and, by monotonicity of $\mathcal{L}(f)$, $P(y, z; \rho) \cup \{j\} \cup \{i\} \in \mathcal{L}(f)$. But likewise, $P(y, z; \rho) \cup \{j\} \in \mathcal{L}(f)$. Therefore $i$ is a dummy voter with respect to $\{y, z\}$ at $\rho$: contradiction.

*Claim 7*: Let $y, z \in \partial Q(x)$ with $z \in I_i(y)$ for some $i \in N \backslash \{j\}$, $i$ as strong as $j$ with respect to $\{y, z\}$ at $\rho$: then $z \in I_\ell(y)$ for some $\ell \in N \backslash \{i, j\}$.

*Proof:* Since both $yI_iz$ and $yI_jz$, if $j$ is not a dummy voter (with respect to $\{y, z\}$ at $\rho$) then $i$ as strong as $j$ implies that $i$ cannot be a dummy voter and, therefore, the result follows from Claim 6. So suppose $j$ is a dummy voter and suppose that, $\forall \ell \in N\backslash\{i, j\}$, $z \notin I_\ell(y)$. Then $\exists B(z, \epsilon)$ such that, $\forall \ell \neq i, j$, either $B(z, \epsilon) \subseteq P_\ell(y)$ or $B(z, \epsilon) \subseteq P_\ell^{-1}(y)$. Since $z \in I_i(y)$, $\exists v \in \partial Q(x) \cap P_i(y) \cap B(z, \epsilon)$ and $\exists w \in \partial Q(x) \cap P_i^{-1}(y) \cap B(z, \epsilon)$. By Claim 2, $vIy$ and $wIy$. Now repeating the argument for Claim 6, derive $P(y, z; \rho) \cup \{j\} \in \mathcal{L}(f)$. And by Claim 2 and $y, z \in \partial Q(x)$, $P(y, z; \rho) \notin \mathcal{L}(f)$. Hence, $j \notin P(y, z; \rho)$ and $N\backslash P(z, y; \rho) = P(y, z; \rho) \cup \{i, j\}$ imply $j$ is not a dummy voter with respect to $\{y, z\}$ at $\rho$: contradiction.□

Theorem 6.3 states that if, for any alternative $x \in X$, the boundary of the set of points reachable from $x$ via the asymmetric part of a strong simple rule $f$, $\partial Q(x)$, is not empty, then the preference profile $\rho \in \mathcal{R}_{cs}^n$ must satisfy a set of extremely restrictive conditions. Specifically, the boundary $\partial Q(x)$ must be contained in an indifference curve for some given individual and, if there is any other individual whose indifference curve contains some pair of boundary points, then there has to be a third individual with an indifference curve that also contains both these two points. Since there is a finite number of individuals, if ever such a configuration of preferences existed then virtually any arbitrary perturbation of the list of preferences to a new profile would lead to the conditions being violated so long as the rule $f$ is not collegial. Figure 6.7 illustrates these observations for a society $N = \{1, 2, 3\}$, $X = \Re^2$ and $f$ simple majority rule. In Figure 6.7(a), each individual $i \in N$ has Euclidean preferences on $\Re^2$ and their ideal points $\{x_i\}_N$ are colinear. Then the boundary $\partial Q(w) = I_2(w)$ and condition (2) holds for every pair $\{y, z\} \subset \partial Q(w)$. Figure 6.7(b) describes the same situation except that individual 3's ideal point is perturbed off the line through $x_1$ and $x_2$. In this case, both conditions (1) and (2) fail and it can be checked (using, for example, the construction in Example 6.7 below) that $\partial Q(w) = \emptyset$.

The import of Theorem 6.3, therefore, is that it suggests that for any noncollegial strong simple rule, the set of profiles for which *every* alternative $x$ in $X$ is such that the boundary $\partial Q(x)$ is empty is, to all intents and purposes, generic in $\mathcal{R}_{cs}^n$. And when it is true that $\partial Q(x)$ is empty for all $x$ in $X$, either the core is nonempty or the top-cycle set coincides with the entire set of alternatives, $X$. To see this, consider any $x \in X$ and assume $\partial Q(x) = \emptyset$. Suppose that $Q(x)$ is not empty and is a proper subset of $X$. Then there exist alternatives $y, z$ such that $y \in Q(x)$ and $z \in X\backslash Q(x)$. But $X$ convex and definition of the boundary of $Q(x)$ imply, that for some

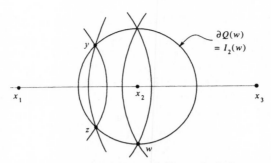

(a) conditions (1) and (2) satisfied at $w$

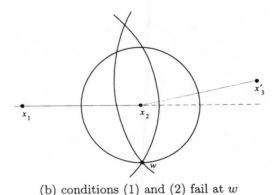

(b) conditions (1) and (2) fail at $w$

Figure 6.7: Illustration of Theorem 6.3

$\lambda \in (0, 1)$, $\lambda z + (1 - \lambda)y \in \partial Q(x)$; contradiction. Hence, $\partial Q(x)$ empty implies that either $Q(x) = \emptyset$ in which case $x$ is a core point, or $Q(x) = X$ in which case all points are reachable from $x$. Now suppose the core is empty; then $Q(x) = X$ holds for all $x \in X$, implying that all alternatives are reachable from all others, i.e. the top cycle set is $X$. Therefore, when social preference "breaks down", in the sense of not admitting a core, it breaks down completely in that one can get from any one alternative in the space to any other via the social preference relation.

To illustrate the preceding observations, consider the following class of individual preferences: say that individual $i$'s preference ordering $R_i \in \mathcal{R}_{cs}$ is *weighted Euclidean* on $X$ if there exists a point $x_i \in X$ and a symmetric positive definite $k \times k$ matrix $A_i$ such that

$$\forall y, z \in X, \; yR_iz \Leftrightarrow -(x_i - y)'A_i(x_i - y) \geq -(x_i - z)'A_i(x_i - z).$$

Thus the indifference surfaces of a weighted Euclidean preference ordering in $X$ are ellipsoids. And note that if $A_i$ is the identity matrix, then $R_i$ is simply Euclidean.

**Lemma 6.3** *Let $X = \Re^k$, $f$ be a strong simple rule and suppose, for all $i \in N$, $R_i$ is weighted Euclidean with $x_i \neq x_j$, all $i \neq j$. Then $\partial Q(x) = \emptyset$ for all $x \in X$.*

**Proof.** Since $x_i \neq x_j$ all $i \neq j$ and preferences are weighted Euclidean, $\rho$ satisfies diversity. Suppose $\partial Q(x) \neq \emptyset$ for some $x \in X$. By Theorem 6.3, $\exists j \in N$ such that, $\forall y \in \partial Q(x)$, $\partial Q(x) \subseteq I_j(y)$. Let $x_j$ be $j$'s most preferred alternative in $X$; since $R_j$ is weighted Euclidean, $x_j$ exists and, since $\forall y \in \partial Q(x)$, $\partial Q(x) \subseteq I_j(y)$, $x_j \in Q(x)$. Furthermore, $I_j(\cdot)$ is a closed and bounded set in $X$; hence $\partial Q(x)$ is closed and bounded. Because $Q(x)$ is open, the definition of $Q(x)$ implies $\exists y \in Q(x)$ such that $yPx_j$. Without loss of generality, set $x_j = 0$. Let $L \equiv P(y, 0; \rho) \in \mathcal{L}(f)$. By $\rho \in \mathcal{R}_{cs}^n$ and $X = \Re^k$, $\exists v \in \cap_{i \in L} P_i(0)$ with $(-v) \in \cap_{i \in L} P_i^{-1}(0)$. Hence, $\forall i \in L$, $vP_i(-v)$: see Figure 6.8.

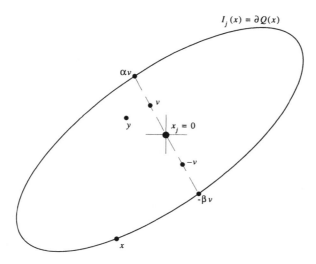

Figure 6.8: Argument for Lemma 6.3

Since, by Claim 3 of the proof to Theorem 6.3, $Q(x)$ is convex and $\partial Q(x)$ is closed and bounded, $\exists \alpha, \beta \in \Re_{++}$ such that $\{\alpha v, -\beta v\} \subset \partial Q(x)$. By $R_j$ weighted Euclidean, $\alpha = \beta$. Therefore, by $R_i$ weighted Euclidean, $\forall i \in L$,

$(\alpha v) P_i(-\alpha v)$. But since $L \in \mathcal{L}(f)$, this contradicts Claim 2 of the proof to Theorem 6.3. Therefore, $\partial Q(x) \neq \emptyset$ is impossible and the result follows.$\square$

Together, Lemma 6.3 and the argument above yield,

**Theorem 6.4** *Let* $X = \Re^k$, $f$ *be a strong simple rule and suppose, for all* $i \in N$, $R_i$ *is weighted Euclidean with* $x_i \neq x_j$, *all* $i \neq j$. *Then either* $C_f(\rho) \neq \emptyset$ *or* $T_f(\rho) = X$.

The theorem asserts that under weighted Euclidean preferences, if the core of a strong simple rule is empty then the top cycle set of the rule is all of $X$; so for *any* two points in the feasible set of alternatives, there exists a finite social preference path from one to the other and back again. It follows that the social preference relation alone places *no* restrictions on the outcomes that might be chosen. In particular, the top cycle set is not constrained to some subset of the Pareto undominated alternatives.

Majority preference is strong only if $n$ is odd; strictly speaking, therefore, Theorems 6.3 and 6.4 cover majority preference only for $n$ odd. However, McKelvey [48] proved that under the assumption of Euclidean preferences the result holds for majority rule irrespective of whether $n$ is odd or even. Unlike the argument for Theorem 6.3, McKelvey's proof for this case is constructive and provides a good intuition for the result, so it is useful to sketch how it works with an example.

**Example 6.7** Let $N = \{1, 2, 3\}$ and $X = \Re^2$. Ideal points $\{x_i\}_{i \in N}$ are described in Figure 6.9. A *median line* in $X$ is a line such that no more than half the population's ideal points lie on any one side of the line. With this definition, any line through $x_i$ that intersects the line connecting $x_j$ and $x_k$ between $x_j$ and $x_k$ is a median line, $i \neq j$, $i \neq k$. In particular, the lines through $x_1$ and $x_2$, through $x_2$ and $x_3$, and through $x_1$ and $x_3$ are median lines; call these lines $H_1$, $H_2$, and $H_3$ respectively. Clearly, there is no single point that lies on all of these lines and this is a defining characteristic of the situation when the core is empty. Now consider any pair of alternatives $y$, $z \in X$; to fix ideas, suppose (as illustrated) $y$ is in the Pareto set $PS_N(\rho)$ and $z \notin PS_N(\rho)$.

We claim that we can reach $z$ from $y$ via a finite sequence of majority preference steps. To do this, consider a point $a_1$ on the perpendicular to $H_1$ through $y$, lying on the opposite side of $H_1$ to $y$, such that the distance between $a_1$ and $H_1$ is slightly less than that between $y$ and $H_1$. By Euclidean preferences, individuals 1 and 2 strictly prefer $a_1$ to $y$. Now consider a point

$a_2$ on the perpendicular to $H_2$ through $a_1$, lying on the opposite side of $H_2$ to $a_1$, such that the distance between $a_2$ and $H_2$ is slightly less than that between $a_1$ and $H_2$. By Euclidean preferences, individuals 2 and 3 strictly prefer $a_2$ to $a_1$. Now construct $a_3$ similarly by dropping the perpendicular from $a_2$ across $H_3$ so that individuals 3 and 1 strictly prefer $a_3$ to $a_2$; and so on. Notice that at each step $t$ in this sequence, $\|y - a_t\| < \|y - a_{t+1}\|$. So by moving around the medians $H_1$, $H_2$, and $H_3$ in this way repeatedly, we generate a sequence of alternatives $a_1, a_2, \ldots$ such that $a_{t+1} P a_t$ for every $t$ and $\|y - a_t\|$ is growing ever larger with $t$. Therefore, there must exist a finite $t$, say $t = r - 1$, such that $\|a_{r-1} - x_i\| > \|z - x_i\|$ for at least two individuals. Given such an alternative, set $a_r = z$; then by Euclidean preferences a majority strictly prefers $z$ to $a_{r-1}$ and the claim is established.

It is apparent that nothing in this argument depends on $y \in PS_N(\rho)$ and $z \notin PS_N(\rho)$; we could easily have started at, say, $a_3$ and used the same construction to arrive at any other point in $X$. Therefore, there exists a finite majority preference sequence connecting *any* two points in $X$ and so $T_{fm}(\rho) = X$ for this case.$\square$

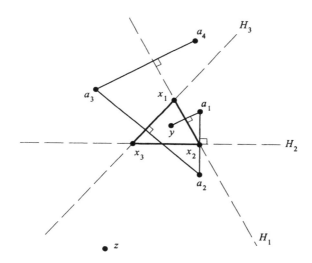

Figure 6.9: Construction for Example 6.7

It is worth noting that although Theorems 6.3 and 6.4 are proved only for strong simple rules, similar sorts of results also hold for any arbitrary simple rule $f$. In effect, Theorem 6.3 and the subsequent discussion say that, for any strong simple rule $\hat{f}$, the typical situation for any alternative $x \in X$ is either that there is no alternative strictly preferred to $x$, or that every alternative $y \in X$ is reachable from $x$ via the *strict* collective preference relation $P_{\hat{f}}$. The extension of these results to arbitrary simple rules is of the following form: if the core of $f$ is empty at $\rho$ then, for all $x \in X$, every alternative $y \in X$ is reachable from $x$ via the *weak* collective preference relation $R_{f(\rho)}$; moreover, the consequent of this claim may obtain even when the core of $f$ at $\rho$ is nonempty.

**Definition 6.4** *For any aggregation rule $f$ and profile $\rho \in \mathcal{R}^n$, the weak top cycle set for $(f, \rho)$ in $X$ is given by*

$$T_f^w(\rho) = \{x \in X : \forall y \in X \backslash \{x\}, \exists \{a_0, a_1, \ldots, a_r\} \subset X \text{ such that}$$
$$a_0 = x, a_r = y, r < \infty \text{ and, } \forall t \leq r - 1, \ a_t R a_{t+1}\}.$$

Let $f$ and $\hat{f}$ be two distinct simple rules. Recall that $\hat{f}$ is said to be *more resolute* than $f$ if, for all $x, y \in X$, for all $\rho \in \mathcal{R}^n$, $x P_{f(\rho)} y$ implies $x P_{\hat{f}(\rho)} y$. By definition, if $\hat{f}$ is more resolute than $f$, then $x R_{\hat{f}(\rho)} y$ implies $x R_{f(\rho)} y$.

**Theorem 6.5** *Let $X = \Re^k$, $\rho \in \mathcal{R}_{cs}^n$, $f$ be any simple rule and $\hat{f}$ be a strong simple rule more resolute than $f$. If, for all $x \in X$, $\partial Q_{\hat{f}(\rho)}(x) = \emptyset$ then $C_f(\rho) = \emptyset$ implies $T_f^w(\rho) = X$.*

**Proof.** If $f$ is strong, the claim follows from the discussion after Theorem 6.3. Assume $f$ is not strong and let $\hat{f}$ be the relevant strong rule, more resolute than $f$. By assumption, $\forall x \in X, \partial Q_{\hat{f}(\rho)}(x) = \emptyset$. So either $C_{\hat{f}}(\rho) \neq \emptyset$ or $T_{\hat{f}}(\rho) = X$. But since $\hat{f}$ is more resolute than $f$,

$$C_{\hat{f}}(\rho) \subseteq C_f(\rho) \text{ and } T_f(\rho) \subseteq T_{\hat{f}}(\rho) \subseteq T_f^w(\rho).$$

Therefore, $C_f(\rho) = \emptyset$ implies $T_f^w(\rho) = X$, as required.$\square$

Theorem 6.3 suggests that (typically) if a simple rule is strong and the core is empty, then the top cycle set includes all of the alternatives in $X$. When the rule is simple but not strong this may not be possible. However, Theorem 6.5 shows that the price paid for having less than all-inclusive *strict* preference cycles is that instead we have all-inclusive *weak* preference cycles. The following example illustrates the result.

**Example 6.8** Suppose $n$ is odd and let $f$ be any $q$-rule with $q_m < q < n$. Then majority rule, $f_m$ (where $q = q_m$) is a strong rule and $f_m$ is more resolute than $f$. By Theorem 6.4, if preferences are weighted Euclidean and no two individuals share the same ideal point, then either $C_{f_m}(\rho) \neq \emptyset$ or $T_{f_m}(\rho) = X$. By Theorem 6.5, therefore, $C_f(\rho) \neq \emptyset$ or $T_f^w(\rho) = X$.$\square$

Of course, the preceding results are predicated on the existence of a suitable more resolute rule $\hat{f}$ for any simple rule $f$. The next result insures such existence.

**Theorem 6.6** *For any noncollegial simple rule $f$, there exists a noncollegial strong simple rule $\hat{f}$ that is more resolute than $f$.*

**Proof.** If $f$ is strong then the result is trivial. So assume $f$ is not strong. Let
$$\mathcal{M} = \{L \subset N : L \notin \mathcal{L}(f) \ \& \ N \backslash L \notin \mathcal{L}(f)\}.$$
Since $f$ is not strong, $\mathcal{M} \neq \emptyset$ and $|\mathcal{M}| = 2t$ for some integer $t \geq 1$. Partition $\mathcal{M}$ into two subsets $\mathcal{M}_1$ and $\mathcal{M}_2$ such that:
$$\forall i = 1, 2, \ |\mathcal{M}_i| = t;$$
$$L \in \mathcal{M}_1 \Leftrightarrow N \backslash L \in \mathcal{M}_2;$$
$$L \in \mathcal{M}_1 \Rightarrow |L| \geq |N \backslash L|.$$
By definition of $\mathcal{M}$, $\mathcal{L}(f) \cap \mathcal{M}_i = \emptyset$, $i = 1, 2$. Define the preference aggregation rule $\hat{f}$ by:
$$\forall x, y \in X, \ \forall \rho \in \mathcal{R}^n, \ x P_{\hat{f}} y \Leftrightarrow [\exists L \in \mathcal{L}(f) \cup \mathcal{M}_1 : L \subseteq P(x, y; \rho)].$$
By definition, $\mathcal{L}(f) \cup \mathcal{M}_1$ is monotonic and both $\mathcal{L}(f)$ and $\mathcal{M}_1$ are proper. Suppose $\mathcal{L}(f) \cup \mathcal{M}_1$ is not proper. Then there exists $L \in \mathcal{L}(f)$ and $M \in \mathcal{M}_1$ such that $L \cap M = \emptyset$; hence, $M \subseteq N \backslash L$. By $M \in \mathcal{L}(f) \cup \mathcal{M}_1$ and $\mathcal{L}(f) \cup \mathcal{M}_1$ monotonic, $M \subseteq N \backslash L$ implies $N \backslash L \in \mathcal{L}(f) \cup \mathcal{M}_1$. By definition of $\mathcal{M}_1$, $N \backslash L \notin \mathcal{M}_1$; so $N \backslash L \in \mathcal{L}(f)$. But since $L \in \mathcal{L}(f)$, this contradicts $\mathcal{L}(f)$ proper. Therefore, $\mathcal{L}(f) \cup \mathcal{M}_1$ is proper. And since, by definition, $\hat{f}$ is neutral and decisive, Theorem 3.1 implies $\hat{f}$ is a simple rule. Moreover, by construction, $\hat{f}$ is strong, noncollegial, and more resolute than $f$ as required.$\square$

Finally, unlike with strong simple rules it is, as we observed above, possible here to have $T_f^w(\rho) = X$ *and* $C_f(\rho) \neq \emptyset$; that is, the core is nonempty yet every alternative is reachable from every other alternative via $R_{f(\rho)}$ in a finite number of steps. In other words, core nonemptiness is achieved by all alternatives being ranked at least indirectly as good as each other: for all $x, y \in X$, there exists a finite sequence of alternatives $(a_1, \ldots, a_r)$ in $X$ such that $x R_{f(\rho)} a_1, \ a_1 R_{f(\rho)} a_2, \ldots, \ a_r R_{f(\rho)} y$. Theorem 6.7 makes the observation precise and Exercise 6.3 provides an example.

**Theorem 6.7** *Let $f$ be a noncollegial simple rule. If $2 \leq k \leq s(f) - 2$ then there exist profiles $\rho \in \mathcal{R}_{cs}^n$ such that $C_f(\rho) \neq \emptyset$ and $T_f^w(\rho) = X$.*

**Proof.** Let $f$ be a noncollegial simple rule with Nakamura number $s(f) \geq k + 2$. By Theorem 6.6, there exists a noncollegial strong simple rule $\hat{f}$ more resolute than $f$. By Lemma 3.2(1), $s(\hat{f}) = 3$. So by Theorem 5.4, $k \geq 2$ implies there exists $\rho \in \mathcal{R}_{cs}^n$ such that $C_{\hat{f}}(\rho) = \emptyset$; in particular, the proof for Theorem 5.4 shows that we can always choose such a profile $\rho$ to be Euclidean and to satisfy diversity. By Theorem 6.4, therefore, we can choose the profile $\rho$ such that $T_{\hat{f}}(\rho) = X$. By definition, $T_{\hat{f}}(\rho) \subseteq T_f^w(\rho)$; so $T_f^w(\rho) = X$. But $k \leq s(f) - 2$ implies $C_f(\rho) \neq \emptyset$ and the result is proved.□

## 6.4   Discussion

The results of this chapter paint a particularly bleak picture of how "rational" any noncollegial simple rule can be in that, in high enough dimensions, core outcomes exist only in very special circumstances (Theorems 6.1 and 6.2) and, when they fail to exist, collective preference can wander almost anywhere in the space (Theorems 6.3 and 6.4), an implication somewhat unfortunately termed a chaos theorem.

Although the core-emptiness results are, from a positive perspective, fundamental, the cycling results (when coupled with those on the existence of the core) are normatively significant: the theorems say that, in sufficiently high dimensional spaces, collective preferences *per se* place no constraints on collective choices, a conclusion that is independent of any assumption on the selfishness or otherwise of individual preferences. However, as in the discussion of Arrow's Theorem in Chapter 2, it is important to emphasize that these instability and chaos theorems are results on the consistency of the various means of aggregating individual *preferences*. As such they are not results on individual *behavior* or the aggregation of such behavior, they are facts about the formal properties of preference aggregation rules on given sets of profiles. In particular, the results do not predict that political behavior is chaotic or that "anything can happen". Instead, they demonstrate that we can *not* view or explain collective behavior as simply an exercise in selecting the best alternative according to some social preference relation. Put in the language of Chapter 1, the negative results on the core imply that we cannot rationalize any observed collective choices as being supported by, for example, the "will of the majority".

## 6.5   Exercises

**6.1** Prove that if a simple rule $f$ is anonymous, then any individual is as strong as any other at every profile and every pair of alternatives.

**6.2** Let $f$ be a preference aggregation rule and assume $f(\rho)$ is asymmetric on a finite set $X$.

(a) Prove that $T_f(\rho) \neq \emptyset$, and that if $C_f(\rho) \neq \emptyset$ then $T_f(\rho) = C_f(\rho)$.

(b) Let $T_f^*(\rho)$ be the smallest (by set inclusion) set $Y \subseteq X$ such that for all $x \notin Y$, for all $y \in Y$, $yP_{f(\rho)}x$. Prove that $T_f^*(\rho) \equiv T_f(\rho)$.

**6.3** (a) Suppose $n = 5$ and $X \subseteq \Re^2$. Assume that all individuals have Euclidean preferences on $X$ and that the preference aggregation rule $f$ is a $q$-rule with $q = 4$. Construct an example to show that *both* $C_f(\rho) \neq \emptyset$ *and* $T_f^w(\rho) = X$. Is it possible to have $C_f(\rho) = T_f^w(\rho) = X$ for some Euclidean profile $\rho$ with all ideal points in the interior of $X$?

(b) Suppose profiles are smooth and $n$ is odd. Discuss the implications of Theorems 6.2, 6.5, 6.6, and 6.7 for the properties of noncollegial $q$-rules.

**6.4** For any $x \in X$, say that there is an $\epsilon$-*local cycle* about $x$ if there is an open neighborhood $B(x, \epsilon)$ and a finite sequence $(x \equiv a_0, a_1, \ldots, a_r \equiv x)$ such that $a_t \in B(x, \epsilon)$ all $t$ and $a_{t+1}Pa_t$ all $t = 0, \ldots, r - 1$. For any set $X$, $Y_f(\rho) \subseteq X$ is the *local cycle set* for $(f, \rho)$ in $X$,

$$Y_f(\rho) = \{x \in X : \forall \epsilon > 0, \exists \epsilon - local\ cycle\ about\ x\}.$$

(a) Prove that if $\rho \in \mathcal{R}_{ds}^n$, if $f$ is a simple rule, and if $X = \Re^2$, then $Y_f(\rho) \subseteq PS_N(\rho)$.

(b) Briefly discuss the relationship between this result and Example 6.7.

(c) What can you say about $Y_{f_m}(\rho)$ if $X = \Re^k$ and $k > 2$?

## 6.6   Further reading

Building on the results of Schofield [71] and McKelvey and Schofield [50], Banks [6] proves Theorem 6.1 and Corollary 6.1. Theorem 6.2 is an implication of a result due to Saari [67], who provides necessary and sufficient bounds for generic core existence for $q$-rules and any population size $n$. Rubinstein [66] and Le Breton [42] prove generic core emptiness results for preference profiles, rather than (as here and in Cox [20]) smooth utility profiles.

The seminal global cycling results are due to McKelvey [48][49] and Schofield [70]; alternative versions are given by Cohen [18] and Cohen and Matthews [19]. Schofield [69][70][72][76] studies continuous cycles; in this setting, cycling under a simple rule can only occur in the Pareto set when the dimension of the space is the Nakamura number less one, but can occur everywhere when it is higher. The interpretation of the cycling and stability results as predicting "anything can happen" is due largely to Riker [61]. Elsewhere, Riker [60] considers at length the implications of these theorems for democratic theory in general.

# Chapter 7

# Summary and Conclusions

The principle focus of this book is the collective preference approach to political or social decision making. The key ingredients in any such approach are:

(1) the set of outcomes, $X$, under consideration;

(2) the set of individuals, $N = \{1, ..., n\}$, relevant for the decision;

(3) the preferences, $\rho = (R_1, ..., R_n)$, of the individuals over the set $X$; and

(4) the aggregation rule $f$ assigning a collective preference relation on the set $X$ based on the individual preferences $\rho$.

Collective decisions at a preference profile $\rho$ are taken to be the maximal or "best" outcomes according to the preference relation $f(\rho)$, outcomes referred to as the *core* of $f$ at $\rho$. A fundamental issue, then, concerns when the core is nonempty, since otherwise the collective preference approach cannot even begin to provide an explanation for any sort of empirical regularity in which we might be interested.

To keep the exercise manageable we need to impose some conditions on the inputs (1)-(4) above. Minimal restrictions will do for the sets $X$ and $N$. For the latter, simply assume that $n$ is at least two, so that we have more than a single-person choice problem. For the former, consider two environments: in the *finite model*, where $|X| = r < \infty$, assume that $r$ is at least two, so that there actually is a choice to be made; in the *spatial model*, $X$ is assumed to be a compact and convex subset of $\Re^k$, $k$-dimensional Euclidean space (where $1 \leq k < \infty$), implying that any subsequent negative results are not being driven by a "badly-shaped" outcome set. However, while the constraints on the sets $X$ and $N$ are minimal, many of the principle results found in the book are intimately related to the "size" parameters $r$ (or $k$) and $n$.

For preferences, the idea is again to guarantee that any negative results regarding collective preferences are not simply a function of "badly-behaved" individual preferences (i.e. to avoid "garbage in, garbage out"). Rather than listing appropriate regularity conditions explicitly (e.g. complete, transitive, convex), for each of the statements below we implicitly assume that preferences satisfy the required properties. By an abuse of notation, we let $\mathcal{R}^n$ denote the appropriate set of profiles in each case. Thus we can write the aggregation rule $f$ as a function, $f : \mathcal{R}^n \to \mathcal{B}$, where $\mathcal{B}$ denotes the set of reflexive and complete binary relations on $X$.

Recall that for any binary relation $R \in \mathcal{B}$ the set of maximal elements in $X$ is denoted $M(R, X)$. Since in what follows we are only concerned with choosing from the set $X$ itself, we write $m(R) = M(R, X)$. Then we can describe a collective preference model as the composition of $f$ and $m$ or, diagrammatically, by

$$\mathcal{R}^n \xrightarrow{\ f\ } \mathcal{B} \xrightarrow{\ m\ } X.$$

The core of $f$ at $\rho$ is therefore given by $C_f(\rho) = m(f(\rho))$.

For any aggregation rule $f$ let $\mathcal{L}(f)$ denote the set of decisive coalitions associated with $f$, i.e. those sets of individuals which can dictate strict social preference over any pair of alternatives when they all agree in their strict preference. The one requirement we place on $f$ here is that $\mathcal{L}(f)$ is nonempty; equivalently, since the set $\mathcal{L}(f)$ is necessarily monotonic (Lemma 2.2), we require that $f$ be *weakly Paretian*: $N \in \mathcal{L}(f)$. (This condition is left implicit in the statements to follow.) Consider two classes of aggregation rules in particular: collegial rules and simple rules. An aggregation rule $f$ is *collegial* if $\cap_{L \in \mathcal{L}(f)} L \neq \emptyset$, that is, if there exist some individuals in all decisive coalitions; an aggregation rule $f$ is *simple* if $f_{\mathcal{L}(f)} = f$, that is, if the rule is completely characterized by its decisive coalitions (Theorem 3.1 shows these to be the rules that are decisive, neutral, and monotonic). For any simple rule $f$ we let $s(f)$ denote the rule's *Nakamura number*, defined as the number of coalitions in the smallest noncollegial subfamily of $\mathcal{L}(f)$. This number is set equal to infinity if $f$ is collegial, and otherwise falls between 3 and $n$ (Lemma 3.1).

For the finite model we know from Theorem 1.1 that the acyclicity of the social preference relation $f(\rho)$ is fundamental in determining the nonemptiness of the core and, therefore, we have the following general results.

*If $f$ is noncollegial and $r \geq n$, then there exists a preference profile $\rho \in \mathcal{R}^n$ such that the core of $f$ at $\rho$ is empty (Theorem 2.4).*

Thus when there are at least as many alternatives as there are individuals, core outcomes cannot be guaranteed unless the rule is collegial. For simple rules we obtain an even tighter condition on core existence.

*If f is noncollegial and simple, then the core of f is nonempty for all $\rho \in \mathcal{R}^n$ if and only if $r < s(f)$* (Theorem 3.2).

For instance if $f$ is *strong* (e.g. majority rule with $n$ odd) then $s(f) = 3$ and so whenever there are at least three alternatives we can always find a profile for which the core is empty (e.g. the Condorcet paradox).

Therefore without additional restrictions core points can only be guaranteed when either $f$ is collegial, and so places a certain amount of veto power in the hands of some (or possibly all) individuals, or else the size of $X$ is suitably constrained. An alternative to restricting the set $X$ is to restrict the set of admissible preference profiles. Let $\mathcal{S} \subset \mathcal{R}^n$ denote the set of *single-peaked* preference profiles: for each profile $\rho \in \mathcal{S}$ there is an ordering of alternatives from left to right such that as one moves away from each individual's preferred outcome one moves down that individual's preference ordering. Then we have the following:

*If f is simple and $\rho \in \mathcal{S}$, then the core of f at $\rho$ is nonempty* (Theorem 4.2).

In particular, if $f$ is majority rule (with $n$ odd) and $\rho \in \mathcal{S}$ we get Black's well-known characterization of the majority rule core as the median of the individuals' ideal points.

Alternatively, let $\mathcal{O} \subset \mathcal{R}^n$ denote the set of *order-restricted* preference profiles, where for each $\rho \in \mathcal{O}$ there exists an ordering of individuals from left to right such that for any pair of alternatives $x, y$ in $X$, the set of individuals strictly preferring (say) $x$ to $y$ are all to the left of those indifferent between $x$ and $y$, who are themselves to the left of those who strictly prefer $y$ to $x$.

*If f is simple and $\rho \in \mathcal{O}$, then the core of f at $\rho$ is nonempty* (Theorem 4.6).

As with the finite model, we have a core nonexistence result in the spatial model which is intimately related to the "size" of $X$ and of $N$.

*If f is noncollegial and $k \geq n - 1$, then there exists a preference profile $\rho \in \mathcal{R}^n$ such that the core of f at $\rho$ is empty* (Theorem 5.4).

And we can as before say more when the rule is assumed to be simple.

*If f is noncollegial and simple, then the core of f is nonempty for all $\rho \in \mathcal{R}^n$ if and only if $k < s(f) - 1$* (Theorem 5.3).

Therefore we have matching core nonexistence results in the finite and spatial model, with the critical number in each differing only by one (think "two (non-equal) points determine a line, which is one-dimensional; three (non-colinear) points determine a plane, which is two-dimensional; etc."). Additionally, in the spatial model we can say how likely it is that core points exist in high dimensional spaces.

*If $f$ is noncollegial and $k > 2(n-2)$, then for almost all preference profiles $\rho \in \mathcal{R}^n$ the core of $f$ at $\rho$ is empty* (Corollary 6.1; see also Corollary 6.2).

On a more positive note, the fact that $s(f) \geq 3$ for all simple rules implies that we have the following:

*If $f$ is simple and $k = 1$, then the core of $f$ at $\rho$ is nonempty for all $\rho \in \mathcal{R}^n$* (Theorem 5.3; see also Corollary 4.5).

Taken together these results show that the collective preference approach to social decision making requires *either* the set of outcomes or the set of admissible preference profiles not to be too "large", thereby limiting the scope of any such approach; *or* the rule $f$ is required to be collegial, thereby placing a certain amount of veto power in the hands of some of the individuals. Given such results, it might appear as if the collective preference approach has little to offer in the way of a general theory of collective decision making and that possibly an alternative such as game theory (the topic of our companion volume) might better serve this purpose. However, we argue in the next section that these results are germane to *any* individual preference-based approach to collective decision making and, consequently, any attempt to avoid them through some other approach is futile. Instead, the results should be viewed as limitations on the type of conclusion rational choice models can draw, as opposed to being fundamental empirical laws.

## 7.1   Social choice

Suppose we generalize the collective preference approach above and describe a preference-based theory of collective or social choice as simply a mapping from preference profiles $\mathcal{R}^n$ into the set of outcomes $X$. Let $c$ denote a generic theory of this sort, so that $c(\rho) \subseteq X$ describes the set of outcomes selected by the collective $N$ at the preference profile $\rho$. Furthermore, we allow $c(\rho)$ to be empty; that is, the theory does not make a prediction at the profile $\rho$. We can think of the core associated with an aggregation rule $f$ as just such a mapping since, as the composition of $f$ together with $m$, the core assigns to each preference profile either a nonempty subset of $X$ or the empty set. We will argue in the next section that any game theory model of social choice also generates such a mapping.

Consider next the following condition on the mapping $c$: say that $c$ is *minimally democratic* at the profile $\rho \in \mathcal{R}^n$ if it is the case that $x \in X$ is not in $c(\rho)$ whenever there exists $y \in X$ such that all but at most one individual prefers $y$ to $x$. Thus if $c$ is minimally democratic an outcome is not chosen when there exists another that is preferred to the former by all, or all but one, of the individuals. (We are concerned here with the *positive* implications of this condition and not its *normative* implications and so conveniently (and thankfully) sidestep the latter.) Alternatively, if $c$ is *not* minimally democratic then the collective choice either $(i)$ invests in at least one individual a certain amount of veto power over this choice, in that while $n-1$ of the individuals prefer $y$ to $x$ the influence of the remaining individual, who prefers $x$ to $y$, is sufficient to render $x$ a collective outcome; or $(ii)$ ignores the *unanimous* consent of individuals for $y$ over $x$ by allowing $x$ to be a chosen outcome (i.e. in a social choice sense, the mapping is not Paretian).

The results above regarding existence of core alternatives for aggregation rules can then be translated into results about social choice.

**Theorem 7.1** *In the finite model, if $r \geq n$ then there exists a preference profile $\rho \in \mathcal{R}^n$ such that either $c(\rho)$ is empty or else $c$ does not satisfy minimal democracy at $\rho$.*

The proof follows by noting that the Nakamura number of a $q$-rule when $q = n-1$ is equal to $n$ and so from above we know that the core for this rule will be empty for some profile $\rho^* \in \mathcal{R}^n$ when $r \geq n$. Therefore at such a profile each outcome $x$ has associated with it another outcome $y$ for which $yP_i^* x$ for at least $n-1$ of the individuals and, therefore, if $c(\rho^*)$ is nonempty it must necessarily be choosing such an $x$, thereby violating minimal democracy.

Using an analogous logic, we obtain:

**Theorem 7.2** *In the spatial model, if $k \geq n-1$ then there exists a preference profile $\rho \in \mathcal{R}^n$ such that either $c(\rho)$ is empty or else $c$ does not satisfy minimal democracy at $\rho$; and if $k > 2(n-2)$ then for almost all $\rho \in \mathcal{R}^n$ either $c(\rho)$ is empty or else $c$ does not satisfy minimal democracy at $\rho$.*

Thus there exists a fundamental trade-off in preference-based theories of collective decision making, in that without restrictions on the domain of the problem (i.e. restrictions on either $X$ or $\rho$) either existence of solutions or the notion of minimal democracy must be sacrificed at some, and at times most, preference profiles. From this perspective, the principle "negative" results of the collective preference approach can be viewed as sacrificing existence in the name of minimal democracy, in that rules satisfying the latter (e.g. majority rule) fail to have core points without restrictions on either $X$ or $\rho$. At the other extreme, if existence of solutions is to be insisted upon, then there is a price that must be paid in terms of constraints on collective influence over the resulting outcomes.

## 7.2   Game theory

To see how other approaches to collective decision making deal with this trade-off, consider a game theoretic approach. In its most basic description, such an approach begins as above with the sets $X$ of outcomes, $N$ of individuals, and $\mathcal{R}^n$ of admissible preference profiles. To these we now add two things. First, for each $i \in N$ a set of *strategies* $S_i$, where a strategy is understood as a complete description of how an individual behaves in every logically possible circumstance she might confront. Analogous to a preference profile, we label a specific list of strategies $s = (s_1, ..., s_n)$ a *strategy profile*, and denote by $S$ the set of all possible strategy profiles. And second, an *outcome function* $g : S \to X$, which assigns to each possible strategy profile a single outcome; thus $g(s) \in X$ is the outcome associated with the strategy profile $s$. Taken together, $(S, g)$ is known as a *game form*; adding a preference profile yields a *game* $(S, g, \rho)$.

We can view a game form as analogous to an aggregation rule in the collective preference approach insofar as both impose a particular kind of structure on the social choice process. For the latter we then added the hypothesis of (collective) preference maximization to close the model and generate a social choice mapping from preference profiles into outcomes. Under a game theoretic approach, the additional hypothesis concerns how individuals select strategies, in that, given a behavioral hypothesis $b : \mathcal{R}^n \to S$, we can compose this mapping with the outcome function $g$ to generate a mapping from preference profiles into outcomes:

$$\mathcal{R}^n \xrightarrow{b} S \xrightarrow{g} X.$$

The most commonly employed behavioral hypothesis is that of *Nash equilibrium*, in which each individual is choosing a preference-maximizing strategy holding fixed the others' strategies. That is, a strategy profile $s^* =$

$(s_1^*, ..., s_n^*)$ constitutes a Nash equilibrium if no individual $i \in N$ can unilaterally change her strategy from $s_i^*$ to something else, say $s_i'$, and generate an outcome she strictly prefers to $g(s^*)$, the outcome associated with $s^*$. (We are not concerned here with either the details of this definition or alternative behavioral hypotheses; such things are covered in Volume II.) Note that, just as with the "maximization" mapping $m$ in the collective preference approach, the behavioral mapping $b$ may well be multivalued (i.e. there may be multiple equilibria), but this is not a concern here.

As with the collective preference approach, a fundamental question in any game theoretic approach is whether the composite mapping $g(b(\rho))$, i.e. the set of Nash equilibrium outcomes, is necessarily nonempty; equivalently, when does there exist a Nash equilibrium? The answer to this question, not surprisingly, depends on the specifics of the game form $(S, g)$ just as the answer under the collective preference approach depends on the specifics of the aggregation rule $f$. However, for a (seemingly) wide class of game forms, at least with respect to the spatial model, existence of Nash equilibria is generally assured. While we leave the details of the argument for Volume II, we sketch the idea here: individual preferences over the set $X$, together with the outcome function $g$, induce preferences over the set of strategy profiles $S$ by equating a strategy profile with the outcome it ultimately produces. Thus a strategy profile $s \in S$ is preferred by $i \in N$ to another $s'$ if and only if $g(s)$ is preferred by $i$ to $g(s')$. Now suppose that each strategy set $S_i$ is, like the set $X$, a compact and convex subset of $k_i$-dimensional Euclidean space and that all players' induced preferences over $S$ satisfy the same regularity conditions we impose on their primitive preferences over $X$ - specifically here, that $R_i$ is a continuous and convex weak order for all $i \in N$. (Note that if these conditions are satisfied on $X$, the requirement that they are in addition satisfied on $S$ implicitly puts restrictions on the outcome function $g$.) Then there exists a Nash equilibrium to the game.

Thus it would appear as if the game-theoretic approach solves the existence problem found in the collective preference approach. Upon further reflection, though, this turns out not to be true, for we know that the Nash equilibrium outcome correspondence is simply another example of a social choice mapping as defined above. Specifically, whereas the collective preference approach induces the social choice mapping $c_{cp} = m \circ f$, the game-theoretic approach induces the social choice mapping $c_{gt} = g \circ b$. Hence the negative implications of Theorem 7.2 above must hold for the game theory approach just as they do for the collective preference approach, namely, existence comes at a price. We state this formally as a corollary to Theorem 7.2.

**Corollary 7.1** *Let $(S, g)$ be any game form in which, for all $\rho \in \mathcal{R}^n$, the set of equilibrium outcomes is nonempty. If $k \geq n-1$ then for some $\rho' \in \mathcal{R}^n$ there exist alternatives $x, y \in X$ such that $x$ is an equilibrium outcome at $\rho'$ and $y$ is strictly preferred to $x$ by at least $n-1$ individuals; and if $k > 2(n-2)$ this statement holds true for almost all $\rho' \in \mathcal{R}^n$.*

(Note that as stated this result holds for *any* behavioral theory, not just Nash, and we could just as well state an analogous corollary to Theorem 7.1 for the finite model.)

From a Nash perspective, Corollary 7.1 implies that at the equilibrium outcome $x$, those (at least) $n - 1$ individuals are unable to change the outcome to $y$, either because (1) $y$ is the outcome associated with *no* strategy profile (implying $g$ has only a limited range), (2) $y$ is associated with a strategy profile that would require simultaneous and coordinated changes in the players' strategies, or (3) it is only the *remaining* player who has the ability unilaterally to change $x$ into $y$. Thus, in effect a game theoretic approach generates existence by constraining the ability of groups of individuals to alter the collective outcome, either by behavioral assumption (i.e. point (2)) or by structural assumption (i.e. points (1) or (3)).

More generally, we know from Theorem 7.2 above that if a game form is necessarily associated with existence of equilibria, it must be that minimal democracy is sacrificed. Indeed, by its focus on individual behavior and hence individual influence over collective decisions, the very essence of game-theoretic analysis calls out for such a sacrifice. Therefore, the collective preference and game theory approaches to the study of collective decision making differ not with respect to existence of solutions *per se* but rather with respect to the implicit trade-off each makes between existence and minimal democracy. We know that *no* approach can have both properties without additional constraints on either the set of outcomes under consideration or the set of allowable preference profiles, i.e. without restricting the domain of the problems to be analyzed.

# Bibliography

[1] Arrow, K.J. 1951. *Social Choice and Individual Values*. New York: Wiley.

[2] Arrow, K.J. 1959. Rational functions and orderings. *Economica, 26:121-127.*

[3] Arrow, K.J. 1963. *Social Choice and Individual Values (2nd. ed.)*. New Haven: Yale University Press.

[4] Austen-Smith, D. and J.S. Banks 1998. Social choice theory, game theory and positive political theory. In: N. Polsby (ed.), *Annual Review of Political Science, Volume 1*. Palo Alto: Annual Reviews Inc.

[5] Banks, J.S. 1995a. Acyclic choice from finite sets. *Social Choice and Welfare, 12:293-310.*

[6] Banks, J.S. 1995b. Singularity theory and core existence in the spatial models. *Journal of Mathematical Economics, 24:523-536.*

[7] Bergstrom, T.C. 1975. The existence of maximal elements and equilibria in the absence of transitivity. *Mimeo. Department of Economics, University of Michigan.*

[8] Black, D. 1958. *The Theory of Committees and Elections*. London: Cambridge University Press.

[9] Blair, D.H., G. Bordes, J.S. Kelly, and K. Suzumura. 1976. Impossibility theorems without collective rationality. *Journal of Economic Theory, 13:361-379.*

[10] Blair, D.H. and R.A. Pollak. 1982. Acyclic collective choice rules. *Econometrica, 50:931-943.*

[11] Blau, J.H. 1957. The existence of a social welfare function. *Econometrica, 25:302-313.*

[12] Blau, J.H. 1979. Semiorders and collective choice. *Journal of Economic Theory, 21:195-206.*

[13] Blau, J.H. and R. Deb. 1978. Social decision functions and the veto. *Econometrica, 45:471-482.*

[14] Border, K.C. 1985. *Fixed Point Theorems with Applications to Economics and Game Theory.* London: Cambridge University Press.

[15] Brown, D.J. 1973. Acyclic choice. *Cowles Foundation Discussion Paper 393, Yale University.*

[16] Brown, D.J. 1975. Aggregation of preferences. *Quarterly Journal of Economics, 89:456-469.*

[17] Chernoff, H. 1954. Rational selection of decision functions. *Econometrica, 22:422-443.*

[18] Cohen, L. 1979. Cyclic sets in multidimensional voting models. *Journal of Economic Theory, 20:1-12.*

[19] Cohen, L. and S.A. Matthews. 1980. Constrained Plott equilibria, directional equilibria and global cycling sets. *Review of Economic Studies, 47:975-986.*

[20] Cox, G.W. 1984. Noncollegial simple games and the nowhere denseness of the set of preference profiles having a core. *Social Choice and Welfare, 1:159-164.*

[21] Cox, G.W. 1987. The uncovered set and the core. *American Journal of Political Science, 31:408-422.*

[22] Davis, O.A. and M.J. Hinich. 1966. A mathematical model of policy formation in a democratic society. In: J. Bernd (ed.), *Mathematical Applications in Political Science II.* Dallas: Southern Methodist University Press.

[23] Davis, O.A., M.H. DeGroot, and M.J. Hinich. 1972. Social preference orderings and majority rule. *Econometrica, 40:147-157.*

[24] Denicolo, V. 1985. Independent social choice correspondences are dictatorial. *Economics Letters, 19:9-12.*

[25] Downs, A. 1957. *An Economic Theory of Democracy*. New York: Harper.

[26] Fan, K. 1961. A generalization of Tychonoff's fixed point theorem. *Math Annalen, 42:305-310.*

[27] Ferejohn, J.A. 1977. Decisive coalitions in the theory of social choice. *Journal of Economic Theory, 15:301-306.*

[28] Ferejohn, J.A. and P.C. Fishburn. 1979. Representations of binary decision rules by generalized decisive structures. *Journal of Economic Theory, 21:28-45.*

[29] Ferejohn, J.A. and D. Grether. 1974. On a class of rational social decision procedures. *Journal of Economic Theory, 8:471-482.*

[30] Ferejohn, J.A. and D. Grether. 1977. Weak path independence. *Journal of Economic Theory, 14:19-31.*

[31] Gans, J. and M. Smart. 1996. Majority voting with single-crossing preferences. *Journal of Public Economics, 59:219-237.*

[32] Gibbard, A. 1969. Social choice and the Arrow conditions. *Discussion Paper, Department of Philosophy, University of Michigan.*

[33] Golubitsky, M. and V. Guillemin. 1973. *Stable Mappings and Their Singularites*. New York: Springer.

[34] Grandmont, J-M. 1978. Intermediate preferences and majority rule. *Econometrica, 46:317-330.*

[35] Greenberg, J. 1979. Consistent majority rules over compact sets of alternatives. *Econometrica, 47:627-636.*

[36] Guha, A.S. 1972. Neutrality, monotonicity and the right of veto. *Econometrica, 40:821-826.*

[37] Hansson, B. 1976. The existence of group preferences. *Public Choice, 28:89-98.*

[38] Herzberger, H.G. 1973. Ordinal preferences and rational choice. *Econometrica, 41:187-237.*

[39] Houthakker, H.S. 1950. Revealed preference and the utility function. *Economica, 17:159-174.*

[40] Inada, K. 1969. On the simple majority decision rule. *Econometrica, 37:490-506.*

[41] Kirman, A.P. and D. Sondermann. 1972. Arrow's theorem, many agents and invisible dictators. *Journal of Economic Theory, 5:267-277.*

[42] Le Breton, M. 1987. On the core of voting games. *Social Choice and Welfare, 4:295-306.*

[43] Levine, H. 1971. Singularities of differentiable mappings. In: C.T.C. Wall (ed), *Proceedings of the Liverpool Singularities Symposium I.* New York: Springer.

[44] Mas-Colell, A. and H.F. Sonnenschein. 1972. General possibility theorems for group decisions. *Review of Economic Studies, 39:185-192.*

[45] Matthews, S.A. 1980. Pairwise symmetry conditions for voting equilibria. *International Journal of Game Theory, 9:141-156.*

[46] May, K.O. 1952. A set of independent necessary and sufficient conditions for simple majority decision. *Econometrica, 20:680-684.*

[47] McLean, I. 1990. The Borda and Condorcet principles: Three medieval applications. *Social Choice and Welfare, 7:99-108.*

[48] McKelvey, R.D. 1976. Intransitivities in multidimensional voting models and some implications for agenda control. *Journal of Economic Theory, 12:472-482.*

[49] McKelvey, R.D. 1979. General conditions for global intransitivities in formal voting models. *Econometrica, 47:1086-1112.*

[50] McKelvey, R.D. and N.J. Schofield. 1986. Structural instability of the core. *Journal of Mathematical Economics, 15:179-198.*

[51] McKelvey, R.D. and N.J. Schofield. 1987. Generalized symmetry conditions at a core point. *Econometrica, 55:923-934.*

[52] McKelvey, R.D. and R.E. Wendell. 1976. Voting equilibria in multidimensional choice spaces. *Mathematics of Operations Research, 1:144-158.*

[53] Moulin, H. 1985. Choice functions over a finite set: a summary. *Social Choice and Welfare, 2:147-160.*

[54] Nakamura, K. 1979. The vetoers in a simple game with ordinal preferences. *International Journal of Game Theory, 5:55-61*.

[55] Parks, R.P. 1976. Further results on path independence, quasi-transitivity and social choice. *Public Choice, 26:75-87*.

[56] Plott, C.R. 1967. A notion of equilibrium and its possibility under majority rule. *American Economic Review, 57:787-806*.

[57] Plott, C.R. 1973. Path independence, rationality and social choice. *Econometrica, 41:1075-91*.

[58] Plott, C.R. 1976. Axiomatic social choice theory: an overview and interpretation. *American Journal of Political Science, 20:511-96*.

[59] Richter, M.K. 1966. Revealed preference theory. *Econometrica, 34:635-645*

[60] Riker, W.H. 1982. *Liberalism Against Populism: A Confrontation between the Theory of Democracy and the Theory of Social Choice*. San Francisco: W.H. Freeman.

[61] Riker, W.H. 1980. Implications from the disequilibrium of majority rule for the study of institutions. *American Political Science Review, 74:432-46*.

[62] Roberts, K.W.S. 1977. Voting over income tax schedules. *Journal of Public Economics, 8:329-340*.

[63] Romer, T. and H. Rosenthal 1979. The elusive median voter. *Journal of Public Economics, 12:143-170*.

[64] Rothstein, P. 1990. Order restricted preferences and majority rule. *Social Choice and Welfare, 7:331-342*.

[65] Rothstein, P. 1991. Representative voter theorems. *Public Choice, 72:193-212*.

[66] Rubinstein, A. 1979. A note about the nowhere denseness of societies having an equilibrium under majority rule. *Econometrica, 47:512-514*.

[67] Saari, D.G. 1997. The generic existence of a core for $q$-rules. *Economic Theory, 9:219-260*.

[68] Samuelson, P.A. 1938. A note on the pure theory of consumers' behavior. *Economica, 5:61-71.*

[69] Schofield, N.J. 1977. Transitivity of preferences on a smooth manifold of alternatives. *Journal of Economic Theory, 33:59-71.*

[70] Schofield, N.J. 1978. Instability of simple dynamic games. *Review of Economic Studies, 45:575-594.*

[71] Schofield, N.J. 1980. Generic properties of simple Bergson-Samuelson welfare functions. *Journal of Mathematical Economics, 7:175-192.*

[72] Schofield, N.J. 1983. Generic instability of majority rule. *Review of Economic Studies, 50:695-705.*

[73] Schofield, N.J. 1984a. Social equilibrium and cycles on compact sets. *Journal of Economic Theory, 33:59-71.*

[74] Schofield, N.J. 1984b. Existence of equilibrium on a manifold. *Mathematics of Operations Research, 9:545-557.*

[75] Schofield, N.J. 1984c. Classification theorem for smooth social choice on a manifold. *Social Choice and Welfare, 1:187-210.*

[76] Schofield, N.J. 1985. *Social Choice and Democracy.* Berlin: Springer.

[77] Sen, A.K. 1970. *Collective Choice and Social Welfare.* Amsterdam: North Holland.

[78] Sen, A.K. 1971. Choice functions and revealed preference. *Review of Economic Studies, 38:307-317.*

[79] Sen, A.K. 1977a. Social choice theory: a reexamination. *Econometrica, 45:53-89.*

[80] Sen, A.K. 1977b. On weights and measures: informational constraints in social welfare analysis. *Econometrica, 45:1539-1572.*

[81] Sen, A.K. 1986. Social choice theory. In: K.J. Arrow and M. Intriligator (eds.), *Handbook of Mathematical Economics vol. III.* Amsterdam: North Holland.

[82] Sen, A.K. 1993. Internal consistency of choice. *Econometrica, 61:495-522.*

[83] Sen, A.K. and P.K. Pattanaik. 1969. Necessary and sufficient conditions for rational choice under majority decision. *Journal of Economic Theory, 1:178-202.*

[84] Smale, S. 1973. Global analysis and economics 1: Pareto optimum and a generalization of Morse theory. In: M. Piexoto (ed.), *Dynamical Systems.* New York: Academic Press.

[85] Sonnenschein, H. 1971. Demand theory without transitive preferences with applications to the theory of competitive equilibrium. In: J. Chipman *et al* (eds.), *Preferences, Utility and Demand.* New York: Harcourt, Brace, Jovanovich.

[86] Strnad, J. 1985. The structure of continuous valued neutral monotonic soical functions. *Social Choice and Welfare, 2:181-196.*

[87] Sundaram, R. 1996. *A First Course in Optimization Theory.* New York: Cambridge University Press.

[88] Suzumura, K. 1983. *Rational Choice, Collective Decisions and Social Welfare.* London: Cambridge University Press.

[89] Von Neumann, J. and O. Morgenstern. 1944. *Theory of Games and Economic Behavior.* Princeton: Princeton University Press.

[90] Wilson, R.B. 1972. Social choice theory without the Pareto principle. *Journal of Economic Theory, 5:478-486.*

# Index

acyclic
    preference aggregation rule, 30
    preference relation, 4
anonymity, 78
Arrow axiom, 16
Arrow's General Possibility Theorem, 30, 48
Arrow, K.J., 23, 26, 55, 118
as strong as, *see* dummy voter
asymmetric relation, *see* binary relation

Banks, J.S., 91, 185
base relation, 8
Bergstrom, T.C., 153
binary relation, 2
    acyclic, 4
    asymmetric, 2
    complete, 3
    condition F, 123
    continuous, 123
    indifference, 2
    lower continuous, 123
    preference, 2
    quasi-transitive, 4
    reflexive, 3
    strict preference, 2
    symmetric, 2
    transitive, 4
    triple-acyclic, 22
    upper continuous, 123
    weak order, 4

Black, D., 101, 118
Blair, D.H., 56
Blau, J.H., 55, 56
blocked coalition, 143
blocking condition, 145
Borda rule, 27
Border, K., 126, 128, 138
Bordes, G., 56
boundary of a set, 173
Brown, D.J., 56, 91

Caratheodory's Theorem, 128
Chernoff, H., 23
choice function, 6
    Arrow axiom, 16
    condition alpha, 8
    condition alpha-2, 22
    condition beta, 15
    condition beta +, 22
    condition epsilon, 22
    condition gamma, 10
    condition gamma-2, 22
    partition path independence, 22
    path independent (PI), 13
    quasi-transitive rationalizability, 14
    rationalizability theorem, 11
    rationalizable, 7
    resolute, 7
    transitive rationalizability, 16, 17